RETURNING HOME AIN'T EASY
BUT IT SURE IS A BLESSING!

This book is about a Nubian sister born in America and her family returning to their ancestral homeland. It speaks to the challenges, joys, tears & blessings of that return.

Seestah IMAHKUS Nzingah Ababio

Publisher
One Africa Tours & Speciality Services, Ltd.
P. O. Box CC 1251 – Cape Coast
Ghana, West Afrika

Tele/Fax: 233-42-40258
E-mail: oneafrica_ghana@yahoo.
Website: oneafricaghana.com

Artwork for Back Cover Design: Emmanuel Rock Nyarko Hanson

Photo for Front Cover Design: Mukadeem El Shabazz

ISBN: 978-1-4251-4763-1 (sc)

ISBN: 978-1-4269-1270-2 (dj)

ISBN: 978-1-4251-8147-5 (e-book)

We at Trafford believe that it is the responsibility of us all, as both individuals and corporations, to make choices that are environmentally and socially sound. You, in turn, are supporting this responsible conduct each time you purchase a Trafford book, or make use of our publishing services. To find out how you are helping, please visit www.trafford.com/responsiblepublishing.html

Our mission is to efficiently provide the world's finest, most comprehensive book publishing service, enabling every author to experience success. To find out how to publish your book, your way, and have it available worldwide, visit us online at www.trafford.com

Trafford rev.6/3/2009

 **Trafford** PUBLISHING® www.trafford.com

North America & international
toll-free: 1 888 232 4444 (USA & Canada)
phone: 250 383 6864 ♦ fax: 250 383 6804 ♦ email: info@trafford.com

The United Kingdom & Europe
phone: +44 (0)1865 487 395 ♦ local rate: 0845 230 9601
facsimile: +44 (0)1865 481 507 ♦ email: info.uk@trafford.com

10 9 8 7 6 5 4 3 2 1

AUTHOR'S NOTE

Returning Home Ain't Easy But It Sure Is A Blessing is the true story of IMAHKUS and her husband's return to their ancestral homeland. All the events presented are factual, based on IMAHKUS' recollection. While all the people portrayed in "Returning Home Ain't Easy But It Sure Is A Blessing" are real, pseudonyms have been used for some of them to protect their privacy. However, some characters are composites of people living and/or deceased.

FIRST AND FOREMOST GIVING ALL THANKS, PRAISE, HONOR AND GLORY TO OUR MOTHER/FATHER CREATOR AND TO THE MEMORY OF OUR GREAT AFRIKAN ANCESTORS.

A MEDITATION

AS AN AFRIKAN PERSON I CALL UPON THE SPIRIT AND WISDOM OF OUR ANCESTORS AND THE COSMIC FORCES OF TRUTH AND JUSTICE TO BE WITH US, TO UNITE US, TO STRENGTHEN OUR SENSE OF RESPONSIBILITY AND HELP US TO RE-CAPTURE OUR MINDS, TO STORE THE KNOWLEDGE AND THE LOVE OF SELF, TO LEARN, TO STUDY, TO CREATE, TO BUILD, TO PLAN AND TO WORK TOGETHER FOR OUR SURVIVAL AS INDIVIDUALS & COMMUNITY.
MAY THE INSPIRATION OF OUR GLORIOUS AFRIKAN PAST AND THE DIVINE LIGHT OF COSMIC ENERGIES SURROUND AND PROTECT US FROM ALL NEGATIVE VIBRATIONS, THOUGHTS, FEELINGS AND ACTIONS AS WE RE-DEDICATE AND COMMIT OURSELVES TO RE-AFFIRMING AND RE-CLAIMING OUR HUMANITY AND OUR HERITAGE. AND AS BEFORE, ONCE AGAIN BECOME AN ALMIGHTY FORCE IN THE RESTORATION OF TRUTH, PEACE AND JUSTICE ON THIS PLANET.

HOTEP MAAT
(Provided by Seestah Fannie S. Clark)

4

DEDICATIONS

This book is dedicated to my dad, Alfred D. Hines Jr., gifted writer, artist and friend who joined the ancestors the day I turned 21 years of age. He continues to inspire me throughout the years; my mom always said I was just like him (I pray so). And to my mom, Virginia Hines, who I love and pay tribute but who didn't accept or understand our leaving Amerika and joined the ancestors after we returned home to Mother Afrika in 1990.

To my late Seestah friend and neighbor, Margaret Fryson, who joined the ancestors in February 1987. Her untimely demise came at a time when we were planning on making our first pilgrimage home to Mother Afrika. Through her love of Afrikan peoples, art and culture, she sparked a flame in our hearts that caused us to re-direct our thinking as Afrikan people who had been cast away in a strange land and who did not realize that we could actually return "home" to Mother Afrika.

To my other beloved family members, my sister Traci whom I love toooooooo much and her family, my wonderful, favorite Senior Mother Aunt Ruby and her family, my other foxy, favorite Senior Mother Aunt Florence, affectionately called "Pookie" and her crew, my childhood friend and confidant Gertrude and my other daughter Cece and all our other relatives and friends.

To our children Kendu, Michele, Kelley, Linda, Terri, Glory and the late Michelle Martin; our grandchildren Shanaquia, Tristen Itai, Andraya Vienna, Zakayaa, Eban, Nerissa, Serapher, JD, Jasmine, Brandon, Allah Kenduvi, God Kendu Allah, Princess Kindra Iture, Princess Kindasia, Yshanaqua Unique, Pansy and great grandchildren Zakiyaa Michele & King Dayquaun.

To my elder brethren Bongo Shorty & Sister D thanks for the love and the many years we spent up the beach, under the big tree in Jamaica, W.I., reasoning & visualizing our return home to Mother Afrika, until it became a reality.

To my Seestahs and Mastermind Partners, Prof. Paulette Caldwell, Esq. Mildred O. Saunders and Seestah Evelyn. Over the many years we have prayed together and stayed together; distance nor time, nor life's many challenges have thawted our vision or our love and respect for one another.

To Ema Yarnah (Ruby) Woodley, Rastafari's first daughter, who has been my true seestah from that time 'til this time...the love and respect still grows.

To my spiritual son, William Jones, Jr. and Claudia Kleinbudde. Meda Se Pe for your love, support and invaluable assistance during the first stages of this work.

A very special thanks to Sister Fannie Clark, affectionately known as "Nurse Clark; who kept me focused on the How, When, Why, Where and What of writing when I tended to wander all over the place. She and Sybil Williams-Clarke, my other elder Seestah have been totally supportive of my efforts spiritually, financially and otherwise. Their chastising wisdom as strong as their love. Real livers and doers of the Kwanzaa principles.

To Seestahs Elimisha Jaliwah Alhasan & Shannon Gidney who allowed me to Lap Top (baby) sit with their precious computers, which enabled me to continue this work as I suffered through "no typewriter, no lights, out dated & non-working computers...you gals came through like bright shining stars in the darkest night.

To Seestahs Mwanda Kumunu-Clavell, Nancy Ivy and Brother Dell Jones (the WAR CORRESPODENT) for reading and encouraging the publishing of my book. And a very special thanks to Seesath Remel Moore (Nana Ama) for rushing down from Accra at the last moment and saving my book from what could have been a disaster without her fine-tune editing during the last hour.

To Seestahs April Amissah and Nana Ata Nkum I for their loving contributions to this work.

To Seestah Janet Butler for what she called her "labor of love". Her final, fine-tuned edit and proofreading was the icing on the cake. To Dr. Stella J. Horton for her love and confidence in this work and that final push over the financial wall.

To Bro. John Victor Owusu who initially welcomed us home in 1987 at the Cape Coast Castle Dungeon.

To "Sun" Bazz thank you for being all that you can be. Your loving spirit, continuous helping hands and giving heart fills the empty spaces of my being. You have truly demonstrated in works, deeds and dedication the sincere attributes of the loving son. I Love You Black!

To my Elder Seestah Talaata M'Bake N'Diaye. "Thank you" just doesn't seem to be enough for all that you do; lovingly supporting the efforts of our people spiritually, morally and financially as you continue to demonstrate what "Pan Afrika" means as you walk the walk and talk the talk of Afrikan liberation. You give us hope for the future as one who walks in the light of the Honorable Marcus Mosiah Garvey and Queen Mother Moore and lives by the principles of "Kwanzaa". We the living and the spirit of the ancestor pays tribute to you for boldly and bravely following our ancestors path back across the watery graveyard of The Middle Passage, home to the "Mother" land... by ship. Ayekoo ... Ayekoo ... Ayekoo!

A special medase pii (Thank You) to Ruth Amponsah, Ruth Mensah and Faustina Yandoh who cheerfully, patiently and effi-ciently took my book from the computer to its perfect finish.

I love ya'll. Returning Home Ain't Easy But It Sure Is A Blessing.

A VERY SPECIAL DEDICATION

This is a special dedication to my Kingman, my Soul Mate, Lover, Best Friend; Father, Grandfather and Great Grand-Father, Nana Okofo Iture Kwaku I Ababio.   He has always been there for me; helping me to make decisions, my many cases of wander lust and "great" and sometimes not so great ideas, whether it was our moving to Afrika or living on the seaside, he has been there. He has always loved me, my family and my friends, unconditionally. Thank you Nana, I love you tooooooooooooo much!

ABOUT THE AUTHOR

An Akan proverb stipulates that a stranger has big eyes but sees nothing. One can apply the same criticism to a denizen since familiarity can as well blunt and blur one's vision. It is a sign of IMAHKUS' maturity that she recognizes the fact that adversity always awaits in ambush for the unwary in every unfamiliar situation. Because of this one should exercise circumspection and an acute sense of judgment wherever one finds oneself.

To re-locate is not a simple matter. It requires a determination to succeed, a firm faith in God The Almighty, a willingness and patience to learn and re-learn. IMAHKUS, a great achiever, has all these attributes and is lucky enough to have for her husband, Nana Okofo an understanding and encouraging man. IMAHKUS' wisdom, extreme sensibility, and her sense of humour have helped the "One Africa" couple to settle and make their home in Ghana. Her open-mindedness has done this for her and husband.

This book can also help those who may choose to walk the path of "Return." IMAHKUS' book should be read by even those who do not intend to re-locate here because it is a book, which imparts valuable information about a country in Africa, one of the countries that many African-Americans repatriate to...Ghana.

Kwesi Brew (Cape Coast)
Ambassador/Diplomat, Successful Writer & Businessman.

It's a privilege to be Afrikan, but Afrikans must Unite!
Del Jones, War Correspondent

IMAHKUS' Blessing

Sister IMAHKUS' book, "Returning Home Ain't Easy But It Sure is a Blessing," is the creation of a master Afrikan Storyteller. It crackles with sharp observation, interesting sidebars and down home wit that allows us to walk in her shoes.

Not sparing us logic, motivation, emotion and spirituality, she strips her very being to enable us to view deeply inside of her unprotected soul. She knows that those of us wishing to return home must taste the reality, the bitter and the sweet. Many fantasize Afrika as a heaven, Utopia or super "Hood". IMAHKUS doesn't play such games; she knows that it is counter-productive and that Brooklyn and Ghana can be too many miles apart if approached wrong.
Her hand can be gentle, her spirit can be strong, and her truth can be digested with the rest of her reality that does not spare us the struggle. Could a reader ask for more? Once we know what we face we can plan to deal Afrikan style with all the unexpected variations.

She writes: "Returning Home Ain't Easy" chronices how we maintained ourselves, re-connected with our extended family, developed business interests to secure a good future for our families, while trying to make a worthwhile contribution to our community".

But it is even more than that, she is part of a small contigent of social and cultural acrhitects who have helped build bridges to the Motherland through their personal struggles. Now those of us who are prepared or preparing to ease across will be able to sidestep some of the traps, hidden barriers and personal obstacles.

PREFACE

Before I began to read this 'book', I had to stop for just a few moments to collect myself. This is not the type of book you just happened across in some ordinary bookstore and you were attracted to the cover or you think it has a catching title. I am here to let you know it is not like that at all. I really don't know if it is adequate enough to refer to this work as just a book. It is more like a journey in which you are about to embark. A journey that ventures through various aspects of life's transitions and experiences that lead you from one avenue to the next and ultimately lands your feet on the path of our Sacred Ancestral beginnings...The Motherland. All the forces that surround you as you hold on to this journey, are the same Ancestral forces that were involved in all the experiences of this journey and have allowed for it to be composed.

Now that you are paying closer attention and you too have to take a moment to collect yourself, check yourself, you realize that you are intrigued from deeper within your spirit and it is by no coincidence that you are about to read and experience this adventure. Those same ancestral forces have purposely called you to pick up this material. Your own Spirit has a longing and attraction for a connection with our Ancestral kindred.

"Returning Home Isn't Easy But It Sure Is A Blessing" is your passport; do you have your ticket yet?
Lastly, before you begin this journey. I must end this flight orientation with just a few words about the author. Only a few words because you are about to get all that and then some. In fact, I would like for you to paint a mental picture. When you see the face of Mother Afrika what does she look like? We always use the terms Mother Afrika, Motherland and even Mother Nature. So I'm asking you for a picture of that Mother.

Do you see a picture of an Elder whose face is aged by the lines of wisdom and life's experiences, dark skinned, profoundly wise, white haired, soft spoken, etc...etc... Ok fine. All that may be true of our Mother Afrika's picture from the viewpoint of our Afrikan Descendant period.

Now as we rise in our consciousness to become the Afrikan Ascendants that we are, we begin to see past the distortion and the negative propaganda the world has portrayed on Afrika, Afrikan people and our individual self. Then, do we also see a different enlightened picture of our Mother Afrika? Can you see her now as being a woman whose age you are really not sure of? She has skin that is smooth and always tanned by the kiss of just enough sun.

Her head is crowned by crystal-silverish, gray black locks that run down her back. She wears the smile of a grandmother but as you see her arms and legs you surely know this version of Mother Afrika can still knock someone out.

We affectionately call her Mamahkus!!! Nuff said!!!

El Shabazz

TABLE OF CONTENTS

INTRODUCTION

Ahead of us loomed this enormous, foreboding structure. The sight caused me to tremble; I almost didn't want to go inside. The outer walls were dingy white, chipped, faded and moldy. The sea had eaten away some of the mortar. It was gray and dismal as we climbed the steep steps, following the sign leading to the reception area. When we entered the reception area of the Cape Coast Castle Dungeons a smallish man with a bright smiling face met us. His name was Mr. Owusu and he had been working there as a receptionist and sometimes Guide, for many years.

After introductions were made all around, Mr. Owusu, our Guide, began the tour around the Castle. Entering the inner part of the castle overlooking a large courtyard, our guide gave us the background history of the Cape Coast Castle Dungeons. This was one of the more than sixty castle dungeons, forts, and lodges that had been constructed by European Traders with the permission of local rulers (the Chieftaincy) and stretched for 300 miles along the West Coast of Afrika to store captured Afrikans, until a shipload of enslaved Afrikans could be assembled, for shipment to the West. Unbelievably, twenty-seven of those houses of misery were located in Ghana.

Various European oppressors had occupied the Cape Coast Castle Dungeons during the Trans-Atlantic European Slave Trade. It began with the Portuguese in the 1500's, followed by the Dutch, then the Swedes, the Danes and finally the English who occupied it in 1665. It remained under their control, serving as the seat of the British Administration in the Gold Coast (Cape Coast) until they re-located their racist regime to Christianborg Castle in Accra in 1877.

Our next stop was the Palaver (which means talking/discussing) Hall, the meeting place of slave merchants, which also served as the hall used in auctioning off our ancestors. The room was huge, the only light coming from the windows which lined both sides of the walls; one side facing the ocean, the other side overlooking the town; a bare room, echoing the voice of our Guide, a haunting echo, which reverberated off the walls, as the Guide explained how they bargained and sold us. When slave auctions were not going on, Palaver Hall was used as a meeting place for the Governor, Chiefs and other visitors. We then moved on to the Governor's apartment and the church, which I felt like burning down!

But nothing could prepare me for what we would experience next. We descended the stairs into a large cobble-stoned courtyard and walked through large double wooden doors, which lead into a long, dark, damp tunnel.

The stench of musty bodies, fear and death hung in the air. There was no noise except the thunderous crashing of the waves against the outer walls and the roaring sound of the water. Deeper we walked, into large, dark rooms which had served as a warehouse for enslaved Afrikan people awaiting shipment to the Americas and Caribbean.

This was the Men's Dungeon. As we stood in that large cavernous room the air was still, the little ventilation that was available came from small openings near the 20-foot high ceilings. Our ancestors had been kept underground, chained to the walls and each other, making escape impossible.

The mood of the group was hushed, as several people started crying. We were standing in hellholes of the most horrific conditions imaginable. There were no words to express the suffering that must have gone on in these dungeons. I became caught up, thrown back in time. I was suddenly one of the many who were shackled, beaten and starved. But I was one of the fortunate souls to have survived the forced exodus from their homelands to be sold, branded and thrown into those hellholes, meant to hold (600) people but which held more than 1,000 captured Afrikans at one time. The men separated from the women, as they awaited shipment to the Americas. According to our Guide, the chalk marks on the walls of the Men's Dungeon indicated the level of the floor prior to the excavation of the floor, which had built up over years of slavery with feces, bones, filth etc.

As the Guide continued to describe the horrors of these pits of hell I began to shake violently; I needed to get out of there. I was being smothered. I turned and ran up the steep incline of the tunnel, to the castle courtyard, the winds from the sea whipping my face, bringing me back to the present. I couldn't believe what I had just experienced. How could anyone be so cruel and inhuman? Following the guide we proceeded across the massive courtyard and down another passage way to the Women's Dungeon, a smaller version of the Men's Dungeon but not so deep underground, it had held over 300 women at any given time.

As we entered that dark, musty, damp room, the sound of the crashing waves was like muffled, rolling thunder. A dimly lit, uncovered light bulb hung from the ceiling on a thin, frayed wire. After standing silently for a time in this tomb, the Guide began to lead the group out. I was the last person left in the room when the Guide turned and said he was continuing the tour.

"Please," I said, "I'm not ready to leave, just turn off the light for me and I will join the group shortly."

As the group walked silently away, the tears would not stop flowing. I dropped to my knees, trembling and crying even harder. With the light off, the only light in that dungeon came through one small window near the very high ceiling, reflecting down as though it were a muted spotlight. Darkness hung in every corner. As I rocked back and forth on the dirt floor, I could hear weeping and wailing...anguished screams coming from the distance.

Suddenly the room was packed with women...some naked, some with babies, some sick and lying in the dirt, while others stood against the walls around the dungeon's walls, terror filled their faces.

"My God, what had we done to wind up here, crammed together like animals?" Pain and suffering racked their bodies, a look of hopelessness and despair on their faces...but with a strong will to survive.

"Oh God, what have we done to deserve this kind of treatment?" Cold terror gripped my body. Tears blinded me and the screams wouldn't stop. As I sat there violently weeping I began to feel a sense of warmth, many hands were touching my body, caressing me, soothing me as a calmness began to come over me. I began to feel almost safe as voices whispered in my ears assuring me that everything was all right.

"Don't cry," they said. "You've come home. You've returned to

16

your homeland, to re-open the Door of No Return."

Gradually the voices and the women faded into the darkness; it was then that I realized that some of the screams I'd heard were my own. The eerie light beaming down from the window was growing dimmer as day began fading into night. As I got up from the dungeon floor I knew that I would never be the same again!

"After years of wandering and searching, I have finally found home. And one day, I wouldn't be leaving again."

The book that you hold in your hands, "Returning Home Ain't Easy But It Sure Is A Blessing," speaks to the visions of our ancestors and demonstrates the efforts both positive and negative, the humor, the tears and the frustrations of a Diasporan Afrikan family diligently working and struggling within the blessings of being back in our ancestral homeland. It faces the startling realities plagued by those of us who are trying to return home. Realities of the fact that many of our continental Afrikan born brothers and sisters have very little knowledge of the Afrikan people born and raised in the Diaspora that resulted from the Trans-Atlantic Arab European Slave Trade.

Ironically, every Ghanaian we spoke with wanted to go to the United States. We were coming and they wanted to go. We were like ships in the night, passing each other unseeing and uncaring.

My story contrasts these with those realities of life on the other side.

Brothers struggling to survive were being killed on a regular basis while driving taxis in New York City. A few years before we repatriated to Ghana, two men held up my husband with a shotgun, while he was working his taxicab. When they entered the cab and sat down, the man with the gun, who spoke no English, put it to my husband's head, as the other man announced in broken English,

"Dis es ah stickup, don' turn roun' or jew dead, Mon."

They then tied and bound him, before throwing him in the trunk of the taxi.

Riding around the Bronx and Manhattan they ended up dumping him on a dark street in the early morning. At a deserted Terminal Market in the Bronx, they ordered him to stay still and not move for 15 minutes.

Thank God, he was unhurt that time, but what about next time?

Certainly no one could doubt there would be a next time the way things were happening in New York City.

Children were being gunned down playing in the streets and in playgrounds. Safety was a problem even in the school system. These chaotic conditions, among other problems caused us to run like hell from New York, out of the United States and straight home to Afrika.

Here we found our family of four could live in comfort on my husband's pension from the New York City Fire Department. We set about pursuing economic empowerment for ourselves and the development and betterment of our Afrikan family on the continent.

However, since arriving here we have found that there are many jobs that are either reserved exclusively for Ghanaians or require certain monetary stipulations designed for big corporations. My husband, who owned and operated his own taxicab/car service in New York, would have to have a minimum of 10 cars to go into the car service business here. If we could afford to purchase 10 cars, would we need to open a car service? We owned our own Travel Agency in the United States but in Ghana we would have needed $60,000.00 US Dollars operating capital and a Ghanaian partner, or $200,000.00 U.S. Dollars to do it alone. In the absence of that kind of up-front cash, we have had to call upon our God given creativity.

Returning Home Ain't Easy chronicles how we maintained ourselves, re-connected with our extended family, developed business interests to secure a good future for our families, while trying to make a worthwhile contribution to our community.

It has been more than ten years since our family repatriated to "Mother" Afrika leaving behind mayhem, racism, creeping anarchy, bedlam, etc. (That's not to say things aren't far from that or are perfect here in Ghana). We've been tricked, accused of being racist, called Obruni (White man & foreigner), but we've also been loved and welcomed home by many of our Ghanaian brothers and sisters. They are anxious to learn about us, as we are about them. Each of us wants to know who the other has become. Who, we have become while we were separated from our "Mother" land.

This healthy exchange makes a stronger bond between us.

Together we can set about correcting those wrongs committed against us and remember the strength and greatness of us as Afrikan people. Just as a two-chord rope is stronger than a one-chord rope, our knowledge of the truth of our separation from one another will enable us to go forward as a stronger, united Afrikan front, a power source to be reckoned with spiritually, economically and politically.

One of our great Afrikan Leaders and Statesman, the late Osageyfo Dr. Kwame Nkrumah, 1st President of the Republic of Ghana from 1957 to 1966 said,

"All peoples of Afrikan descent whether they live in North or South America, the Caribbean or in other parts of the world are Afrikans and belong to the Afrikan nation."

That being so, it is with the blessing & fulfillment of *Prophesy that we have returned home on the **"wings of the wind.

*Genesis 15 verse 13:

"And he said to Abram, know of a surety that thy seed shall be a stranger in a land that is not theirs, and shall serve them; and they shall afflict them four hundred years."

**Biblical expression found in Revelations and true today as airplanes fly through the skies.

AFENA

A ceremonial sword that always accompanies a chief.
It is also used as summon to the chief's palace.

CHAPTER ONE

PREPARING FOR CHANGE

We had both been married before and had seven children between us, including grandchildren coming, so we were not exactly teenagers. We were blessed! Our cup was running over. But even within those blessings we continued to work and struggle, while helplessly watching the moral and economic decline of our community. Crime was on the rise, heavy drugs were in the area and police protection was a dismal failure. People were becoming more and more afraid of venturing out, especially at night. The sight of young thugs and hoodlums hanging out around the front of our store frightened potential customers away.

Work and struggle was the name of the game. Struggle to pay the mortgage, the utilities, the car note, the bank loan, credit cards, life insurance policies (really death policies), etc. and then work while trying to put something away for your old age; that is – if you made it to old age. And there were all the other expenses connected to the operation of our Travel Agency/Boutique and Car Service.

We were located in New York's Northeast Bronx where things were bad enough but they got a lot worse when the city re-zoned our neighborhood because Blacks and Latinos had infiltrated this "predominately white" community.

Property insurance and rent skyrocketed and our expenses shot through the roof. It was during this period of time that we had opened our own business. For years, insurance for stores fluctuated between virtually non-existent to so high that we couldn't afford it. All we could do was pray for the best and keep on working and struggling.

For example, most businesses in the area used a Trash Collection Company that held a monopoly on trash pick-up in the Bronx; these folks kept pestering us for our business at $100.00 dollars a month. Hell, it took us longer than a month to accumulate a small trash basket of waste paper. Because we were just starting out, business was not booming. Consequently, we didn't sign up. So faithfully, every month someone from the Trash Company would stop into our Agency and ask,

"Where is your window sticker for your garbage pick-up?"

And each time the response was the same...

"We don't have any garbage."

What little we did have, we took home and discarded it from there, $100.00 dollars was too much money to pay for hauling away two dollars worth of trash especially when we needed the money for so many other "important" things.

Although my husband Ben received a Pension as a retired New York City Fireman and I earned a decent salary as an Assistant Personnel Director for a major teaching hospital; working from nine to nine, sometimes six days a week for overtime, and most of the money I earned after taxes went towards running the business. Ben would cover the agency during the day and I'd rush home after work at the hospital to relieve him so that he could go out and drive the taxi. It was after one of those days from hell, Ben said,

"Vienna, we desperately need help."

But it was virtually impossible to hire staff; we couldn't afford it. Ben and I were the staff.

One day, a young woman from the community who had recently graduated from one of those Travel Agency Courses, stopped into the agency in search of work. She hadn't been able to find work because she had no experience, but she couldn't gain experience if no one hired her. A real catch-22 for her - a blessing in disguise for us! We hired her, with a small stipend and the opportunity to gain the necessary experience in managing a Travel Agency. She agreed. This arrangement freed Ben to drive his taxicab during the day, eliminating the need for him to continue working nights.

Our friends and neighbors, Robert and Margaret had talked us into leaving our in-house business. They ran an Art Gallery and, like us, they had been running a business out of their home, until they acquired a store in the neighborhood on a busy main street. When another store became available, they convinced us to move our business to a more public location, in fact, right next door to them.

"We can help each other," they said.

This was the first time either of us was operating a business outside of our homes and other than managing our not-yet-paid-for taxicab, Ben and I had always worked for someone else. Margaret also worked for a major teaching hospital as a Surgical Nurse, running home, after work, to their business. Now that we were together, both families supported each other's efforts spiritually and sometimes financially.

And, we dreamed. We dreamed about the success of our businesses and we dreamed and reasoned about Afrika. A few people we knew had taken a trip or two to the Motherland. The information they brought back was just enough to whet our appetites, even though I was not interested in seeing lions and tigers outside of the Bronx Zoo.

Our first attempt at going to Afrika was to organize a tour group to Egypt. I researched the information: we made up flyers and sent out notices. However, the response was very poor. Most of the people we approached asked, rather skeptically,

"What's in Afrika and why should I spend that kind of money to go there?"

The tour was rather expensive, even though we did everything possible to keep the cost down. But we didn't give up.

Because Margaret and Robert were dealing in Afrikan art, our discussions were constantly on the continent of Afrika, the arts, crafts and artifacts, the beautiful fabrics that we had seen and or obtained from visitors from the continent, the customs and the people. Years before I had changed my mode of dress from western looking attire to a more Afrikan motif.

"Girl, I can just see myself in that village, carrying a load on my head," I laughed, talking with Margaret one day as we were sitting around the Gallery.

"Yeah, just like that painting hanging over there," she said wistfully.

We started laughing as I jumped up and attempted to carry a

book on my head, but succeeded in looking like a seal doing a balancing act.

"In time girl, in time. It's in the genes, I'm just a little out of touch," I added, "but it will come. Just watch me girl, just like that picture."

We had a good laugh and continued to plan.

Determined, we put together a second tour to Afrika, but in the midst of our plans Margaret fell ill.

Coming in from work one evening I stopped into the Gallery. Margaret was sitting at the counter with the strangest look on her face.

"Hey girl," I joked, "was" up? Why the look of gloom-and-doom?"

She seemed to look right through me and in a very quiet voice said, "Vienna, I have cancer and there's nothing they can do about it. Girlfriend, I'm going to die."

I could only stand there with my mouth wide open. "What?" I softly screamed.

Again, with a forceful finality she repeated, "I'm going to die!"

"Oh God, no," I cried out. "Where's Robert?"

"I'm here V," came the subdued response from the rear of the gallery, as we all started to cry again.

Robert and Margaret had been together since childhood. They had lived in the same neighborhood, attended the same schools, graduated and gotten married. They had five children. By this time Robert had joined us in the front of the gallery and the three of us just sat there looking at one another, bawling like babies. That's how Ben found us, sitting in the gallery as still as statues, with the hot tears cascading down our faces. Ben asked a similar question to mine, inquiring whether or not Margaret was sure.

For months unbeknown to us, Margaret had been going to doctors, because of pain in her stomach, taking a battery of tests and praying hard. This final test revealed just how serious her illness was, it was cancer.

"The doctors said my life could possibly be extended for a longer period of time with chemotherapy," Margaret said softly. "But, I don't want no part of that! I know how awful the treatment is and I don't want to subject my family or myself to it. I've seen many patients suffer through the therapy at the hospital and it's not a pretty sight. I saw the X-rays and there is nothing that they can do to save me. The cancer has already metastasized," she concluded, beginning to weep again.

She had discussed her decision with the family; sadly they accepted her decision.

Margaret eventually got to the place that she could not come into the Gallery anymore. So we spent a lot of time with her at home in prayer and reasoning. But, she wouldn't give up either.

One day she and Robert approached us about the possibility of her going to Jamaica, West Indies to see an Herbal doctor who was well-known for his successful treatments of serious illnesses, including cancer. I had previously lived in Jamaica and knew a few people who had been treated by him and had been told of many others who had traveled from various parts of the world to be treated by him. I agreed to look into the possibility of him seeing and treating her. When I presented all of the information to Robert and Margaret they were anxious for her to travel to Jamaica and Margaret wanted me to go with her. I asked Ben to accompany us for I knew that we would need help.

Robert remained in New York to raise the necessary funds for treatment and to keep the business going because that was their only source of income, aside from her disability payments. Our financial situation was not much better but she was our friend and she needed our help.

I took an extended vacation and emergency leave from my job in January '87 and we left for Jamaica. The trip to Jamaica was not easy as Margaret was now confined to a wheelchair or forced to lie down. Although she was taking her medication, she still suffered a lot of pain. The look on her face, when the pain took hold of her made you want to weep.

"What can I do?" I'd ask helplessly, when I'd seen the look of pain on her face.

But she'd just tightly grip my hand, gritting her teeth.

"I'm OK V, the pain will soon pass. I'm fine," she said trying to reassure me.

We arrived in Jamaica after some delay. After clearing Customs and checking into our residence, we informed the doctor of our arrival. Dr. Moses was an elderly, highly respected, Rastafarian, herbal physician in the country, who was very knowledgeable of the treatment of illnesses using Herb's. The first thing he did after examining her and pin-pointing her problem was to change her diet. He put her on a diet of raw foods and a broth made from various types of fish and herbs. He used many types of different herbs in his treatments to which she responded favorably during the three weeks I was there with her. I saw a marked improvement in her condition she was able to stand again and take a few steps without help.

Unfortunately, her mind was not at peace. She kept worrying.

"How am I going to pay the doctor?" She repeatedly asked. "How much is he going to charge me for the treatment?"

"Sister, please try not to worry. Just think about getting well," Ben and I told her. But she continued to worry, and worry and worry.

One day during her treatment she questioned Dr. Moses, again. "How much are you going to charge me for this treatment? I hope that I can afford it!"

"Don't worry about money, your primary concern should be on getting better," Dr. Moses told her.

Finally, one day when she again asked him of his charge, Dr. Moses responded, with a hint of impatience, the locks of his precepts shaking as he spoke.

"My Sistren, how much would you pay for your funeral?"

Margaret replied, "From three to five thousand dollars."

"Well then, he said, is that also not a fair price to pay to save your life? After all, I have come to save life, not to take it away. But I cannot do it without your total co-operation. So please no more worries and conversations about money!"

For a time Margaret was fine, but she again began to fret and worry, calling New York regularly to see how the Gallery was coming along and checking to see when and if money was being sent to her. Just before I returned to New York, three weeks after we arrived, one of her sons who was studying medicine in New York, joined her in Jamaica. He jumped right in, joining the doctor in his mother's treatments and optimistic about her progress and what he was learning from Doctor Moses. He and my husband worked closely together trying to keep her spirits up.

Leaving Ben behind I returned to New York after three weeks, feeling optimistic about Margaret's recovery.

When the news of her death came a few weeks later we were totally devastated. Within three months of learning of her illness, Margaret was dead and so was our dream of going to Afrika together.

* * * * * * *

But getting Margaret's body released from the authorities became a problem. She had died suddenly, on the weekend, while the doctor was out of town and there was no one who could sign the death certificate. There was the additional delay associated with a person dying on foreign soil. Ben and Margaret's son ran up and down between the American Embassy and the local authorities. In the meantime funeral arrangements were being made in New York. They finally managed to get through the bureaucracy and red tape and her son escorted Margaret back to New York.

I spent a lot of time with Robert and the family at their house, trying to do whatever I could to help. There were people to notify and Robert was not in a very good state. Her death had devastated him. He tried holding it all together for the children but he was having a hard time of it.

"Why V? Why?" he'd ask me, tears falling from his eyes.

But I had no answers.

The funeral was very sad. Margaret's co-workers and many other friends, relatives and business associates attended the funeral service, for Margaret was well-known and well-liked.

Once the funeral arrangements were completed, we sadly settled back into our daily routine. But the gap created by Margaret's passing was very wide and deep. Robert was very sad and listless.

When the Gallery was opened again, I would stop in to reason with Robert, he would look mournfully at me, his eyes filling with tears. Ben would talk with him. Sometimes he'd whisper, "Why, V, why? I miss her so much. We were going to do so much."

Other times he would just sit and stare. The work orders were beginning to pile up. But he just wasn't up to handling it. I felt so helpless. So I prayed...prayed for Robert, prayed for the children and prayed for us.

One day Robert bounced into our agency with a little spring in his step and a new glow on his face. Smiling broadly, he asked, "Where's Brother Ben? I have something to share with you two."

Before I could answer, Ben walked in and the two of them exchanged greetings, hugging and laughing and carrying on like two schoolboys.

"Welcome back, my man," Ben replied, "It's been a real rough storm but you've made it."

"You can say that again," answered Robert. "Yeah man, I can't hold on to the past but I'll never stop loving her. I'm outta here though. I'm moving to Florida with the children and setting up the business down there. After all, Margaret and I often talked about one day doing that."

Two weeks later he was gone.

It was a little strange at first, seeing the Gallery deserted and empty, gates drawn across the windows and doors. Gone were the beautiful Afrikan paintings that adorned the windows, lit up by large spotlights. Gone were the beautiful Afrikan carvings & clothe, the smell of incense burning, and the sound of drums and Afrikan music playing from within the Gallery. Gone were our dreams of traveling home to Afrika together. There was an air of loneliness and desolation!

I missed my friends, and all the discussions and planning for our collective futures. For weeks after Robert left, I still half expected to see him walk through the door. It was difficult dealing with the pain of Margaret's passing and Robert's leaving but gradually it began to subside, but would always leave a soft spot in my heart. Focusing once again on my life's priorities, I threw myself back into the business of day-to-day survival.

The Children: *Michele, Kendu, Kelley & Linda, Terri, Glory Dawn, Shey & El Shabazz.* ***Some of the Grandchildren:*** *JD, Serapher, Zakiyaa, Nerissa, Eban, Shanaqua, (with Pop), Kenduvi, Tristen Itai, Jasper, Jasmine, Andraya Vienna, Shanaquia and Tynisha.* ***One of the Great grandchildren:*** *Zakiyah Michele.*

FIHANKRA

This symbol denotes security,
safety and solidarity and emphasises the necessity
of serving as one another's keeper.

CHAPTER TWO

AFRIKA BECOMES A REALITY

It was a sweltering July day, the air conditioner was not working and my mind was not on the Travel Agency. So I was sort of day dreaming, when this smallish looking, dark skinned brother, with cat eyes and an air of superiority claiming to be a chief from Ghana, West Afrika walked into our Travel Agency.

An Afrikan Chief? Right! I thought to myself, and I'm Pocahontas. Just what I need first thing this morning, some nut to raise my temperature even further. But I put on my best professional face and smiled.

"Good morning brother," I said smiling, "what can I do for you?"

The first thing he said was, "You don't believe I'm a Chief, do you?"

"Well my brother," I responded laughingly, "Whatever turns you on." Whatever rocks your boat, I thought. "Is there something that I can help you with?"

He then proceeded to give me a brief "history lesson" on Afrika and Ghana.

"You Afrikan-Americans do not know much about your history. We are the same people and we need to get together. We have a lot to learn from each other. The white man has kept us separated too long, etc., etc., etc."

I must admit, the conversation had taken an interesting slant and had touched a very sensitive spot in me. He now had my undivided attention.

"I'm going to be enstooled as the Chief of my family. My uncle has died and I'm next in line for the Chiefs' Stool according to our custom and tradition. This is legitimate," he continued, "there are some other Afrikan Americans also going to see my enstoolment."

Oh oh, here it comes, I thought, the real reason for his visit.

"I have a fantastic opportunity for you," he said.

All he needed was for me to give him five thousand dollars and he could make all the arrangements in Ghana for me and anyone else that our agency could find to attend this ceremony.

It did sound kind of interesting though.

"But who are you? Who knows you?" I asked. "I don't know you from Adam's House Cat; and where do you think we can get that kind of money to give to you, a perfect stranger, to take us to God only knows where?"

The brother had certainly brightened up my day but not enough to make me want to throw open the vault.

"I'll be in touch, Chief," I said, "Just leave your particulars and I'll get back to you."

Not looking too pleased but leaving a flyer on my desk, the "Chief" went on his way. After the "Chief" left, I contacted the number on the flyer. It was then that I found out that another Travel Agency in Mount Vernon was also already making these same arrangements. The story he had told me about his chieftaincy was in fact true. They had already signed up some people for the trip and there was still space available if I wanted to join them. I was beginning to feel a little excited.

Was I really going to have the opportunity to go to Afrika?" I thought.

By the time Ben came in I was "bursting at the seams" as I told him all about my morning with an "Afrikan Chief." The thought of seeing someone made a Chief in Afrika sounded exciting to both of us.

"It's not a bad idea," Ben agreed. "But as you're unfamiliar with the brother and Ghana, why don't we make this a familiarization trip for the agency before we start making arrangements to take others there. After all, haven't we been working and planning to go to Afrika before Margaret died?"

He was right. This trip would afford me the opportunity to get some first hand knowledge. Plus, I figured we could do a much better job of promoting Ghana to travelers if I went there, and liked it. We agreed that Ben would stay behind and manage the business, while I "checked out" Ghana. We immediately made the necessary arrangements with the other Travel Agency. I could barely contain myself! I was really going to Afrika!

A few days before departure a reception and Bon Voyage party were held for the trip participants in Mount Vernon, New York. It was given by the Bereshith Cultural Institute, an Afro-centric School and Cultural Center, independently owned and operated by Afrikan-American brothers and sisters who also had an interest in going to Afrika. This was also the first time that I would meet brothers and sisters practicing Hebrew, Old Testament teachings in a Hebrew Israelite community.

The reception was held in the courtyard of the school. Brothers and sisters dressed to the nines in colorful Afrikan garments were milling around, laughing and talking. A group of brothers were making some fine music on the drums. During the reception we saw the Ghanaian "Chief" who had visited our agency.

"Welcome," he said, walking up and shaking Ben's hand, laughingly he continued. "Your wife did not believe that I was a Chief; she is very cautious sister. I want you to meet my wife, Gloria."

He was married to an Afrikan-American sister who was the niece of one of the founders of the institute.

"My wife will also be going," he continued. "Just make yourself at home. I'll introduce you to the other people and members of the institute who are also going to Ghana to witness my enstoolment. My name will no longer be Isaac Simmons, after my enstoolment," he said seriously. "I will take the name of my uncle Nana Gypie."

Shortly thereafter we received our final orientation in preparation for the trip and were given our airline tickets. It was a real festive evening. My appetite was really whetted and I was ready. After getting all the particulars we returned home for my last minute packing.

I was too excited! There were butterflies in my stomach and I didn't sleep much that night.

When we arrived at John F. Kennedy International Airport the following day, the sight that greeted us was enough to make a person change their mind about going to Afrika. People were milling around all over the place. There was no order, limited seating and absolute chaos. I didn't see the check-in counter that was normally available for check in before boarding the plane and it was as hot as

Hell. I had traveled extensively, to many parts of the world, but I had never seen anything quite like this and of all places, here at John F. Kennedy Airport, in New York City.

I must confess that it was also the first time that I had ever flown on an Afrikan airline, "Nigerian Airlines." What an unforgettable experience that was! It was stifling hot, people were shouting, there were no chairs, so folks were milling around or sitting on the floor as children ran up and down as though playing in the playground. Total chaos!

As I stood in the midst of that confusion, looking for my traveling companions, a crackling announcement came over a barely, audible loudspeaker, announcing the boarding of the flight. People started rushing towards the Boarding Gate, shoving and screaming. I found myself flattened against the wall, trying to keep from being trampled. Suddenly, a white woman in a blue uniform stood upon a table in front of us and began screaming at the top of her lungs.

"Get back, get back. You people get back or I'm going to call the police!"

Suddenly, a couple of "Rent-a-Cops" appeared and started pushing people around, threatening them with sticks, while the fool-ass woman kept shouting at the top of her lungs.

"Get back, get back! You people are not getting on this plane, if you don't stop pushing; get back, get back!"

The area was hot and airless, the sweat was pouring off me as I wished I were somewhere else. As I drew closer to the screaming woman, I saw that she was physically manhandling people. By this time, I was hot, sticky, irritable and tired of being pushed around. To say the least, I was not, a happy camper. So when she got to me, with her hands raised, I glared at her and told her in a tone that she had no trouble understanding.

"Do not.... put your hands on me," and refused to move.

She then turned and directed her lunatic wrath onto someone else. Working my way out of that melee I went through a very narrow door and met one of the brothers in my party.

"Shalom," he said, smiling warmly, "I'm Kohain Nathanyah HaLevi."

I immediately liked him and we both had something in common. This was also his first trip to West Afrika and both of us wondered, "Is this the way you travel to Afrika?"

Surprisingly, amidst all that confusion they were somehow managing to move a few people at a time inside a small room, down an elevator, and onto the field, where we were boarded on buses. We were taken some distance out onto the airfield to the waiting plane. It took a good while to load the plane before we could depart. It didn't help matters that the plane itself was none too comfortable nor the hostesses too friendly. They behaved as if we were annoying them, and, that they would rather be doing something else besides serving us. This was going to be one helluva trip. So I squeezed back into an almost too little seat and buckled my seat belt and said, "Whatever... I'm on my way to Afrika."

Once we settled in I had an opportunity to meet the other 15 people in our tour group. We exchanged pleasantries and talked about the "riot control" tactics that had just been employed at the airport. None of us had ever experienced that before. I, as a Travel Agent, was certainly going to report this to the airline authorities when I returned to the United States.

The attitude of the hostesses was so bad that you didn't want to call them for anything. A call for a blanket was met with a glare and a very sharp, biting response.

"Excuse me," I said after she finally answered the call bell. "May I have a blanket, please?"

First she glared at me before sharply answering. "You will have to wait. We're very busy just now."

Whooowe, I thought to myself, *what's her problem? Forget the blanket!*

Then, there was some discrepancy regarding the food because some members of the group had ordered Kosher meals but received something different. Again, the hostesses were anything but helpful. What the hell! I was so tired that I went right to sleep. When I woke up they were preparing to serve breakfast and looking a little less hostile. We would be landing in Nigeria before long. I just couldn't believe it. I was almost in Afrika not knowing what to expect but happy to be coming home to Afrika.

After eight and one half-hours, we arrived in Lagos, Nigeria. Initially, I thought we'd reached our destination, but we were told that we were just changing planes and would be continuing shortly on to Accra, Ghana.

Conditions were bad in Nigeria and the people were not friendly. We were advised by the airline employees not to worry about our luggage because it would be put onto the Ghana Airlines flight and we would pick it up when we arrived at our destination.

While the group was getting together, some man claiming to be a Customs Officer approached us and said that he would be processing our papers; he had to collect all our passports and our airline tickets. He was going to check us through to Accra because we were not leaving until 4:30 PM. We'd arrived at 6:30 AM.

Why such a long wait? I wondered.

As the group leader was getting the documents together, I did not feel too comfortable with these arrangements. *Was he really a Customs Officer and where was his Identification? Somethin' in the milk ain't clean,* I thought to myself.

When they requested my passport and ticket, I refused to give them up without first seeing the alleged Custom's Officer's proper identification. Besides, since when did you just give your documents to some stranger who couldn't prove who he was? As we were debating this, the man started to quietly ease away with some of the documents. Observing this, we called him back and reclaimed the documents telling him that someone would accompany him to complete the processing. He became very annoyed, insisting that it wasn't necessary, because he was airport personnel and security. However, he never produced the ID we kept insisting upon. Suddenly, he pushed the documents back into the Tour Leader's hands, said something we didn't understand and quickly disappeared into the crowd.

Baby, some of us were well-trained in spotting a con artist, having come out Harlem and the South Bronx. As I watched him disappear, I noticed one of my suitcases on the conveyor belt being removed by another unknown person, with no identification.

"Where are you taking those suitcases?" I inquired.

The man removing the suitcases stared coldly at me, did not answer and continued to remove the bags. After a few minutes I got really annoyed and shouted at him.

"Those are my bags, so take your hands off them."

It was then that I realized that all of our bags were being unloaded, some placed to the side on the floor and some stacked on several baggage carts. Because we were so persistent about the handling of our bags, they were suddenly abandoned and the men who were not in uniform and helping themselves to our luggage, disappeared. Upon further inquiry, we were told that we would have to carry our own luggage to the next flight with Ghana Airlines, which was fine with me.

As we struggled with our own luggage, other men appeared to help us, but this time we watched them very closely. They assisted us to the elevator and loaded on our suitcases. When they were finished they demanded payment. Not knowing any better, we collected thirty dollars between us and paid them. When the elevator arrived at the upper level, the elevator operator refused to take the bags off the elevator, claiming that it was not his job and if we wanted them removed, we'd have to pay him. Just then, some other men appeared and they began to unload the elevator, and when they were finished, they also demanded payment. We paid again, expecting them to take the luggage to the place where we would be boarding our next flight. Much to our astonishment, they refused, saying that it would cost us extra to carry them further. We had finally had enough of this foolish rudeness and total lack of cooperation of these people. We decided to carry them ourselves and had to literally fight to keep people away from our bags.

When we arrived at the departure area, we were told that the flight would not leave until 4:00 p.m. We settled in to wait, even though these were not the arrangements that had been made by the Travel Agent. No one had told us about a layover in Nigeria.

We were all getting a little hungry...because we hadn't eaten anything since breakfast. The delay continued. It was now after 3:00 p.m. After much discussion, arguments back and forth, we were finally able to get Ghana Airlines to provide us with a meal as the delay was not of our doing and there was no place to get anything to eat. When they finally brought us something to eat, it was cold, hard sandwiches and soft bananas, which they served from a couple of cardboard boxes that had been dropped on the floor near us. We had no place to sit and eat, except on the floor, in the waiting area.

We cracked jokes and made light of the situation, while one of the elders in the group, Elder Lee was taking pictures of everything and everybody. Suddenly, a couple of policemen appeared out of nowhere threatening to take his camera and arrest him for taking pictures in a restricted area.

"I'm sorry," Elder Lee told the police, "I wasn't aware of any restrictions, I won't take anymore pictures here."

But they were insisting on arresting him. After much pleading and protesting, they finally agreed not to arrest him and to let him keep his camera but he had to remove the film and give it to them. It was a small price to pay, to keep from going to jail in Afrika. The Lagos Airport was a government facility and taking pictures here was a big "no-no." That was a close call! No one had informed us of any restrictions in advance and in the United States you could take pictures of "almost" anything. But this was Nigeria and that crap did not wash here. Another lesson learned in coming home.

Since picture taking was a no-no, and we couldn't leave the airport, to kill time some of us decided to shop for souvenirs at the airport gift shop. But we needed to exchange our dollars for Nigerian Naira in order to make purchases. Since everyone was not able to leave the area, a couple of us left the group and went to the Forex Bureau to exchange our money. Unfortunately, when we were ready to leave Nigeria, the Forex Bureau would not change the money that we had just exchanged back into dollars. This was crazy! But no one was paying our protests any mind.

Shortly thereafter, several other members of the group joined us. They had been in Nigeria for several days before we arrived and they also had horror stories to tell about unfriendly people, being cheated out of their money and so on. The journey home was not easy and I was beginning to wonder about this trip. After much delay we finally left for Ghana, after nine o'clock in the pm. Tired, musty and more than a little disgusted we boarded the plane for the final leg of our journey, praying it would get better.

We finally arrived in Ghana, a couple of hours later, but not before stopping at Dakar, Monrovia and other locations along the way, but this time we did not get off the plane. At one location soldiers even prevented us from coming out of the airplane to look around.

Welcome home, I thought dismally, *this be Afrika!*

But still I was happy. I had finally reached my ancestral homeland; at long last I was home in Afrika, after over 500 years in a strange land and nothing was going to spoil that.

CHAPTER THREE

AKWAABA MEANS WELCOME

So, this was it. Ghana...tropical climate, population of approximately 15 million people of various ethnic backgrounds. Previously known as the Gold Coast until 1957 when the late President, Osageyfo Dr. Kwame Nkrumah led the one-time British Colony to independence and re-named it Ghana after an ancient kingdom that included parts of Mali, Mauritania and Senegal. Ghana...the home of my ancestors.

We arrived at Kotoka International Airport in Accra, on the 23rd of August at 11:00pm. We would be here until the 4th of September. Once again we were going through Customs Clearance, document checks and securing our luggage. Things seemed to move a little more smoothly in Accra and the attitude of the people was much better and they were friendlier. People smiled and offered to help you.

"Welcome home," could be heard from some of the people (Porters, Customs Officers) as they greeted us. And much to my surprise (contrary to our earlier Afrikan welcome) representatives from the Ghana Tourist Board also met us. They brought a large, comfortable bus to convey us to Takoradi.

Great! I thought.

The Tourist Board Representatives said we should come with them. However, the brother who invited us was there to meet us and had also made arrangements for our transportation and got into a shouting match with the Tourist Board.

"Get lost!" He told them as they argued back and forth, like they were bartering for us.

After much ado, our Group Leader convinced the Tourist Board

Rep. that we felt safe and would go along with the young man who had invited us. We really didn't have a lot of choices, this was a strange land, it was after midnight and we were exhausted. I never did find out who had arranged for the Tourist Board to meet us.

There were two smaller buses to convey us to Cape Coast. As the first bus took off into the dark night, I had no idea where I was, nor did I know where the other bus had disappeared. It had been behind us until we got to the Police Barrier. As we were having our bus checked, a feeling of terror came over me, at the sight of these Black men in black military uniforms, coming out of the dark carrying automatic weapons and demanding information on our destination. The driver spoke rapidly to the soldiers in Fante. It sounded like they were arguing but I didn't have a clue as to what they were saying. The driver referred the soldiers to the second bus that was carrying our host. But, it was nowhere to be seen.

Next, the soldiers boarded our bus, their machine guns under their arms, shining their flashlights in our faces.

"Where are you from?" they demanded, to no one in particular.

Someone responded, "From America, what's the problem?"

The soldier only glared at us as they marched up and down the tight isle of the bus.

"What is in the cases?" they demanded.

Again, another voice! "It's our clothes and personal belongings."

Oh Lord, I prayed to myself, *please don't let them shoot us.*

I was scared, as were most of us. This was a totally new experience for us. I was shaking and almost pissed in my drawers. But then again as I thought about it, *why was I so frightened at the sight of Black men, in black uniforms and carrying automatic weapons?" Didn't White men, in black uniforms, carrying automatic weapons and Billy Clubs "protect" and kill innocent Black people in "self defense" in the United States, all the time?*

Now that is fear! Feeling a little more relaxed, I sort of chilled out.

After a little more delay we were permitted to continue on our journey. Everyone began talking at the same time.

"Man, what the hell was that all about," one brother asked the driver.

"They just wanted a dash," he said.

"Dash?" someone else asked, "What is dash?"

"Yes, they want you to give them something. It happens to the drivers all the time," he continued. "I gave him something small so he would let us go. When they saw foreigners, they know you have plenty of money."

We all laughed at that for in America it was called a bribe or stick-up and as far as "plenty money," everyone on the bus had saved a long time for this trip. It had been a sacrifice for most of us to even make this journey. In fact, there was little left to do much with. We were riding on our "plenty money."

It was dark and there was nothing to see, so settling in again, most of us went to sleep. We traveled quietly for approximately three hours until we reached our destination in Cape Coast. The driver took us directly to our hotel. We pulled off the road into a dark driveway. I didn't have a clue as to where we were but I knew that we were near the ocean because I could hear the sound of crashing waves. As we descended from the bus, there were no lights on in the place, only a small lantern.

"The lights have gone off," said a lady sitting nearby what looked like a bar, "but we are using kerosene lanterns."

"No problem," I said, "we're just beat and want to lay down. Can you please show us to our rooms?" I asked tiredly.

It was difficult to see our surrounding very well. I soon found out the name of the place was called Apotech. However, the first room we were shown was painted a sickly green and had no linen on the bed. The room was only big enough for one person and the bed was made of concrete and covered with a small, thin, damp, foam rubber mattress.

"You don't expect anyone to stay in there," one of the brothers said, "let's see something else."

But all of the rooms were the same, some a little worse. Some of the people in the group were getting very upset because they had paid a lot of money for this trip and this was not what they expected. To make bad matters worse the second bus with our Host and the Tour Leader had still not arrived. Since I was a "somewhat" seasoned Travel Agent I set about trying to calm folk's nerves.

"Please don't be too upset," I reasoned with the group, "I'm sure there is an explanation. We'll just have to wait for the other bus to arrive."

But folks were rumbling and grumbling and ready to go to war. Shortly thereafter, the other members of our tour group arrived. They had stopped for a cold beer along the way and were in quite a jovial mood when they arrived.

However, that quickly changed when they saw where they were expected to sleep. Seventeen irate brothers and sisters from America went completely off. Shouting, some of them were ready to strangle our host. They had paid their hard-earned money for this trip and they expected decent, air conditioned, accommodations. These arrangements were totally unacceptable to everyone and they demanded to be taken elsewhere. If there had been sheets on the beds I could probably have made it through the night. I was used to roughing it having been a camper and having backpacked through South America. However, the rest of the folks were not having any of this!

When the smoke cleared we wound up at Dan's Paradise, a Hotel in the middle of town. The rooms were clean and some of them were air conditioned, but there was no running water, so each room was given a bucket of water. We were too tired to argue any further. It was now three in the morning and some of us had been on the move for more than 24 hours. Elder B., Kohains' dad, and I were the only ones who had not been assigned to a room and there was only one left. He started joking about the sleeping arrangements and said it would cost me but he'd be nice to me, this time, and let me have "his" room and bunk with some of the guys. I could not go any further. I went to the room "gifted" to me and crashed.

"Good night and welcome home!"

After a refreshing nap in my clothes, I arose to a bright and sunny morning. After washing the "fuzzy" monster out of my mouth, I ventured outside. I was the only one awake at that time. The air smelled so good and a gentle breeze was blowing. In the distance you could hear the sounds of the crashing waves and the "swish swish" sound of people sweeping. This was really Afrika! I still couldn't believe I was here. Gradually, the others began to make their way out of their rooms. Folks appeared to be feeling a little better, though still pissed off! The conversation centered on the previous night and the dissatisfaction with our current arrangements. Unfortunately, the only thing that we could do was wait for our host.

He'd better come with some good news, I thought to myself, or someone is subject to stomp a "mud hole" in his ass.

While we were waiting for him, two of the other Tour Leaders, Sister Yedidah from Mount Vernon, who had been living in Ghana for the past six months and Sister Tamakeyah, a resident Ghanaian, went in search for a better place for us to stay – something closer to the ocean, and with running water.

In the meantime we made the best of our situation, enjoying ourselves over breakfast. Across from our hotel, on top of a hill was a Primary school and little children in brown and beige uniforms were running up and down in the yard playing.

Having eaten my breakfast and no longer wanting to discuss the previous night any further a couple of us decided to visit the school.

As I was climbing up the side of a small rocky mountain, covered with tall grass and thorns, talking to myself, I couldn't imagine having to do this everyday but I was also not ten years old either. Puffing and blowing I made my way up the uneven terrain.

"How did the teachers get up here?" I asked no one in particular.

One brother, Eugene Redd commented jokingly, "This was your idea sister, so don't complain. I'm as crazy as you are for following you!"

But he and his wife kept climbing, puffing and blowing all the way. However, the climb was worth it. Once at the top, it offered a fantastic, breath-taking view of the town and overlooked the hotel.

And the children were all so wonderful.

"Take my picture, take my picture," they chimed in together. "Take my name and address. Write me when you go back to America."

Some of them, a little frightened of us, ran a distance away from us. There were so many beautiful Black faces, smiling, laughing and respectful. No cursing and swearing or disrespect for their teachers and visitors. Some of the classes were in session and when we walked into a classroom, children stood up and greeted us in unison.

"Good morning, Madam, Good morning Sir."

The teacher invited us in and welcomed us to Ghana. These school children were a real pleasure. Other members of our group joined and we had a great time posing for pictures and interacting with the students and teachers. Everywhere I looked I saw young, bright and beautiful Afrikan faces; plenty of Black folks here and it felt so good! It felt so good to be home!

* * * * * * *

Our host finally arrived and we departed to our new location; I prayed our accommodations would be better because anything worse would have resulted in the lynching of our host. However, we were pleasantly surprised. The hotel was clean, recently completed and on the Gulf of Guinea. It afforded us a clear view of the Elmina Castle Dungeons in the distance.

It's difficult to describe my feelings at that time. I was happy because I was in Afrika for the first time; but I missed being able to share this momentous occasion with my husband and I so wanted to share it with him. I was also overwhelmed and sad at the thought of my ancestors being housed in that ominous and forbeboding looking building called the Elmina Castle Dungeons.

I was equally sad because Margaret had never gotten the opportunity to make this journey with me. I spent some time in prayer and meditation. I couldn't stop the tears from flowing. Coming to Afrika for the first time is an emotional experience, for some of us it can be a real heart wrencher but regardless I was home...I was really home. I just couldn't believe it and I was determined to make the best of it.

After getting registered and settled in our room, which was small, clean and comfortable, the thing that struck me strange were the heavy, ugly drapes with Abraham Lincoln and George Washington on them. I would have expected a more Afrikan, cultural motif.

"It's a helluvah lot better than our previous accommodations," I told my room-mate "and it's on the ocean. And water is my weakness."

After everyone was settled in their rooms, we took off again, this time to the Cape Coast Castle Dungeons. As we rode, we passed by villages and saw houses made out of mud with thatch roofs. There were mounds of chopped wood neatly stacked together along side stacks of dried coconut shells (I was told that this was used for the cooking fire). Everything was so orderly. These were the Ewe people's village; they had migrated from the Volta Region, which is in the northern part of Ghana. Many were now living in the Central Region. They caught and smoked fish, which was sent back to the Volta Region for sale.

They had no electricity or running water or toilets: none of the conveniences we took for granted back in the United States. As I watched the villages as we rode past them, I couldn't help wondering how it must be for our people, living in this kind of environment and I wanted to visit with them.

On entering the town of Cape Coast we saw women carrying large pans and parcels upon their heads, a regular mode of transport it seemed. They carried everything on their heads from cords/sticks of wood and food, to a table setting for six, on their heads. They moved so gracefully with their backs straight, never stumbling or missing a beat. They reminded me of graceful Swans. I loved it. I wondered if I could do that!

Small stores called kiosks lined the streets and the stench from open sewers hung in the air in certain places. There was hustle and bustle everywhere. New York hustled and bustled but this was different, everyone was Black, some even looking like family. I was really feeling at home. The warmth and friendliness of the people, the happy laughing children, running up and down and playing and also begging. As we walked through town people called to us.

"My brothers, my sisters, you from where? African American, Jamaican, Rasta? Akwaaba. Akwaaba Obruni!"

I waved and laughed, experiencing a joy and excitement I'd never felt before.

"Obruni, Obruni," they called.

I soon found out that it meant, "Welcome white man or foreigner," and I was none too pleased by that. I had come this far for my own people to see me as a "white or a foreigner?" Something was terribly wrong with that picture and it saddened me. We really needed to get to know one another again.

As we strolled down the middle of the street, like we owned the place, a man rushed up to us and said, "You are all wanted at the palace. You must come now."

"A palace," someone responded, "what kind of palace and what for, why should we go with you?"

At this point Kohain, who had walked ahead of the group returned to see what was holding us up. Once again, the man repeated his request but this time with a little more specifics.

"My Chief, Nana Mbra, wants to see all of you at the palace, now!"

"All right," Kohain responded, "where is the palace?"

The man then turned and pointed to an old 2-story building, located in the center of town. Not knowing what to expect and having never met a King, we proceeded to follow the man. Upon arrival at the palace we were instructed to wait in the reception area until we were summoned to come upstairs.

While we were waiting several of the brothers in the group noticed these huge drums and in their excitement proceeded to try their hand.

Boom, boom, boom sounded the bass drums. Boom, boom, boom.

And the brothers were on a roll! The sounds of the drums echoed throughout the room, reverberating off the walls and into the street.

Boom, boom, boom, baboomboomboom, the drums sounded repeatedly.

Suddenly, someone from the palace came running up, very excited.

"Daabi, Daabi! Stop, stop!" the person demanded. "You cannot touch the drums of the Chief. They are talking drums and call the people to the palace. No one, other than those who are permitted, may touch them and only at the command of the Chief."

Everyone started apologizing at once. But in the midst of the confusion, we were told that the Chief was awaiting us. We all felt a little foolish and a little nervous for violated someone's space, coupled with the fact that we had never met an Afrikan Chief before and couldn't begin to imagine why he had sent for us. Quietly and a little apprehensive, we mounted the stairs to his quarters.

Upon entering, there sat a rather large, majestic but friendly looking man draped in kente cloth, surrounded by elders and other men in attendance.

"Please be seated," said the man who escorted us upstairs to the Chiefs quarters. "You are welcome."

We quietly took seats around the room and anxiously waited for someone to say something.

"Akwaaba," said the man standing next to the Chief, "Akwaaba." He then instructed us to rise, and greet the Chief, shaking hands with him and those in attendance. Once that was done we returned to our seats.

Once again, the man, standing next to the Chief, spoke. He was called the Okyeame, who translated and spoke for the Chief, who according to custom did not speak directly to the people.

"Akwaaba, my brothers and sisters, Akwaaba. Welcome to the palace of Nana Osabarimba Kodwo Mbra V, the Traditional Ruler of the Oguaa Traditional Area. My Chief has seen you walking down the street of Cape Coast and wanted to know who are these strangers. Who are these strange Afrikans that he has never met. And what is your mission?"

As Kohain was the leader of our group, he spoke, explaining that we were in Cape Coast for the enstoolment of our friend and that we were not aware of the custom, which required us to come and greet the Chief.

"This is our first time in Afrika," Kohain explained "and we did not intend to offend anyone. Now that we are aware you can be assured that it will never happen again."

The ice was broken and everyone laughed and relaxed as Kohain gave Nana Mbra a little background history on our group. Everyone even got an opportunity to say something. It was wonderful. We had really met a king.

He was so friendly and reminded us of an old family member, especially when it was explained how Nana loved to sit at his window and watch his people and activity that went on in the middle of his town. He reminded me of my grandmother who used to also sit at the window in her Harlem, NY apartment. She saw everything that went on in the block.

Nana said he was very happy to see us and invited us to return home to Afrika where we belonged. He called us his children and said that land was available for us if we wanted it. He said we were Afrika's children and this was our homeland. Needless to say we were overjoyed.

Shortly thereafter, happy and elated about this meeting, we assured Nana Mbra that he would be seeing us again and said our good-byes.

The following year, in 1988 Nana Mbra along with his entourage of Chiefs visited with us in the United States: Ben & I were Nana Mbra's official Limousine Service, personally driving he and his entourage around as they visited our homes, our schools and our community in Mt. Vernon and other parts of the country and inaugurated the first official observance of JUNETEENTH in a major city, in the State of New York. It was at this historic occasion that Nana Mbra once again, invited his sons and daughters in America to come home to Ghana; and later requested that this celebration be observed in Cape Coast in solidarity with those brothers and sisters in the Diaspora.

JUNETEENTH was celebrated for the first time in Ghana on 19th June 1992 in the Cape Coast Castle/Dungeons and dedicated to the late Nana Osabarimba Kodwo Mbra V, Omanhene.

Background Photo: *what remained of the South Bronx where IMAHKÜS grew up,* **Top photos:** *IMAHKÜS' parents, Alfred & Virginia Hines, IMAHKÜS (center), with Sister Traci & Brother Alfred in 1955. IMAHKÜS & Nana Okofo with Pres. Rawlings during Ghana's 1st Emancipation Day celebration in August 1998.*

49

Nana Osabarimba Kodwo Mbra V, Omanhen of the Oguaa Traditional Area, Cape Coast, Ghana – West Afrika, who reigned for more than 45 years; IMHOTEP Gary Byrd, his Queen Zanobia & Nana Gypie III; Nana Mbra and his entourage when they visited America in 1988. **From left to right:** Nana Ebow Tando V, Nana Kofi Ebu III, Nana Kofi Obiri-Egyir II, reception team members, Lawyer Aponsadadzi & Brother Eugene Redd **2nd Row:** reception team member, & the Umbrella Bearer, Nana Mbra, Bart Addison, & Nana Egyir Gyepi III. Nana Okofo's limousine used to transport Nana Mbra & entourage while in America. Bottom Row: Nana Mbra's funeral – **left to right:** Brother Ahveekhy, niece of Sister KIniya, Sister KIniya Awaal, IMAHKÜS, Nana Okofo, Sister Lucy Hagar-Grant, Kohain HaLevi, Rabbi, Sister Mabel HaLevi, and Sister Tamakeyah Frimpong.

CHAPTER FOUR

"THE RETURN –
THRU THE DOOR OF NO RETURN"

We continued to work our way slowly through the streets towards the Cape Coast Castle Dungeons, savoring the pleasure of being home and interacting with folks along the way. Even though we didn't understand the language, we were still enjoying ourselves, while making new friends.

Ahead of us loomed this enormous, foreboding structure. The sight caused me to tremble; I almost didn't want to go inside. The outer walls were chipped with a faded and moldy white exterior. The sea had eaten away some of the mortar. It was gray and dismal as we climbed the steep steps, following the sign leading to the reception area. When we entered the reception area of the Cape Coast Castle Dungeons a smallish man with a bright smiling face met us. His name was Mr. Owusu and he had been working there as a receptionist and sometimes Guide, for many years.

"Akwaaba," he said, "we are happy that you have come home. We don't get many African-American visitors, only white people, they come all the time," he continued.

We all laughed and told him that we were equally, if not more happy than he was, for we had worked, planned and saved for many years to make this journey. Most of us will be in debt to the Credit Card companies, VISA and Master Charge. "Plus some of us borrowed money from friends who we will have to re-pay when we get back to our homes in the United States," I told him. But for years many of us had spoken of Afrika, our "Mother" land and finally all our discussions and dreams had become a reality.

Debt-be-damned, nothing is greater than this, I said to no one in particular.

After introductions were made all around, Mr. Owusu, our Guide began the tour around the Castle. Entering the inner part of the castle overlooking a large courtyard, our guide gave us the background history of the Cape Coast Castle Dungeons. This was one of the more than sixty castle dungeons, forts, and lodges that had been constructed by European Traders with the permission of local rulers (the Chieftaincy) and stretched for 300 miles along the West Coast of Afrika to store kidnapped Afrikans, until a shipload of enslaved Afrikans could be assembled. Twenty-seven of those houses of misery were located in Ghana.

Various European oppressors had occupied the Cape Coast Castle Dungeons during the Trans-Atlantic European Slave Trade. It began with the Portuguese in the 1500's, followed by the Dutch, then the Swedes, the Danes and finally the English who occupied it in 1665. It remained under their control, serving as the seat of the British Administration in the Gold Coast (Cape Coast) until they relocated their racist regime to Christianborg Castle in Accra in 1877.

Our next stop was the Palaver (which means talking/discussing) Hall, the meeting place of slave merchants, which also served as the hall used in auctioning off our ancestors. The room was huge, the only light coming from the windows which lined both sides of the walls; one side facing the ocean, the other side overlooking the town; a bare room, echoing the voice of our Guide, a haunting echo, which reverberated off the walls, as the Guide explained how they bargained and sold us. When slave auctions were not going on, Palaver Hall was used as a meeting place for the Governor, Chiefs and other visitors.

We then moved on to the Governor's apartment and the church, which I felt like burning down!

But nothing could prepare me for what we would experience next. We descended the stairs into a large cobble-stoned courtyard and walked through large double wooden doors, which lead into a long, dark, damp tunnel. The stench of musty bodies, fear and death hung in the air. There was no noise except the thunderous crashing of the waves against the outer walls and the roaring sound of the water. Deeper we walked, into large, dark rooms which had served as a warehouse for enslaved Afrikan people awaiting shipment to the America's and Caribbean.

This was the Men's Dungeon. As we stood in that large cavernous room the air was still, the little ventilation that was available came from small openings near the 20-foot high ceilings. Our ancestors had been kept underground, chained to the walls and each other, making escape impossible. The mood of the group was hushed, as several people started crying. We were standing in hell-holes of the most horrific conditions imaginable. There were no words to express the suffering that must have gone on in these dungeons.

I became caught up, thrown back in time. I was suddenly one of the many who were shackled, beaten and starved. But I was one of the fortunate souls to have survived the forced exodus from their homelands to be sold, branded and thrown into those hellholes, meant to hold 600 people but which held more than 1,000 enslaved Afrikans at one time. The men separated from the women, as they awaited shipment to the Americas. According to our Guide, the chalk marks on the walls of the Men's Dungeon indicated the level of the floor prior to the excavation of the floor, which had built up over years of slavery with feces, bones, filth, etc.

As the Guide continued to describe the horrors of these pits of hell I began to shake violently; I needed to get out of there. I was being smothered. I turned and ran up the steep incline of the tunnel, to the castle courtyard, the winds from the sea whipping my face, bringing me back to the present. I couldn't believe what I had just experienced. How could anyone be so cruel and inhuman?

Gradually, the others began emerging from the dungeon, subdued looks on their faces; many tear-stained...no one was talking. Following the Guide we proceeded across the massive courtyard and down another passage way to the Women's Dungeon, a smaller version of the Men's Dungeon but not so deep underground, it had held over 300 women at any given time. As we entered that dark, musty, damp room, the sound of the crashing waves was like muffled, rolling thunder. A dimly lit, uncovered light bulb hung from the ceiling on a thin, frayed wire. After standing silently for a time in this tomb, the Guide began to lead the group out. I was the last person left in the room when the Guide turned and said he was continuing the tour.

"Please," I said, "I'm not ready to leave, just turn off the light for me and I will join the group shortly."

As the group walked silently away, the tears would not stop flowing. I dropped to my knees, trembling and crying even harder. With the light off, the only light in that dungeon came through one small window near the very high ceiling, reflecting down as though it were a muted spotlight. Darkness hung in every corner. As I rocked back and forth on the dirt floor, I could hear weeping and wailing...anguished screams coming from the distance. Suddenly the room was packed with women...some naked, some with babies, some sick and lying in the dirt, while others stood against the walls around the dungeon's walls, terror filled their faces.

"My God, what had we done to wind up here, crammed together like animals?"

Pain and suffering racked their bodies, a look of hopelessness and despair on their faces...but with a strong will to survive.

"Oh God, what have we done to deserve this kind of treatment?"

Cold terror gripped my body. Tears blinded me and the screams wouldn't stop. As I sat there violently weeping I began to feel a sense of warmth, many hands were touching my body, caressing me, soothing me as a calmness began to come over me. I began to feel almost safe as voices whispered in my ears assuring me that everything was all right.

"Don't cry," they said, "You've come home. You've returned to your homeland, to re-open the Door of No Return."

Gradually the voices and the women faded into the darkness; it was then that I realized that some of the screams I'd heard were my own. The eerie light beaming down from the window was growing dimmer as day began fading into night. As I got up from the dungeon floor I knew that I would never be the same again!

After years of wandering and searching, I had finally found home. And one day, I wouldn't be leaving again.

My ancestors were truly a strong, courageous and determined people to have survived that holocaust but they had warmly received me.

As I slowly made my way back to the group, I reflected on my experience in the dungeons.

There was no question...I would be returning: next time with Ben.

As I drew near the group, it was startling; the expressions on everyone's face was the same...sorrowful...and angry. We would never forget this day.

When we were leaving the castle, the receptionist asked us to sign the Visitors Book, which we sadly but gratefully did, for we had just made history in returning home to the land of our ancestors – the first in our family to return.

I wrote in the book on August 30, 1987.

"The story is yet to be told! I praise God for returning me to the land of my ancestors. There is much work to be done. The spirit of the ancestors moves within these walls and touches my soul. Praise God!"

After our visit to the Cape Coast Castle Dungeons most of us were wiped out so we returned to our hotel to chill out for a while.

I was too keyed-up to sleep but didn't feel like talking so I found a quiet place on the wall outside my room. As I sat there, with the misty spray from the ocean wetting my face, I couldn't help thinking how angry these waters of the Atlantic Ocean were, they literally roared and thundered: the waves looking like billowing clouds or an avalanche of snow as the waters crashed against the shores of the route of the Trans-Atlantic Arab European Slave Trade.

Angry...Crying...Screaming...Heart Wrenching Anger: the Gulf of Guinea, the Gold Coast.

"We are Africans

not because we are born in Africa,

but because Africa is born in us.

Look around you and behold us in one greatness.

Greatness is an African possibility,

you can make it yours".

Chester Higgins, Jr.:
Feeling the spirit
Bantam Books 1994

CHAPTER FIVE

THERE'S NO PLACE LIKE HOME

Shortly after our arrival at the hotel we were met with another problem. The hotel was demanding payment for the rooms or eviction.

Now what? I reasoned to myself. But what kind of foolishness was this?

Many of the group had already paid, their accommodations were included in the package and they were not about to pay again. Naturally, everyone was asking for our host, who somehow managed not to be around when we were having troubles. He especially avoided those people who had given him their money in the United States. After much ado, the Manager finally agreed to hold off evicting us until we caught up with our host.

Several of us went into town searching for him and found him at his palace in Cape Coast. But we were told that we couldn't see him because he was in seclusion as was the custom for someone who was about to become a Chief. We had been with him when he was snatched by a group of people in the town. When a person is selected to become a Chief (Nana), the group or company that he/she belongs to grabs the prospective Nana as they walk through the streets of the town and carries him/her shoulder high through the town, laughing and shouting. The person then goes into seclusion for a designated period of time. The only person they can see is a selected and limited number of people. Under normal circumstances that would have been fine but we were all facing eviction and our host was the only one that could straighten out this mess that he had gotten us into.

"Sorry," said a family member, "he will be out in a few days."

"Madam, we don't have a few days," I said patiently, adding my two cents worth.

"Either he comes out of there or we're going to go in and get him," a brother shouted angrily.

"We're sick of this crap," another brother interjected heatedly.

The air was charged, voices raised, people shouting in Fante (the local language) and English.

"You people do not understand our customs," they said.

"The Chief is in seclusion and cannot be disturbed by outsiders. You must 'wait small,' he will come, etc., etc., etc.,"

"But y'all don't understand either," someone from our group interjected. "The people at the hotel want to put us out, unless they get their money."

It was looking like we were going to have a real, old fashion, Harlem, street showdown.

"All we want is for someone in the family or in authority to go to the hotel and square things with the hotel Manager," Kohain interjected.

Once again voices began to rise. Suddenly the door opened to the room where our host was secluded and he came forward. The noise, which had died down began to raise again...everyone talking at the same time. Two brothers in the group were threatening our host.

"Do something or else, man."

Finally a family representative was dispatched to accompany us to the hotel to meet with the manager and to insure payment of the hotel bills. Finally some semblance of order was restored now that the problem was satisfactorily resolved.

That evening during dinner we laughed and joked about the events of the day. It reminded me of some argument or fight that you might have with your brother or sister, when you returned home from college or the army, after being away for a time. When all was said and done you ended up laughing about it. This was some vacation!

"Well, let's pray that the rest of the trip will be without problems," I said to the group.

I wondered if other people have the same kind of problems when they visited Afrika? We seemed to be going from one problem to another. But in spite of everything, everyone or at least most of us were still in a happy frame of mind, determined not to let anything or anyone get in the way of our blessing.

That night, before we retired we had a unity circle outside of our rooms over looking the Gulf of Guinea. The mood of the group was pensive as we held hands, offering prayers of thanksgiving and praise to God and our ancestors for putting us in this place, at this time in our lives. A rolling fog suddenly appeared out of nowhere, encircling us. It was the strangest thing. It seemed to float all around and in between the group, embracing us, as though offering a warm and secure blanket and welcoming us home. I sang a song that I had written a few years ago, entitled, "Thank You Lord for Giving Me This Day."

It seemed appropriate for the occasion and everyone was moved by it. When the circle broke up some of us retired for the night while others just hung around, too charged up to sleep. This was a never-ending dream come true for me and I didn't want to waste a moment lying around in bed.

I awoke early the next morning feeling refreshed. The sound of the waters was soothing. I jumped out of bed and went outside quietly so as not to awaken my roommate. Kohain stood gazing into the waters as I walked up. After greeting him, we stood upon the rocks in front of Oyster Bay, reasoning and watching the Elmina Castle Dungeons in the distance. How utterly unbelievable that we are here in Africa! After a time, Kohain turned his back to the ocean and prepared to return to his room; just then a huge wave rose up out of the waters and as he dashed forward to avoid getting wet, the water caught the hem of his garment as though kissing him lightly, or baptizing him.

"Now, that was close," he said.

Welcome home." I responded laughingly. "Welcome home".

Early mornings before most of the group was awake, I'd walk the road outside of the Oyster Bay Hotel, where we were staying, passing small villages, alive with activities at that early hour. The smell of burning wood and smoking fish filled the air and the sounds of people sweeping. Women and children passed me on the road carrying firewood on their heads, carrying large buckets and pans of water. People looked at me strangely, some smiling and speaking in their native tongue and I didn't have a clue what they were saying. I just know that it sounded good and I wasn't afraid. Children ran up to me laughing, not getting too close, and kind of checking me out. When I would speak to them (all I could say was good morning and thank you), they would laugh harder and run away. Finally a little girl approached me and in broken English asked,

"What is your name?"

"Vienna," I replied.

"Where from you?" she continued.

"I come from the United States." I answered.

"You be my friend?" she asked sweetly.

"I would be happy to be your friend," I responded joyfully. "And what is your name?"

Her name was Gifty and she lived in a small village called Nyiah commonly known as the women's village, nearby the hotel. It was so named because most of the village was comprised of women, the young men were gone, either in search of employment long distances away, (there was no work locally for them) or they just went away and never came back. The only men in the village were elders or the very young males so the women were holding things together.

Gifty offered me her hand and invited me to come to her house and meet her family. As we walked off the road into her compound, it was like being in another world. High walls made of coconut tree boughs surrounded the place. The earth had been cleanly swept, children were playing and preparing themselves for school...washing themselves in small buckets of water. Goats and chicken roamed freely about, occasionally a dog barked. The houses were mud huts covered with thatch roofs, situated behind high, braided coconut bough fences, which surrounded individual family compounds. In Gifty's compound there were at least eight houses, a communal kitchen and a large area where they smoked fish. There was also a large mud oven for baking bread.

As we approached a rather large house Gifty's mother met us.

"Akwaaba," she said and called to a child to bring me a chair.

Once I was seated they offered me water, as is the custom. Consider ... That done, they inquired about my mission.

"What mission?" I asked. "I just came in to say hello."

Everyone laughed. According to the custom they asked your mission and if anyone was in pursuit of you. If you responded "yes" then they would hide you.

"That's good to know for the future," I said, "But no one is chasing me today," I laughed.

I couldn't understand what was being said but as Gifty interpreted how she met me and brought me home, they kept saying, "Oh fine, oh fine, oh fine, you are welcome."

It was then that another women appeared. Gifty introduced us. She said her name was Margaret and she also wanted to be my friend. Suddenly, I froze.

"Margaret?" I said in disbelief. "Is your name really Margaret?"

"Yes," came the reply. My name is Margaret Eshon. I am Ewe. My people come from the Volta Region," she continued.

I was in shock. I couldn't believe I was hearing correctly. What kind of sign was this? Here I was over 7000 miles from the Bronx, talking with Margaret again. It was the spirit of the ancestors again manifesting themselves to me, confirming that this was the place that I was supposed to be. I started to cry — not tears of sadness but tears of joy and thankfulness. When I told them the story of my friend Margaret who had died in the United States, they understood and said,

"You no lose her. You find her at home waiting you. Her spirit is here in our village. She is your new Ewe sister, Margaret."

I was overjoyed and could not wait to get back to the group to tell them what had happened. I left the village promising to return again and to bring some of my friends with me the next time. Holding hands, Gifty walked with me back to the hotel. I was very happy: I had found my new family.

I had been gone for quite a while and when I returned breakfast was being served. I excitedly told them about my little adventure and solicited Sister Josie, a member of our group, to accompany me to the village the next morning. She readily agreed.

After breakfast, the group prepared to go to Accra for sightseeing and shopping. When we initially arrived in Ghana, we had not stopped in Accra but came directly to Cape Coast. So as yet we had not visited the capital. Around nine o'clock we got on the road.

Now we could see the countryside, for we had arrived under the cover of darkness and nothing was visible to us. Everyone was excited, laughing and talking at the same time. And just generally cracking up about our previous days adventures, as every day managed to be another adventure for us.

As we sped along the road to Accra we saw large mounds of red dirt piled high. We were told that they were anthills and could not be easily knocked over by hand. We passed large tracks of mountainous land that glittered like diamonds. Almost simultaneously, people started yelling at the driver,

"Stop the bus, stop the bus," we shouted at the driver, "Stop! We want to get down."

We had heard that there were plenty of gold and diamonds in Ghana and here it was right in front of us, or so we thought. Like little children we scrambled off the bus, running to pick up the glittering pieces of rock, trying to dig them from the walls. It wasn't hard like I knew diamonds to be and flaked up in our hands. But we soon found out that it was not gold or diamonds but a mineral deposit called Mica, which is used for making stainless steel, glass and mirrors. Boy, had we been fooled. Laughing, we got back on the bus and continued our journey.

Two and half-hours later we were in Accra, the capital and largest city in Ghana. Accra, though it is the city, has many tree-lined streets and wooded residential areas. It was hard to believe at first that this city boasted of more than one and a half million people: there were no skyscrapers, the rush hour traffic was mild in comparison to New York City and the pollution level seemed to be very low, except when you got too near some of those buses and trucks belching out black smoke. I didn't think "Emission Control" laws existed here. But although there was hustle and bustle, there was also a relaxed, easy-going atmosphere once you got out of the commercial district.

Accra is surrounded on three sides by hills and is only 64 feet above sea level, which accounts for the frequent floods during the rainy season, which occurs from June through September. The different sections of the city are linked together by four major arterial roads of several kilometers, which open into big crossroads known as circles...and Accra is full of circles! Thank God for our friend and Tour Guide Sister Tamakeyah, who knew her way around. She very coolly moved us from place to place.

The first thing we did was to change our American dollars into Cedis. Wow, did we get a lot of money for our dollars. Three Hundred Sixty Cedis to the Dollar, so for one hundred bucks, I got back Three hundred and Sixty Thousand Cedis. I felt rich! Armed with the local currency we were ready to buy out Accra.

Our first stop was to the famous Makola Market that is spread out over several city blocks. There were plenty of people everywhere. Anything you wanted to buy was there. Hair care products, hardware, food, you name it. Beautiful, bright, multi-colored cloth in yellows, oranges, purples, and greens, a rainbow of Technicolor cotton and brocade fabrics lined the walls of the numerous stalls and activity was brisk. Very politely we began trying to make our way through the densely crowded market.

"Excuse me please, excuse me please," I said.

But that got me nothing but stared at, laughed at, fussed with and/or shoved aside. I soon found out that the best way to get along was to join in with the pushing and shoving to make your way through the masses of people, to find what you wanted. Everywhere we stopped people bartered and bargained: there was no set price for anything. Any price paid was based on the outcome of the agreement between you and the seller. They loved it if you paid whatever price they demanded for the people looked at us as rich foreigners. The sooner you understood the concept of bartering, the better you could do and I did not do too badly, once I got the hang of things. Hard bartering was the name of the game. They even wanted to trade our T-shirts and other items that we had. Coming away slightly exhausted but loaded down with beautiful materials we left the market. That had been fun!

Next we visited the Art Centre on High Street, where we met many other traders, trading in masks, dolls, drums, carvings, cane furniture, baskets, kente cloth, etc. We were having a ball. After purchasing and trading for some of the things I wanted, I returned to the bus worn out. As I sat there chillin' out, some of the brothers returned to the bus, loaded down with everything from masks to marbles and several of them weren't wearing shoes.

"Hey Zar, what happened to your shoes?" I inquired.

"Sister, I traded them. We had big fun," he said.

He and the brothers were clowning, strutting up and down, showing off their purchases and laughing like little boys.

"Man, oh man, we got some good deals. I didn't know we could do it so good." Zar laughed.

"Yeah," another brother cut in. "We even traded our sneakers for drums and carvings. But we had help from an angel."

This was the best shopping spree that any of us had ever been on. Sister Tamaykeyah, our angel, also emerged from the market looking worn and tired, for the group had pulled her in a million different directions, trying to get her to help them shop and barter. She was great!

Our tour then took us to the W.E.B. DuBois Center, the National Museum and other places of interest, and people kept welcoming us home. This was wonderful: we were really home. Home! Boy did that sound good. Home, where people looked like you. Home, with no white people everywhere! No high rise buildings, no untamed jungles and Tarzan swinging through the trees but home in "Mother" Afrika – this was the place where it had begun for us over 500 years ago.

As I walked through the streets of Accra I thought how very similar Accra was to some of the cities in the United States. But here when you drove for two minutes, you found yourself surrounded by lush trees and bushes and in its midst, beautiful homes situated behind high stone walls, with beautiful flowers growing everywhere. As we rode along we saw smaller dwellings, run down shacks, small stores set up along the roadways, people selling things in the streets. But for me it did not matter, I had come home to my ancestral homeland.

I couldn't wait to get back to New York to tell my husband what I had experienced. Now I was even sorrier that he and I had not come together. I guess Nasi, one of the brothers who was in our group was sick and tired of hearing me talk about my husband. But he didn't seem to mind though for our conversations centered on our respective mates and how much we wanted them to like Ghana because we wanted to live here one day.

After lunch we continued our tour of Accra and its surrounding area before we finally returned to Cape Coast...tired but happy. We had a lot less money in our pockets, but we were rich nonetheless and satisfied beyond our expectations.

The following day the group left for Kumasi but I decided to remain behind. I was still tired from the day before and besides, I could visit Kumasi another time, for I was definitely coming back. Sister Josie, another sister who was traveling with the group had also remained behind. She was a Registered Nurse in New York and was traveling with her husband. This was also their first time in Afrika. We had hit it off from the beginning of the trip. I invited her to accompany me to the village. So while the others were away, we had a great time. We spent the next couple of days visiting with my friend Margaret and her family, at their village. We spent the morning bathing some of the children, eating the local food and enjoying life in the village.

One day there was drumming and dancing, as members of the village were preparing for a special program. We got all caught up in the festive mood of the place and sisters pulled us into the circle to join in the merry-making. And "make merry" we did, until we returned to our hotel.

When the group returned from their trip to Kumasi they had more adventure stories to tell and I was even happier that I had followed my first mind and remained behind. As they described the almost eight hour ride over some of the worst road you could imagine, I couldn't help laughing. They had traveled on roads that made New York City "pot holes" seem like a skating on ice. In addition, they had been covered from head to toe with red dirt by the time they reached their destination and their bodies were sore and bruised from being bounced and thrown around in the bus, etc., etc., etc. They had fun, but boy had they suffered. However, they were still laughing.

The following day we went to Cape Coast to visit our host who was being enstooled as a chief. The atmosphere in town was festive as the people were preparing for the "Fetu Afayhe Festival" the (festival of the harvest), which occurs on the 1st Saturday in September. The festival is the occasion for pouring libation and sprinkling yam to our ancestors and the seventy-seven gods of Oguaa (Cape Coast) for the part they played in bringing us abundant yield from both land and sea, and for warding off any misfortune that would have befallen the Oguaa State. It is also a time for family re-unions, settlement of feuds and merry-making in general. Unfortunately, we would not be there to participate in it because our time was almost up and the festival would begin the day we were scheduled to leave.

As we were strolling through town we were approached by a group of brothers, who surrounded us. Suddenly they snatched Zar Zebulon, one of the brothers in our group. He began to struggle with them, trying to get away but they just laughed. We were all taken by surprise.

Was this Ghana's idea of a mugging?

I really didn't have a clue as to what was going on. Zar being a very large and robust brother, the people had a rough time lifting him up onto their shoulders and to make "bad matters worst" he was fiercely struggling. After all he had been caught by surprise and anyone's first instinct is to fight like hell. We soon found out from some of the town's people that no one wanted to harm him. They were taking him to their area (a part of town where they kept their Asafo Shrine) and they expected a struggle. Mildly relieved we began to laugh watching these folks trying to get that big brother on their shoulders. As they carried him along, re-enforcements were called in to assist for he was a big, robust man. We were afraid at one point that they would drop him, but they managed, even though it was not an easy task.

We were taking pictures and having a good time when suddenly another member of our group was snatched and carried away in a different direction. I was beginning to feel a little uncomfortable again. I went looking for Kohain and Tamakeyah for I truly did not understand what was going on. When I finally found them, they explained that the people who had been snatched were being made "Asafo" chiefs of various companies and were being taken away to their respective company's location, in various areas of the town.

There are seven "Asafo" Companies in Cape Coast. In the present day festival, all seven of the Asafo Companies of the Oguaa Traditional Area turn out together to escort the Omanhen (King), his Chiefs, Divisional Chiefs, Sub-Divisional Chiefs, the Supi and Asafohenfo of the various Asafo Companies, as they parade through the streets during the Afahye Festival.

Asafo Company No. 1 is "Omansafe" and their members wear red trimmed in black.

No. 2 Asafo Company is called "Anafo" and is the advance guard, wearing yellow and blue costumes.

No 3. Asafo Company is called Intsin, the Omanhen's main bodyguards, dressed in dark green.

Next in order is Asafo Company No. 4, known as "Nkyidom" the rear guardian. They wear bright yellow and their emblem is the sounding of the bugle.

No. 5 Company is called "Nyimfafo" the right flank fighters and they wear light green with the major emblem being two canons.

Asafo Company No. 6 is called "Akrampafo," the volunteer company. They use the national flag and drum as their emblem.

History has it that in the colonial days, mulattos and the elite's of society formed this company hence their being reminiscent of the colonial governors. They are tasked with the duty to make peace between any of the feuding Company Captains (Asafohenfo) and they are dressed in white uniforms.

The last Company No. 7 is called "Benkum," the army of the left flank. They are dressed in wine colored attire, with miniature Whales as their emblem.

They come last in the procession of Asafo companies, preceding the Omanhen and his retinue. According to tradition every "Asafo" Company in modern military parlance may be construed as militia in defense of the state. So during the Afahye preparations preceding the actual festival, members from the various companies go out in search of people to swell their ranks. They do this by snatching un-suspecting persons and carrying them away. At which time they have a special ceremony or initiation for the new "recruits."

They said that we had nothing to worry about. It seemed harmless enough but I still was not feeling too comfortable, in spite of Kohain and Sister Tamakeyah's explanation.

Sister Josie and I were walking together when she got snatched. Not wanting to leave her alone I followed her and her company. She belonged to the same company as Zar, Company No. 5. People were singing and jumping around.

Men were beating drums, cowbells and blowing horns and the people danced in the streets and chanted,

"Ah Woo, Ah Woo!" (Which means, "This is yours").

They chanted...as they waved their Lappa and other pieces of cloth at the person who had been snatched.

"Ah Woo, Ah Woo!"

This chant was said to drive any evil spirits away from the person who was being made a chief and declaring to everyone that this person now belongs to their Company/tribe.

"Ah Woo, Ah Woo," I shouted and started waving my cloth also.

When I saw Kohain again, he told me four members of our group (Nasi, Sister Josie, Mr. Redd and Zar Zebulon) had all been snatched. Those of us who remained were to split up so that each person snatched would have representation from our group. I followed Nasi and his Company because no one was with him. I joined in the festivities, following the crowd to where they were taking him and making certain that he knew that I was there. When we arrived at the area there was fierce drumming and dancing (a favorite Afrikan proverb says "there is no dancing without drumming") and dance we did. Nasi was set upon a stool three times, given a sword and draped in the Company's colors. Libation was poured and the Linguist for the Company spoke about how happy they were that their big brother from the United States had returned to them and was once more a part of the family.

A very strong drink made from Palm Tree juice or sugar cane juice (the local hooch) was passed around and everyone was expected to take a drink. When the drink was passed to me, I inadvertently took more than I should have; the liquid burned my throat, making me choke and cough fiercely, my eyes ran water and I got hot and cold chills. Mad Dog 20/20 had lost its place in rank: this stuff was rough.

"What is this stuff?" I asked the person standing next to me.

"Akpeteshie," someone responded, "or some say, Kill Me Quick."

Well, they did not have to worry about me drinking that Fire Water again. With my stomach still burning, I left Brother Nasi and went to find some of the others to let them know where we finally wound up.

As I walked along the street, a man approached me and said that they were going to snatch me next. I freaked out.

"Don't touch me," I screamed, "Just leave me alone. I don't wanna be no Chief!"

But the man persisted. I shouted at him again to leave me alone, pulling on my Ghetto street attitude to show that I meant business, however, he just laughed. I suddenly turned and ran like the devil himself was after me.

Where was everyone? Things were getting out of control. *Are these people crazy,* I thought?

I had no idea what was expected of a chief, nor why they wanted me. There were so many questions that I needed answered and with so little information and understanding of the custom, culture and tradition, I wasn't having any of it, this time.

I finally ran into Kohain and some of the other group members who were making the rounds to the other companies and picking up the new chiefs or Nana as they were now to be referred. It had been an exciting time but I was a nervous wreck and I was ready to return to the hotel. In fact, everyone was ready.

On the way back to the hotel, I stopped at the seamstress to pick up my garments that I was having made. Our time was growing short and it would soon be time to return to the United States. Upon returning to the hotel everyone retired to their rooms to rest and refresh themselves before dinner. I rested for a short time but was too excited to lie down for long. I went out to the restaurant and found that I was not alone. People were just too excited to sleep. As we ordered our food and waited for the meal, we talked about all the things we had done and the purchases we had made. After dinner we would display all our things on the tables and take pictures. It took forever for the food to come but it was well worth waiting for, it was the best Cassava fish I had ever tasted.

After dinner I went back to my room to try on my new clothes to make sure that they fit and to put on a little fashion show for the group. The first garment I tried on was a two-piece suit. I couldn't believe it, but one sleeve was much longer than the other was: in fact one sleeve was at my elbow and the other at my wrist. The skirt was hitched up in the front and down in the back and my beautiful green material had been sewn with brown and white thread, with a black zipper.

As I walked around the restaurant, with my arms extended to accentuate the sleeves, while I tugged at my skirt, the group started laughing. I then tried on the next outfit, which was miles too big for me and hung off my shoulders like clothes on a clothes rack. I slowly strolled around – pulling up my skirt that was falling off and trying to keep the dress up on my shoulders, while I described my "space" dress.

By now they were in stitches, laughing but there was also surprise and disbelief. They didn't seem to know whether to laugh or be serious.

As I strolled around the restaurant, clowning and describing my garment, I narrated.

"Ladies and Gents, this little 2 piece number will keep you almost naked. If you're not careful your boobs will be all over the place, if you have any!" Folks were in tears!

"Don't go away, I told them, there is more to come."

Needless to say I was not feeling too pleased about this. My last outfit was even worse. I was barely able to climb the stairs to the restaurant. Everyone was laughing at my efforts.

"Brothers and Sisters, this little three-piece number is so tight that it prevents you from walking properly, so you jump up the stairs like a frog or you can waddle like a duck or an Afrikan 'Geisha Girl.' Notice the flap like wings at the shoulders that make me look like the 'Flying Nun."

By this time the group was hollering and holding their stomachs laughing, while tears ran down their faces. But then the laughter stopped and a more serious note came over the group for some of them had given their material to the same seamstress. When I had picked up my things, she told the others that she had not gotten around to their things yet but would definitely have them ready before our departure date. Those brothers now wanted their material back from her and I certainly wanted my money back for she had ruined my material and I couldn't use any of the things she had made for me.

When I gave her my fabric, I asked her, "Can you sew? Are you a good seamstress?"

"Yes," she had replied confidently.

Furious, I was ready to go back to town. I didn't want to hear anything and the brothers were in agreement.

"If we don't go tonight," Brother Rueben said, "tomorrow might be too late to save our material."

It was about 11 o'clock that night, when we called our driver to take us to Cape Coast. When we arrived at the women's house, everything was dark and quiet. The door was closed but not locked, a large stone held the door to the courtyard closed. I knocked several times but getting no response, we moved the stone and proceeded upstairs to her room. Knocking lightly on her door I woke her up. I tried explaining the situation to her and demanded that she return my money. But getting my point across was difficult because of our language differences. Another woman, her sister, who spoke English a little better, came forward to interpret.

"She doesn't have the money anymore," she said, "but she will fix the clothes for you and return them in a few days."

"This is unacceptable," I told her, "and we will leave in two days!"

"I'm sorry, but she cannot do better," the Auntie explained.

"She's sorry!" I shouted, "she's sorry, but what am I suppose to do."

By now I was furious and frustrated. I couldn't get my money back, my clothes were in a mess, I couldn't speak the language and the people just smiled at my dilemma as I ranted and raved. Realizing that I was not getting anywhere, I demanded, "Please, just return the material that she is holding for the other members of the group."

With tears in my eyes I collected all the material, and stormed out of the house to the waiting van.

"Did you get our material? Did she cut our material yet?"

The brothers wanted to know when I got back on the bus.

"You're the fortunate ones in this drama." I assured them. "All of your material is in tact."

Feeling better, with their material in their hands, they thanked me and told me not to worry.

"Hey Sister Vienna, something will be worked out," they assured me.

Easy for them to say, I thought to myself, they've got their material safely in their hands. They'd be singing a different tune, if the shoe was on the other foot.

I wasn't feeling too optimistic, but what could I do at this time? It was after midnight when we returned to our hotel. This was one night that I wanted to go to bed, so that I could cry and sulk in private.

The following morning when Sister Tamakeyah came to the hotel, we related our latest adventure story to her: the "midnight ride" of some disgruntled Afrikans. I was in a better mood this morning and could laugh about the night before.

"Not to worry, Sister Vienna," Sister Tamaykeyah said, "I will take you to my friend, Sister Lucy and maybe she can do something with your clothes."

Sister Lucy lived in Cape Coast and was a Seamstress and Designer, who ran a small sewing school. She had about fifteen (15) young women in attendance.

I immediately liked her. She took my measurements and after looking at my ruined garments, told me that she would do the best that she could do and "not to worry." There were those words again, "not to worry." Every time we ran into difficulty, someone said, "not to worry." I was beginning to wonder and "worry" a little too, but I left her my garments. It couldn't get any worse.

"Sister Lucy, if you can fix this mess, I'll be your customer for life," I said.

I did a few last minute things around town and enjoyed my last day in Cape Coast. I was going to miss being in Ghana.

The night before our departure, we went to Sister Lucy for our things as she had also made garments for the other folks in the group. When she showed me my garments, I couldn't believe they were the same clothes. The girl was a magician, a miracle worker with a sewing machine! My garments were fabulous. She had made me a beautiful two-piece suit; gone were the "Flying Nun" shoulders, replaced by a short sleeved, double-breasted jacket. The suit that was miles too big for me was made into a unique three-piece Walking Suit with an "A" line skirt and head wrap. Everything else was fabulous also. I hugged and kissed Sister Lucy, dancing around. I was happy and extremely grateful.

Until this day, Sister Lucy still makes my clothes, making me one of the best-dressed women around. In fact, even today people try to buy my clothes off my back. The girl is *that* good!

The following morning we departed for Kotoka International Airport in Accra. Our time in Ghana had come to a close, for now. But I was definitely coming back. I couldn't wait to get home and tell Ben about our trip. I was so happy. I had really come home.

However, our adventure was not yet over. We had plenty of stuff to check in at the airport and we had another problem. Folks had bought so much stuff that we were overweight. And that meant some folks had to pay extra. Not everyone in the group had shopped to that point though. But in order that some folks did not have to pay too heavily, everything was checked in together and still we had to pay. Not as much, but something. The problem though was that those with the most goods did not have money to pay for overweight. Everyone put in something, with the understanding that they would be paid back when we got back to the United States.

It was finally time to board the plane. We sadly said good-by to Sister Tamakeyah, our friend and angel warrior, promising that we would be returning.

When we landed in Nigeria to make our connection to New York we had a rather long layover. After waiting for more than three hours, we were told that the plane was having engine trouble and would not be leaving until the following morning. The airline authorities said they would put us up for the night and allow us to call our families in New York when we arrived at the hotel. A bus was sent to convey us to the hotel. It was dark and you couldn't see much of the landscape but there were still plenty of people in the streets and plenty of cars. At that hour you would think that the streets would be deserted but not so in Lagos, Nigeria. About 30 minutes later we pulled up in front of this tall gate.

"Where are we and what kind of place is this," I inquired. "And where is the hotel?"

"This is the place," answered the driver as he drove into a dimly lit courtyard.

By now folks were grumbling and complaining. The building was also dimly lit with red and green light at the entrance. It did not look "kosher" to me. When we got inside we found that there was no telephone and no way to get to one. The driver of the bus was gone and all of our fussing and complaining got us nothing but stared at. No one seemed to give a damn about this group of irate Afrikan-Americans.

Things were so eerie and the people were not too friendly. Realizing that we would get nothing but more frustrated, we followed the receptionist into the dining room, where they were going to serve us a meal. There was no menu. To add insult to injury the food was terrible. We were given a meal of tough, cold chicken, sour rice, stale bread and warm soda. We ate what we could before being shown to our rooms.

My room was small with a blue light and the bed was hard as a rock and there was no sheet or blanket to cover up with. Since I was traveling alone, I had a room to myself. I didn't sleep much the rest of the night and I never took off my clothes.

At five o'clock in the morning we took off again for the airport. At that early hour the streets continued to be jammed with people, animals and cars.

Our folks back home were worried sick by this time for they had been waiting at the airport and had received no word of our delay. Tired and weary we finally departed for home. Eight hours and one day later we arrived at John F. Kennedy International Airport. It was good to be back in New York.

Ben met me at the airport. He sure looked good to me. It had been a long and exciting trip and I couldn't wait to share it with him.

"You look good – and Black!" He laughed, "Did you have a good time?" he wanted to know.

"Well honey, let's just say that I know where I want to spend the rest of my life," I answered, "and I hope you will too. You have to go there, Ben. It is the most wonderful place I've ever been to."

"You say that about every place you've ever visited," he continued, grinning at me.

"But this is different, this is our homeland and when you visit Ghana, you will see what I mean. You'll love it. I hope as much as I do for I want to one day live there."

You could feel the excitement in the air. I must have talked a mile a minute on the drive home from the airport. And some of my fever was rubbing off on Ben.

The following Saturday, we visited the Bereshith Cultural Center to attend their worship services. After the service, the people who had been on the trip and some other friends got together at the Center to share pictures and talk about our trip.

Ben hit it right off with the brothers in the group. And Bereshith would play a prominent role in our lives. Thereafter, we joined the organization and became active members of this Hebrew Israelite community. The vibes were so positive and everyone seemed so close.

And with all the talk about our trip and those wonderful pictures we had taken, Ben really caught the fever. In December he was on his way to Ghana, alone. He had originally planned to visit Ghana with a couple of buddies but at the last minute they all backed out.

"Oh honey, don't worry about them. You just go. We met some people that had invited us to return and they would be glad to meet you at the airport and take you around," I told him.

So Ben proceeded with his plans and took off for Ghana, alone, where he also celebrated his 51st birthday on 18 December 1987.

SANKOFA

Go back and take it.

This symbol speaks to the importance of going back to the past to bring forward useful tools and values necessary in the present; it teaches us to cherish our very valuable culture.

CHAPTER SIX

CLEAVIN' AND LEAVIN'

Ben and I made several trips to Ghana in the next few years with other members of the Bereshith Hebrew Israelite community.

On one of our trips, we traveled to The Gambia, where we spent four great days. The entire trip was not so great for me because I came down with sun poisoning after falling asleep on the beach, with the hot sun baking my brains.

While Ben and the group moved around I hung out at the hotel close to my bed and the toilet. But before I poisoned myself I did see and experience the people, who were great and culturally conscious: they wore their national dress and sisters in long, flowing Bubu's seemed to float down the road. Even at the river, washing their clothes, they were culturally attired - very few people wore western styled clothes and T shirts. I loved it. This was a very sharp contrast from Ghana. And Ben loved it too. He really loved The Gambia.

"I could live here," he said wistfully.

But we had already decided that Ghana was the place, or it had been decided for us. After four days we headed back to Ghana via Ghana Airways, the Black Star Line as we called her.

Relaxing, I was suddenly aroused by the excitement in Ben's voice.

"IMAH, look at the Pilot. Who does he look like? Who does he remind you of?"

But it was really hard for me to tell for his back was to me. Suddenly, he slowly began to turn, as though he had been summoned. His face was round and Black and he smiled brightly, looking directly at us for a long moment before returning to his original position. Recognition kicked in with a jolt.

"Marcus Garvey!"

And he was flying the "Black Star Line - we were too excited. It was as though confirmation had been given that we were doing the right thing in coming home to Afrika. We were coming home and our Honorable Ancestor and Elder Marcus Mosiah Garvey was taking us there. What greater sign could have been given? It was like a seal of greater approval.

We arrived in Ghana but had decided earlier to stay behind after the rest of the group returned to America. It was also our first traumatic encounter with the Ghana Immigration Service. We had left Ghana to visit The Gambia but did not know that we needed another visa to re-enter Ghana. The Immigration Officer was terrible. He shouted at us, threatening to return us to America on the flight that night. No amount of pleading and explanation would satisfy him. He demanded fifty dollars from each of us. But we really did not have it and the rest of the group was going to be leaving the following day per their reservations. He did not care. He called the airline that the group was scheduled to fly with demanding that we be put on the plane that very night. Where was this attitude coming from? In the midst of all of this confusion, a white man walked up with a similar problem and he suddenly became so nice and helpful, smiling and bowing and scraping.

Turning back to us scowling, he said roughly,

"Go to the airline office, you're all leaving tonight."

He then changed his face again and returned his attention to the white man.

But when we arrived at the airline office the man behind the counter said that he had never received a phone call as the phones were out of order and even if they weren't, we couldn't leave that night because the waiting list which already had twenty-three people on it was closed. We then returned to our "brother" with the news, which he accepted reluctantly.

"You make sure you are here tomorrow," he growled.

He then made us each pay ten dollars and we went on our way.

When we returned to Cape Coast, we went to see a friend of ours who was a lawyer to find out what we had to do to remain in the country. After all, Ben and I were there to make final arrangements for returning home permanently. We were given an invitational letter from Nana Mbra, the Omanhen of Cape Coast who had originally invited us to come home. Once the group left we were on our own.

It was during this time that Ben was asked by the elders of the village of Iture to be their Safohen (Warrior) Chief.

One day Ben was driving past the village of Iture and saw a group of people congregating. He thought they were having a church service, so he stopped and asked if he could join them. The people were delighted and asked him to have a seat in front, with the other invited guests. However, it was not a church service they were conducting but were trying to raise funds to get electricity for their village. They needed someone to help them. Listening to their plight, Ben offered to assist in any way that he could.

As legend has it, the village of Iture is a historic village dating back to 1468, when the Portuguese were building the Elmina Castle Dungeons. A Ghanaian by the name of Iture Kwaku worked with the Portuguese and was as the leader of the "Lime Digging Project" located at the Sweet River and what is known today as Iture. Laborers were required to dig out crabs that were found in the river and attached to the Asopuru Vines, which grow in the river. The crab shells are then burned and ground into a white powder (Lime) that is used to make cement.

Slaves and free men stayed for years, working hard and supplying the Portuguese with the necessary lime and manpower to complete their task. After the completion of the Elmina Castle Dungeons in 1482, Iture Kwaku who was not a slave settled in with some of his men and started families and began farming and developing the village of Iture, which bears his name today.

During the early days of travel between Elmina and the Oguaa Area, (which means "Market Place" and is today known as Cape Coast), there was no bridge across the Sweet River to connect the two areas, so Kweku Iture transported people back and forth by boat for marketing and other business. Iture was adopted as part of Elmina and eventually became one of the first villages developed in Elmina.

After Ben offered to help the village, the elders asked him to be their Safohen Warrior Chief. He told them that he would think about it and let them know. When Ben came back to the house he told me what had happened and said that he would pray on it before responding to the village elders.

He also wanted to speak with Kohain in America but attempts to get through by phone failed. Ben was very excited and the spirit was so strong on him, he decided to accept the offer made by the elders. It was during this time that his name was changed to Nana Okofo Iture Kwaku I. I was unable to stay for his ceremony for I had to return to the United States to take care of some other business. But I left him with specific instructions.

"Honey, find us some property near the ocean. Not right on the beach but kinda up high so that I can see the water every day and with a good view too," I continued. "I'm counting on you."

Lo and behold, just before I returned to the United States, Ben had located our land. When the elders of Iture asked him to be their Safohen, they also gave him a piece of land. It was located on the Gulf of Guinea, high up on some rocks with a picturesque view of the Elmina Castle Dungeons in the distance.

I left for the United States to prepare for our return home. I was ecstatic to say the least.

When I broke the news to our brothers and sisters at Bereshith some of them appeared not to be very happy at Nana's decision to become a Chief. After all, we had agreed at one of our congregational meetings that we should work with the other Asafo Chiefs in Cape Coast to live up to their responsibilities before taking on anything else.

However, I explained that Nana had been caught up and excited about the prospect of becoming a chief and his attempts to reach Bereshith before he made his decision failed, so he had moved ahead.

Additionally, as a group we had been visiting Ghana since 1987 and were always talking about going home but no one was really ready to make that move. Some of them were still talking about buying property in America. We had also wanted to buy another house but Nana and I just weren't interested in America any longer, it was time to go home, so we moved forward.

We informed our children, family and friends of our decision. Needless to say most of them were none too happy about our decision to go to Afrika.

"What's in Afrika?" They wanted to know, and why would anyone in their right mind want to go there. "What about the wild animals? Afrikans don't even like us and on and on."

The negative media hype, Tarzan movies and other unfavorable stereotypes had done an excellent job in turning our people away from their heritage.

They didn't like the idea at all. In fact, they were angry with us for they felt that we were deserting the family and going too far away from them. As much as we tried to explain, the less they wanted to understand.

However, our eldest son Kendu was more agreeable with our decision and excited about the whole thing. He even spoke about joining us one day and getting a job cooking in a hotel, as a Chef. The girls on the other hand saw it differently. But there was nothing we could do to change their minds. It was a little sad for we wanted them to understand and be happy for us, to appreciate the significance of being able to return to one's ancestral homeland. We were going forward to build a place for the family. For whoever decided to come, they would find their Family House, in Ghana. It was time to go!

In June 1990 we repatriated home to Mother Afrika.

Nana left first and I followed after him, staying behind to help some of our brothers and sisters at Bereshith Cultural Institute, who were preparing for their Annual Afrikan Family Day Festival. Believe me I was itching bad to go to Ghana but they asked us several times to at least stay until African Family Day.

"Can't do it," Nana said.

"Maybe there was a hidden agenda and folks were planning something we didn't know about. Plus they needed all the help they could get," I argued.

Afrikan Family Day was a huge undertaking. It was growing each year, with this being their fourth year of observation and celebration.

Besides, I stated, it's only two weeks difference from our original departure date. We'll see a lot of old friends and turn this Afrikan Family Day into a big Bon Voyage party for us.

"No way," he continued. Nana was adamant. "I'm outta here in June Mommy, come hell or high water. Just say good-bye to the folks for me."

And he never broke his stride.

"Baby, I been waiting for this for too long; I'll see you when you get to Ghana."

And off he went...a closed subject, never to be mentioned again!

I was so sad taking him to the airport that day but I couldn't let him see that. I tried joking.

"Two weeks will pass so fast... I really do need a few more days with moms, (which I really did) because she is still royally pissed off that I am going to Afrika and taking you with me," I said.

My mother refused to accept that relocating to Ghana was a joint decision and not just "my idea."

"You're always talking about moving somewhere else," she'd say. "What's wrong with what you've got? You've wandered all over South America and the Caribbean: wandering around like a damn gypsy. And besides," she continued, "you weren't born in no damn Afrika and on and on and on. After you and Ben got married, I thought you would settle down and start acting like someone with good sense. But no, not you! Now you've moving way-the-hell to Ghana."

Sometimes we actually argued and that made me feel terrible.

"If you wanted to go to Afrika, that was fine, but why do you have to take Ben with you?"

"He's my husband, and besides, he wants to go: he has wanted to go for a long time, and now he has the opportunity. You can't blame him," I said.

"I don't blame him, I blame you," she cried.

"So why won't you come to Afrika with us, I pleaded. You could live like a queen off your pension. No mortgage payments ... coolin' off by the ocean. No Master Charge or VISA. No car note?"

"I ain't lost nothing in Afrika," my mother lamented. "Y'all go-on to your so-called "roots" in Afrika. Right here in the United States is my roots, thank you!"

And she wouldn't budge an inch.

So with all that and Nana leaving without me I was trying really hard to be good and strong.

As we were waiting at the airport for his departure, we reasoned together, laughed and joked. When I occasionally looked a little melancholy, he said,

"This was your decision, so you might as well cheer up and be happy. I'll meet you at the airport on the other side."

He was laughing and grinning like a big child trying to keep a secret, until take-off.

Once he left I let my true feelings show ... real sad, hot tears running down my cheeks. After a good cry, I turned it loose and the two weeks literally flew by.

In fact I was having the greatest time. I played my P'NUT BUT-TER the Afrikan-American Clown act during the Afrikan Family Day parade. I was dressed in my huge, bright red Afro wig, orange Kente Cotton Jump Suit, with a Kente Cloth strip with buttons of Malcolm X, Harriet Ross Tubman, Dr. Martin Luther King, Jr. and Mickey Mouse adorning it draped across my shoulder. As I had the children's attention, I used this to teach the children about their history, while we were having fun. I was also wearing size 18 Nike sneakers. I had long gold eyelashes and a big red rubber nose but did not paint my face white for it was important for the children to know that I was an Afrikan. Additionally, there were, very few Black Clowns in the country, they were mostly White Folks.

To top my act off I carried my "Ghetto Blaster" or "Boom Box" as those humongous radios were called. I sang and partied hardy! I had been doing this sort of thing for several years before moving to Ghana.

Everyone naturally asked for Nana Ben. When I told one of our friends that Nana was gone and sent his good-byes, he said,

"Go brother man!"

And shot his clenched fist to the sky.

"I'm outta here tomorrow," I said.

And he really started hollering. He told everybody. It almost wasn't necessary to make a public announcement. Word spread like wild fire. By the time I was called to the stage "there was a party goin' on."

Our friends who had asked us to stay for Afrikan Family Day called me to the microphone and made a presentation of a plaque of appreciation and 75 dollars.

For about 15 minutes I said good-bye to friends, evoking Afrikan hoots and hollerin' and laughter when I told the crowd how Nana had responded when we asked him to delay his departure. That was the party of parties.

"Amandla," I shouted, a Zulu word meaning "Power to the People" "Amandla."

The thunderous response and the chanting continued. The field rocked, the drummers played and the folks danced.

Happy...Happy...Happy.

A few people even put something in my pocket. One girl friend quipped,

"I figure y'all could use the money, can't eat no kente cloth, baby," she said laughingly, as I thanked her.

Happy...Happy...Happier.

It was almost departure time.

I hoped and prayed that my mother would be a little less pissed off with me now that it was really time to go. My friends arrived around 3:00 p.m. to take me to the airport. My mother was sitting on the porch, arms folded solidly across her chest (like Chief Sitting Bull), an angry look on her face.

As my friends approached and greeted her, "Good evening Mrs. Hines." She grunted something, barely acknowledging them. Sensing something was amiss, they quietly returned to their van to wait for me.

"I'm leaving Fatty, (as we affectionately called my mom) I said. Please don't be mad with me, but I've got to go. I love you and I'll write to you."

"Yeah," she replied.

The stoic expression on her face never changed. She was real angry.

"Go on then," she muttered, "Go on back to Afrika, since that's more important to you than me!"

I could feel another argument brewing but I wouldn't give in to that.

"Think about what I said. Think about coming to Ghana with us. Nana will even come back to escort you on the plane."

I was trying so hard to be cheerful. But her expression never changed.

"I love you Fatty,"

I told her as I walked slowly and sadly to the waiting vehicle.

Boy, was she still pissed off with me! It wasn't like there was no one there with her. My sister was nearby, my lazy nephew would move back into the house once I'd left. My aunts, my mother's brother and a host of friends had assured her that she only needed to call them if she needed anything. They would help her to keep my apartment rented (we owned a two family house) and whatever else. None of that mattered to her. No matter what anyone said.

As we pulled away from the house I saw tears running down her round, brown cheeks, her full lips in a big pout. I almost turned back, starting to cry and feeling a little hurt inside because she wasn't happy about our decision and I'd wished I could have left on a better note. But the pull to come home was stronger and more gripping than biological, if you can understand what I mean. It was spiritual: it was the ancestor calling...

"Come on home girl, ain't nuttin' to be scared of. Been waitin' a long time. Come on home, girl!"

It was time to go home again.

My sister and my niece also rode with me to the airport.

"Don't worry about your mother, I'm here," my sister chided. "She just doesn't want you to go, that's all. Hell, I don't want you to go either. But she'll be all right."

When we left America, Nana and I had offered my sister our share of the house.

"Just take over the mortgage and utilities," we told her, "and do whatever is necessary to maintain the house."

Besides, she'd be closer to our mother and she'd have a built in baby sitter because Fatty never went anywhere except to Pathmark Supermarket and the Fish Market. You couldn't bribe her out of the house otherwise.

My sister lived deep in the South Bronx. Ghetto Blasters (radio big boxes) playing all night, the Jamaican brothers blasting their music through huge concert sized speakers on the sidewalks and from their apartment windows. Guys rushing up to stopped cars to sell five dollar bags of marijuana gold, mole, or dot, cocaine, smoke, dope, crack, you name it.

'Niggers with an attitude,' shooting at one another anytime of the day or night, not caring who got shot, children, elders, their mothers, the dog. They just did not care. Calling a policeman could get you killed 'by mistake.'

And then there was the attempted sexual assault of my sister's twelve-year-old daughter in the elevator of her building. My sister had more locks on her door than a bank vault and still the thieves got in. You had to contend with alternate side of the street parking, between certain times of the day and my sister was always getting tickets for parking violations.

I thought those were sufficient reasons for wanting to change one's location. Plus someone was going to give you an equal share in a fine house, fully furnished, if you so desired. There was no hidden cost, just the shared cost of the mortgage for as long as she wanted to live in the house. But I was wrong. My sister said she was buying her apartment now that her building (in the middle of hell-fire) was going co-op. So we rented out our apartment to strangers to cover the cost of our share of the mortgage and other expenses. We even installed $5,000.00 dollars worth of iron gates to the doors and windows of our house to satisfy my mother, who was refusing to live in the house or allow us to leave unless we did so.

But still, my mother was pissed off. I looked back no more. But that was the last time I'd see her alive. Less than five months later she was dead.

"Forward ever, backwards never," the Honorable Osagyefo Dr. Kwame Nkrumah, the first president of Ghana and noted Pan Afrikanist told us.

And as one of our bible references in Genesis stated,

"Therefore shall a man leave his mother and father and shall cleave unto his wife; and they shall be one."

Well, I was cleavin' ... and leavin'.

At nine o'clock that night I kissed my sister and niece farewell and departed from John F. Kennedy International Airport on my way home to Ghana.

It was a good flight, taking about thirteen hours for I was traveling through Europe. I slept most of the time, for I was bone tired and weary. The stewardess woke me up, saying it was time for breakfast.

"Already?" I asked.

I couldn't believe that it was six o'clock in the morning. The night had passed quickly. We made one stop in Amsterdam, Holland, where we changed planes. Six hours later, we were landing at the Kotoka International Airport, in Accra. I was finally home.

When I arrived, Nana and our friend and brother Kwadjo were there to meet me. After I cleared Customs we set out for Cape Coast. It felt so good to be back and Nana was looking great. He had gotten real black in the two weeks that he had been here. Undoubtedly, he was not trying to hide from the sun. I asked him a lot of questions.

"Did you find a place for us to stay?" I wanted to know immediately. "Did you miss me too much? What have you been doing?"

As we rode along I kept pinching myself to see if I were going to wake up. The countryside looked beautiful.

We would be staying with our friend and brother Cole. We were renting a room in his house while we looked for a permanent place to stay.

Additionally we had secured an ideal spot, a piece of beachfront property in Elmina, with a fantastic, unobstructed view of the historical Elmina Castle Dungeons. It was located on the Gulf of Guinea, the Gold Coast, the West Coast of Afrika. The location was perfect.

Nana had been given the property when he was made an honorary Safohen (Warrior Chief) in the village of Iture.

It was also hard to believe that we would be living on this historic piece of land, situated between the Cape Coast and Elmina Castle Dungeons. A land occupied by our ancestors who had helped to build the Elmina Castle Dungeons. This was no coincidence but a further confirmation that we had made the right decision to return home.

We were also searching out the owner of an unfinished and abandoned structure next to the property we had acquired. For several years we'd looked at that house but no one knew the whereabouts of the owner. But our friend and brother Cole, whom we had met during our previous visits to Ghana and were now staying with, said he was going to help us find the owners (so we thought).

It was like a dream come true. Our ancestors were from here. I could feel it. I had felt it the first time I entered the Cape Coast Castle Dungeons in 1987.

As anxious as we were to get started, we weren't quite ready to begin construction. The architectural plans for our new house were being drawn up so we could get our Building Permit and take care of the other details.

In the meantime we bought a 1978 Mercedes Benz from Brother Kwadjo and also found a house to rent. It wasn't what I really wanted because it was not on the ocean, but at least we would be in our own space. Our friend Kwadjo helped us greatly by allowing us to stay with him and his family. This gave us a real and valuable introduction to Ghanaian culture: something extremely important for someone coming from a different cultural background.

We were grateful for this opportunity and to show our gratitude and appreciation we paid more-than-our-fair-share to our host and family, without complaint. One of his children was even named after me. In fact the naming ceremony was conducted when we came home the first time. We enjoyed our new family and the warm Ghanaian hospitality. Although our new family insisted that we remain with them, we really wanted to move into our own space and not wear out our welcome.

The rent on the four bedroom house, with three bathrooms, a living and dining room, behind a high wall with plenty of space, fruit trees and flowers was only fifteen thousand cedis a month. Which was less than $45.00 US Dollars a month. And we'd stay there until our house was completed.

Kwadjo and the architect had told us, that our house could be completed in less than six months if the money and materials were there and the work moved along steadily. Our Building Plans called for a beautiful, three bedroom, house with two bathrooms, a large living room, dining room, kitchen and garage including electricity and the other finishings and was going to cost us ten thousand U.S. Dollars; an unbelievable price for building a house. We were ecstatic.

Kwadjo, "our good friend and brother" assured us that he would help us every step of the way.

"Like a contractor," he said.

After all, he had helped other friends build their houses while they sent money to him from the United States. We even met and talked with one of his friends, who further assured us that everything would be all right.

During this time, I tried reaching out to my mother. I called her several times but each phone call always ended up in an argument. My sister and nephew were giving her the blues. No one could do anything to satisfy her. She didn't like the prospective tenants she had interviewed. Her leg was still troubling her from the blow she received when she hit it against the edge of her bed. My mother was diabetic, obese, hypertensive, smoked almost a carton of cigarettes a week, ate what she wanted and disregarded her doctor's advise. She wouldn't listen to anyone, except herself.

She said, "Just come home, and everything will be all right."

After every phone call I was worn out. Finally I said,

"Fatty, if you're going to argue and complain every time I call, I'm going to stop calling."

I didn't hear her response, for the phone went dead. The next time I called she was being admitted to the hospital for surgery on her leg. She had hit her leg in the same place several times and was still not following the advice of her doctors to lose weight, stop smoking and change her dietary intake. Now surgery was necessary to improve the circulation in her leg, and she wanted me to come back. That was in September. I called my Aunt who is a Registered Nurse to get a clearer, medical understanding of my mother's condition and to see if it was really necessary for me to return to the United States. I really didn't want to go back if it could be. My aunt assured me that my mother would be fine, if she stopped being so stubborn.

"Besides," my aunt said, "your mother has plenty of help here if she just doesn't take undue advantage of it and stop complaining to everyone that you've gone off and deserted her. Don't worry about your mother, she'll be fine."

With that assurance Nana and I proceeded to push forward in preparation of building our first house in our ancestral homeland. Shortly thereafter, I called my family in New York. The operation had been successful and a Visiting Nurse was providing follow-up treatment and post-op care for my mother at home. Several friends and family were available to assist her as was my sister and nephew.

In late November, a few days before Thanksgiving (which I had totally forgotten as Nana and I had not celebrated Thanksgiving in many years) the telephone rang in the middle of the night. Nana answered the phone. I heard him laughing and talking.

"Of course we miss you," he said, "and I love you too. You're my favorite girl! Hold on while I get your daughter."

It was great to hear from my moms but before I could open my mouth well, my mother started in.

"The apartment isn't rented, your nephew is living in the house again, and is still unemployed, his girlfriend is pregnant and unemployed, and your sister isn't helping me. I want you to return to the United States immediately to help me get my life back together," she argued.

"Fatty, I just don't understand you," I said. "How many times have we (the family and friends) advised you to send your grandson and his girlfriend to Social Services, if they didn't have jobs and to seek assistance to pay their share of the rent, as they were staying, in our apartment."

"But why can't he get a job?" I asked. "Why do you continue to make excuses for him?"

I demanded to speak with my nephew but he refused to come to the telephone and my mother wouldn't try to force him. It was going to be one of those discussions again, more arguments and crying. The last words we spoke before she hung up were,

"I love you Fatty," I said softly.

To which she replied,

"I love you too Vee-anna," as she often called me.

I went back to bed more than a little distressed. That was the last time I spoke to my mother.

Two days later the phone rang again in the middle of the night. I waited breathlessly until I heard our host call me to the telephone. What a pleasant surprise, it was my sister calling.

"Hey baby Sis, I said, what's up?"

The next words sounded like they were being screamed into my brain.

"Your mother's dead," replied my sister, curtly. "When are you coming home?"

"Oh no, I screamed", She can't be; She can't be!"

Within moments, Nana was at my side and I was crying uncontrollably. By this time the entire household was awake. Nana finished speaking to my sister assuring her that we would immediately make arrangements to return to New York. When Nana hung up, he said,

"Your sister sounded a little uptight, I guess it's the shock of your mother's passing. But then she said, she had found a Will and nothing could be done until you got there."

"A Will," I said. "What could Fatty have had that required her to make a Will?"

Oh shit, I thought, *trouble!*

We made our preparations to return to the United States to bury our mother.

Nana was taking it quite well but I knew that it had hit him quite hard for he and my mother were very close. They had more than a son-in-law/mother-in-law relationship. He was her son and she his mother and they were very good friends.

I really felt that he should stay in Ghana. He was suffering from malaria and I knew how strongly he was against returning to the United States. I suggested that he let me go alone but he was having none of that.

Our friends that we were staying with were really wonderful during this time and very concerned. They even organized a Wake Keeping for us, doing everything to keep our spirits up.

I'll never forget this beautiful Fante song that was played often throughout the day. The title of the song was "Adofupa," which meant "good lover or good friend, I'm saying good-bye to you." The song said:

"When your good lover passes out,
it's a big problem.
Today, if you see your friend,
look in his eyes for death gives no message.
Today I call you and you do not answer.
A year before you passed, we were sitting here drinking.
And now I'm drinking alone.
I said in this world, death can bring confusion to life.
What did we come in this world for but to trade?
And now we must make an account to God.
All I had to say is over, you've died and all my hope is over.
Good lover/good friend, I'm saying good-bye to you.
Today you let me know that death is walking with us.
And we have to pray that you get a good place to stay."

That song had such deep meaning for me. It was true, for my good friend, my very best friend, my mother was gone.

We finished up some last minute business as best we could. We were also in the process of setting up booth space in Accra for participation in the First Ghana Trade Fair, with items that were being manufactured by us.

Nana and I had gone into partnership with brother Kwadjo, the person we were staying with. He had machines for making snakeskin and leather bags and shoes but he didn't have enough money to start up the business, and then there was the question as to where to put the machines. We discussed everything in detail and after carefully evaluating the entire situation, it was agreed that his garage was the perfect location for the factory.

Nana and I put up part of the money to have the garage converted to a factory; the electricity and machines installed and to pay the salary of two young men from Abidjan, who were experts in making handbags and shoes.

When we left for the United States the work on the garage was still going on. We even took samples of the snakeskin and leather bags with us to test the market for these goods in New York. Kwadjo assured us that he would take care of registering the business in both our names and everything would be operational by the time we returned to Ghana. We left for New York feeling secure in the knowledge that our interest was in good hands.

CHAPTER SEVEN

A SAD REUNION

On the 28th of November 1990 we arrived back in New York amidst plenty of confusion. Why is it that when someone dies, the worse seems to come out in people?

Getting re-settled in the house was difficult. I went into my mother's bedroom half expecting to see her but there was only the empty, blood stained, bed. It was hard to believe that such a simple operation had come to this. A Visiting Nurse had come to see my mother on a regular basis and the last time that she visited my moms and changed her dressing – she was fine except for a little bleeding.

"Nothing to worry about," she said, "your mother was fine."

However, on that fateful day something had gone wrong. My mother had sent for our neighbor, who is also a Registered Nurse but at the time she was having dinner and my nephew did not tell her that it was urgent, that she come immediately. So after dinner she came to the house to see what my mother wanted.

"When I arrived and took one look at your mother, I knew that your mother wouldn't make it because she had lost too much blood. I felt so bad. Why hadn't I been told to come immediately," she asked.

By the time the ambulance was called and they finally came and took my mother to the hospital it was already too late.

I wanted to strangle my nephew but restrained myself. But I informed him that he and his girlfriend would have to find some-place else to hang out, the party was over and I didn't give a damn, or care who didn't like it either.

Later on that evening my Auntie arrived and she began to relate some of the things that had transpired on the day of my mom's death. As my nephew had not gone along with my mother in the ambulance, no one knew what hospital she had been taken to.

"First, I went to Jacobi Hospital; there was no Virginia Hines there," she said sadly.

"Next, I went to North Central Bronx Hospital but they had no record of her there either. How is that possible?" she queried the nurse. "A city ambulance picked up my sister-in-law, less than an hour ago."

"Just a moment," the nurse said and went back into the Emergency Room.

When she returned, she asked my aunt to accompany her to identify a DOA (Dead on Arrival) – it was my mother. Shortly, thereafter, my sister arrived at the hospital.

The more they told me, the worse I felt and the madder I got. How could two grown adults, living in the same house (my nephew, his girlfriend and their new baby were living with my mother) not be aware of the problem and suffering that my mother must have been going through on that fateful day. Hadn't they seen or spoken with her? It seemed almost impossible to imagine. But it was too late now. My mother was gone and I had to begin dealing with a series of other problems that were staring me in the face.

While waiting for us to return from Ghana, my sister had done a thorough search of my mom's belongings. She had previously found an insurance policy and Last Will and Testament that made me the sole beneficiary to mother's estate (such as it was). This caused more trouble than it was worth because my mother didn't have anything much. My Mom and I had purchased a house together about ten year's prior. She was on retirement and receiving her pension, had filed bankruptcy and owned a house full of furniture and appliances. There was no IRA, Savings Account, Stocks or Bonds. There was nothing except the monthly pension check that was deposited into her bank account on the first of each month. And a one thousand dollar insurance policy that her union gave her after working 30 years for Lerner Shops.

We managed to quickly get the money together without having to borrow any. We got an additional blessing through a friend of mine from school days who was a Mortician and agreed to handle all the arrangements for a nominal fee. My sister wanted me to go and identify the body of my mother but I wouldn't do it.

"Did you go and view her?" I asked. "Are you satisfied that the temple remains which you have seen is that of our mother?"

She acknowledged that it was and that was enough for me. I didn't want to see my mother that way. In fact, I had told my moms many times that whatever we were doing the last time we were together, would be my only remembrance of her, if she traveled (passed away) before me. That was acceptable between us and that's all that mattered to me.

We had a beautiful memorial service, with no open casket. Naturally, there were members of our family that did not agree with this but that's the way it was. We also asked that people not send flowers. Instead, we had only one long stem rose, standing next to an enlarged picture of my mother and a white stuffed kitten. My mother loved her cats and my Dad had always given us only "one long stem rose."

He said it represented a deep, single love for the person and said much more than a dozen.

On the day of the funeral, the weather was overcast and dreary. In spite of this, the memorial ceremony went well, with many of our friends and family in attendance. It was raining cats and dogs when we left the funeral home to escort my mother's remains to Pinelawn Memorial Cemetery, to be laid next to my father, as had been her request. She had made me swear that I wouldn't have her remains cremated. The burial ceremony was over quickly but as we were leaving the cemetery, the rain stopped and the sky became a majestic blue, pink and gray. You could almost hear music playing. It was if my mom and dad were letting me know that everything was all right and that they were together again. Several of the others noticed the same thing and had similar thoughts.

Now that the funeral was behind us it was now time to get down to serious business. The ugliness that so often rears its head when someone dies had already started to peek out from behind corners. My sister was upset because our mother had left a Will naming me sole beneficiary and her as second beneficiary, in the event that something happened to me. Our mother did this because I was the eldest and because she did not want any confusion regarding whom our house rightfully belonged to in the event of her death. When my Mom and I had bought the house, no one was interested in going in with us. No one helped us, no one cleaned for us, in fact my mother was always complaining because the family did not visit her often enough.

When I first became aware of a Will, I laughed and asked my mom, "What in the world do you have that warrants spending unnecessary money on a Will? And if you've got it like that, I want mine now, while you're alive because I could use the money, if that's what you're leaving to us."

As far as the house was concerned we both knew that whoever left the planet first, the house would belong solely to the one being left behind. And, I wasn't worried about anyone taking anything from me. But wisdom comes with age, and Fatty knew the players only too well.

I explained to my sister that the Will was very clear; the house belongs solely to me (which is as it was supposed to be). Mom and I bought this house together, with our money. No one helped us and no one wanted to buy the house with us. It has always been understood from the beginning that in the event of either of us checking out, the house would belong to the survivor. The rest of mom's things were to be divided equally between us.

Needless to say, my sister did not like this arrangement, one bit. She still wanted money.

In fact, I told my sister, she could have everything in the house that belongs to Fatty. Other than a few pots and old frying pans, I don't want anything else. I only wanted to get the house sold, collect the money and return to Ghana as quickly as possible.

We exchanged a few more heated words before my sister decided to lie down. But the subject was far from closed, not by a long shot. But I wasn't going to argue, fuss and fight any further over something that was mine and that I had worked for; something that I had rightfully earned, and no one was going to intimidate me or move me off my course.

Now I understood and appreciated why Nana would not allow me to return to New York alone. Getting through all of this would have been tougher without him being there with me. As it was, when the "stuff" started jumping off, he was in Florida. But that was a lot closer than Ghana and he was coming back in a week. It was going to be a rocky road to returning home again. When my sister woke up, we talked again, running into the same stone wall.

Look, I told her, becoming exasperated with this whole conversation, nothing has changed. Everything in the house is yours and the house is mine. Case closed! And I'm sorry if you don't like it. I didn't want to be harassed any more than was necessary, as we prepared for our final departure from The United States.

With the sudden death of my mother forcing us to return to America, we caught hell trying to get out the second time around. What we had experienced the first time was like a preview of coming attractions. But our objectives were very clear: to sell the house and return to Ghana, as quickly as possible.

We notified a Real Estate Agency, who came and assessed the house.

Everyone was opposed to our selling the house, painting a bleak economic picture; saying that we should wait and not sell the house at this time for the market was too bad and we were going to lose money. But we held to our decision.

Hell, the house still belonged to the bank with yet another fifteen years to pay, pay, and pay, before paying off the mortgage. My sister even came up with an idea that had been suggested to her by one of her girlfriends. We would rent the house to the City of New York to be used for homeless people and she would handle the collection of the rent and maintenance of the house and forward the rent to us, minus her commission.

Nana and I discussed all the options and decided that we would put it on the market and get what we could get. Whatever we got was more than we had. The first agent completely turned me off with her very negative I don't want to make you any promises attitude.

"After all, people have had their houses on the market for years with no takers. There are even a few in this neighborhood," she said.

Whoopee, Dhoopee, I thought. You definitely ain't the one.

I explained to her that our ultimate goal was to immediately sell our house so that we can move on. "But since you aren't too optimistic regarding our prospects, I really didn't think you're the one that we want handling our business."

On that note I thanked her for coming and went looking for another agent with a better attitude. The next one was much more positive. I immediately informed her that,

"We know all about the terrible economic market but that's not our problem. I have prayed about it and want to walk away with at least fifty thousand dollars in our hands. It might be a loss for someone else but for us $50,000.00 was a small fortune that could take us far in Ghana. We want the house sold immediately," I continued, laughingly.

"Are you the one that can do it?"

"That's why I'm here," she replied with an air of confidence.

Praying and making my affirmations I wrote:

"I will sell my house and be in Ghana by July. We will have $50,000.00 in hand, after Closing on the house. When I turn 50 years old in November, I will be home in Ghana."

I wrote them on a piece of paper, which included the amount of money I wanted to receive and the period of time in which I wanted to sell the house. I then purchased a large white candle and had it anointed with Frankincense and Myrrh, put it in a saucer of water and put my affirmations under it. A candle stayed lit until we left for Ghana.

One month after putting the house on the market it was sold. The new buyers loved the house and their agent immediately began processing their mortgage loan papers.

In the interim my sister and I sorted out mom's things: giving away, throwing away and setting aside the few things that I would be keeping. One night, two weeks after the house had been sold, as per our agreement, my sister backed a truck up to the house and took everything from the house, refrigerator, freezer, furniture, dishes, books, records and the mirrors on the wall. The place was bare except for the carpeting on the floor.

Nana and I continued to hold regular Garage Sales until the garage was also empty and then the wait began. But the devil was also busy. First, the people had the mortgage and then they didn't; then they did, but the man processing their loan went to another bank and took their papers with him which meant they had to start all over again...more delay. What looked like a short term, sure deal, was stretching into months.

We were sleeping on the floor because believing that we would soon be out of the United States, we had shipped most of our belongings to Ghana. We had given our children our furniture, then sold, gave or threw away everything else and now we were left with an empty house...and the wait continued.

It was now June and more than five months had passed before we finally got a date to go to Closing on the house. The day before we were to go to Closing, another snag popped up delaying us further. It would now be another month before we could go to Closing.

Next, the New York City Department of Roads, Highways and "sidewalks," cited us for a violation, putting a lien on our property thus preventing the sale until we fixed a small crack in the sidewalk (which had been there for years before we had even bought the house) and it was small too. But they insisted that it had to be done. The forces were working hard to keep us in the United States. But we kept fighting, determined to return home to Ghana.

Three thousand dollars and two "Jack Leg" Contractors later, the city inspectors finally approved the work that was done. On the day that they came, we prayed that they would not ask us to open the garage, for the previous contractor had torn up the sidewalk and put all the concrete slabs in the garage and never came back to haul them away – another violation.

However, the delay continued as we waited (not too patiently) for the Closing date to be re-confirmed. Finally, we were given a new date but it was three weeks away. The lawyers were not available until then and a whole host of other reasons were given for the continued delay.

But in the midst of this turmoil, Nana and I were inspired to travel throughout the South. This became a sacred pilgrimage for us. We touched the soil hallowed by the blood, sweat, tears and labor of our ancestors who had been sold into Chattel Slavery. We went to Hilton Head, South Carolina and wanted to visit the Daufuskie Islands, another historical island, being the first sight of land seen by the enslaved Afrikans, after being on the sea for three to four months. Many of them jumped from the Slave Boats and swam to the island but they were not pursued for the waters around the island were Shark infested.

However, the only access to the island was by a Tourist Boat, operated by a fat, red-faced cracker and his prune-faced wife. With no other way to get onto the island, we reluctantly joined the tour boat but we were the only Afrikans on board. As the boat captain narrated during the trip over to the island, my blood boiled even more as he spewed out the history of the surrounding area filled with jokes about an old slave woman who still haunted the place.

"Well suh," he drawled, "after me and the little woman has a few drinks under our belts, we see spooks, haw, haw, haw," he continued.

I tried to block out the sound of his voice by singing to myself and gazing into the moving water.

Once we landed on the island, we rented a golf cart and drove around the island on our own, hoping to meet and speak with some of our people. But our reception was not very warm. A young man we met directed us to a few people but when we approached them they were reluctant to speak with us. One woman stated emphatically, "I ain't got nuttin' to say to you." And slammed the door in our faces. But even with that, the spirit of the place made your body tingle.

The one person who people called "Rasta," and might have spoken openly about the island, unfortunately, had gone to the mainland shopping. So at the end of the tour, having received no worthwhile information and thirty dollars lighter in our pockets, we proceeded on to the Slave Markets in Charleston, South Carolina (which was earmarked for demolition) and to other ports where our people had been auctioned and sold.

At each site, we prayed and talked to our ancestors.

"It's over — we've come full circle - you've paid the price, and we, your children are now able to return home to "Mother Afrika."

Our travel route, unplanned by us had become historically likened to our ancestors escaping from enslavement in the South, heading North to so-called freedom. We realized on our return to New York how important our pilgrimage had been...for we, in doing this, were removing yet another link of our chain of enslavement.

It was time to go to Closing on our house!

It was the middle of September and we had been trying to escape from Babylon for ten long months. We were going home. God had answered our prayers and blessed us bountifully.

When the lawyer turned our check over to us we had $50,000.00 in our hands but now we had to pay the taxes, which ate us up. But it was still cool for we had enough to do what we needed to do.

Next we bought four (4) round trip tickets to Ghana because it was more economically feasible and cheaper than a one-way ticket. Besides if Bongo and Sister D. (our extended family from Jamaica) didn't like Ghana and wanted to return to Jamaica, their tickets were good for one year. Then we bought four round trip tickets to Jamaica, West Indies – the last remaining link in the chain to be broken.

Rejoicing we wasted no time collecting our few remaining things and saying our final good-byes and leaving the United States. We had notified our brother Bongo Shorty and his Queen Sister D that they should be on standby, for as The Creator blessed us, so also were they...and we would be coming for them also.

We had initially met Bongo and Sister D in 1970 when we visited Jamaica for the first time, on our vacation. Bongo was a small but powerful Rasta man with long flowing Dred Locks, bushy precepts and laughing eyes. He was a well-respected brother who was a Fisherman and also the leader of a band called "The Jolly Boys". They had been hired to come to our villa to play for a party. After a wonderful night of music, dancing and drumming we found out that he was one of the most trusted men in Jamaica. He invited us to go fishing the next day.

He picked us up from off the beach in front of our villa and off to sea we went. We had a great time and even caught some fish. When we returned from our fishing trip, he took us to his place in Runaway Bay to meet his queen, Sister D. They were complete opposites. She was a big robust but shy and gentle sister (unless you made her angry) and I loved her immediately. Don't get me wrong, "she didn't take no tea for the fever." Thereafter, whenever we visited Jamaica, which was quite often, our first stop on the way to our villa or hotel was to Bongo and Sister D's.

Over the years our friendship grew stronger and they were more family than mere friends. In fact, I lived with them for over a year, as I had at one time been giving serious thought to re-locating to Jamaica.

We were always talking about Afrika and our desire to return home. And I had always said, "If I ever get my hands on any substantial amount of money I'm going to Afrika and taking y'all with me."

"Mi ah pray for dat, mi seestah," Bongo would respond, speaking in Patois. "Mi ah pray for dat!"

In fact I also prayed often for that day. So after my first visit to Ghana in 1987, the call to my ancestral homeland was even stronger...and Jamaica was just a resting place, a preparation for the big move.

Just before leaving for Jamaica, Nana and I stopped by this vegetarian restaurant run by some Rasta brethren. We had been taking our meals from them regularly as we prepared to Exodus America. And we reasoned often together about Afrika, going home and JAH. It was always a powerful and stimulating reasoning we undertook.

Nana sat outside in our van as I went in to place our final order.

"Hail brethren," I said. "Dis be mi last meal with the I. We're on our way forward, at last."

"Hail Empress," the brethren responded, "JAH guide and protect the I and the I's Kingman. Tis wonderful dis be happenin'. But seestah, stick a pin (wait a minute), mi naw know the I's name."

"Oh, I responded, I'm called EMAHKUS." (Although I've always spelled it "IMAHKUS").

The brethren looked pon I (at me) for a moment and announced,

"No Empress, the name is "IMAHKUS. 'I' One with the Almighty Creator."

I immediately began to feel a real comfort about my new name that I had never felt before, nor had I ever heard it pronounced in that way. I loved it. It was God-given, inspired and orchestrated. It means "I MOTHER AFRIKA QUEEN OF THE EARTH." But please allow me to explain the spiritual significance.

I began changing my name in 1984, in Jamaica, when a young sister, who looked like a daughter we had lost to Lupus in 1980, began calling me "Kush," which is the "land of the burnt faced people" in Ethiopia (the Garden of Eden).

In 1987, I made my first pilgrimage to Ghana with my brothers and sisters from the Hebrew Israelite community out of Mt. Vernon; they called me EMA, which means Mother; Ema Kush or Ema Vienna (my birth name).

In 1990, when Nana and I made up our minds to leave the United States, I formally announced to friends that I no longer wanted to be known as Ema Vienna but as Ima Kush. One day a very special elder sistren, Ema Yarnah questioned me on the spelling of my name and suggested that I change it slightly, putting the "H" after Ema, for the letter "H" represented the number 8, which represented a beginning and/or an ending – a building or destroying. For our move home was representative of ending the old and building the future. After all, Kus, Kush or Cush was still "the land of the burnt faced people." So my name took on a very special meaning for me.

It took 7 years to complete, there are 7 characters in my name, and I was born on the 7th day of the 11th month in the 41st year. (1+1+4+1=7). Four times 7 = 28, 2+8=10, cancel the 0 and it equals 1. It's also spelled with all capital letters. I = One with the Almighty Creator, M = Mother, A = Afrika, H = represents the number eight (8) to build or destroy, KUS = the land of the burnt faced people. The Queen of Ethiopia, the Queen of Sheba. I ran out to our van and told Nana what had happened.

"From this day forward honey, my name is IMAHKUS," I told him.

"Sounds good to me," he replied with a warm smile on his face, "yeah, that's alright honey."

Two days later after closing on our house, with tickets to Ghana in hand, we arrived in Jamaica. As we drove along the beautiful coast line from Montego Bay to Runaway Bay where Bongo and Sister D lived, I could not help reflecting on the 500 years that had passed since the beginning of the Trans-Atlantic European Slave Trade. Here we were in yet another location where enslaved Africans had been dropped off during the worst holocaust known to man.

But we were 'high stepping' this time, we were on our way home.

When we got to Salem, we stopped at our favorite Pub, *Mr. Sutty's Place,* to buy a case of cold Red Stripe beer for our celebration. Although Mr. Sutty was glad to see us, he was a little sad for he knew that we had come to take Bongo and Sister D to Ghana.

"It's a dream come true for dem," he said, "but I'm going to miss Bongo Shorty and I-Man-Queen" (as he affectionately called Sister

D)," but it's a long time dem speak of this day. Just don't forget we here in Jamaica," he continued.

"Not a chance," we assured him, as we left the pub heading for our beach.

We found Bongo and Sister D in the camp (as we called our living place). After greeting all our brethren and extended family members, Nana, Bongo, Sister D and I strolled up the beach to the big tree, where we had spent many days and nights over the years, reasoning about returning to "Mother Afrika."

Today was a real special and blessed day. They were real happy to see us. Every one was laughing and talking all at the same time. Once seated, Nana and I changed up the vibes. We got real serious: I acted a little sad and was trying hard to keep a straight face as I withdrew the tickets and their passports out of my bag.

"This is yours Bongo," I said.

I sat quietly not cracking a smile. Nana also had this somber look on his face.

"I don't know what to say man," Nana said as he looked away.

Everyone's mood was real pensive. As Bongo opened the envelope, a big smile slowly spread across his small but wise face before he jumped up and grabbed Sister D.

"JAH Rastafari, this is it D," he shouted, "This is it! JAH has answered I prayers, I n I be goin' home."

By now all of us were hollering, laughing, screaming and crying. Some friends who were a short distance away heard all the commotion and ran up to see what was going on. They also started to dance and clown, the word spread like wild fire and the beach was alive with activity. There was laughter and there were tears, for Bongo and Sister D were well loved by everyone and as the word spread that they were leaving, folks came from everywhere. The entire night was spent celebrating. Brothers brought out their drums. We sang, we chanted and made music and danced the night away.

The following morning we went shopping for suitcases and a few other things, returning that evening we began packing. Bongo gave away his fishing boat and two outboard motors and everything else that would not fit into his two large bags. It was a frantically happy time.

Nana and I were planning to return to New York to finalize some business after we had gotten Bongo and Sister D all squared away. We were scheduled to leave for Ghana the following Tuesday, October 8th. I was whipped after a full day of shopping, packing and getting ready. We had truly shopped until I was ready to drop.

I slept hard that night, having nightmares. I dreamed I was Lot's wife (from the bible) and had returned to New York to take care of business and turned into a pillar of salt. I was stiff as a board ... and all I could do was stand by and watch everyone leaving me. I woke up in the middle of the night in a cold sweat, shaking. I knew that I was not going back to New York to take care of anything. I woke Nana and told him about my nightmare.

"Please Nana," I asked him, "please go in my place and take care of the final banking business because I'm deathly afraid that something will prevent me from returning home to Ghana."

"That's impossible," he said, "everything is in your name."

"Don't worry," I told him, "I'll just call the bank and work it out with the manager."

I guess I forgot where I was for a moment. First of all New York was not around the corner and finding a working telephone was not the easiest thing to do but we finally got through. At first the Bank Manager said, "Oh that's not possible, you'll have to come yourself."

"What's so unusual about my request," I argued. "Big business does it all the time. I'll be giving my husband enough information to prove who he is as well as a statement if necessary exonerating the bank of any liability, if something should go wrong. Under no circumstances can I return to New York," I continued.

After much debating back and forth we finally worked things out so that Nana could withdraw the funds. He was given all the pertinent information, passwords etc., which would satisfactorily identify him to the bank.

On Sunday, as I drove Nana to the Montego Bay Airport, I thought of how truly blessed I was to have Nana as my life's partner. He had always been there for me and I loved him even more. It was not every man that would be as supportive as he had been, nor as agreeable. Leaving home, family and friends to begin a new life, in another country was not the easiest thing in the world to do but he was doing it...we were doing it together. We would meet again on Tuesday at the Departure Terminal of British Airways, in New York.

When I got back to the beach, the mood had changed slightly and some folks were a little angry that Nana and I were taking Bongo and Sister D away from them. They didn't seem to want to understand or care that this was a joint decision and that no one was being kidnapped.

"Don't worry bout dem, dem will get over it," Bongo assured me.

So on our last night in Jamaica, we did not sleep but spent our night saying our final farewells and loading up the car for our departure the following morning. But as usual, the devil was up to his old tricks again. Many of our friends wanted to accompany us to the airport but the car was too small and could only hold the three of us, and the luggage.

That morning as we prepared to leave, the car was packed and everyone was in the car except me. I was tearing up the house searching for the car keys, which were nowhere to be found. The last place I had seen them was on the shelf, in the room. But now, they were missing, and no one knew where they were, nor did they seem too concerned. We searched everywhere and time was running out as we had a three-hour ride in front of us. Our plane was scheduled to depart at 1:00 p.m. Totally exasperated, I started to cry.

"Ire Star", said Bongo, "we ah come too far and me naw turn back now. Tis' Afrika me a go, JAH know."

With that he took off down the road in a trot. Within fifteen minutes he was back in a red pick up truck belonging to Mr. Sutty and being driven by our friend and brethren, George Young.

"Mon naw can stop dis movement hyah (here)" Bongo laughed, jumping out of the truck.

Once again, our travel route, unplanned by us had become historically likened to our ancestors escaping from enslavement in the South, heading North to so-called freedom. Within five days of our arrival in Jamaica, we were continuing our "Exodus."

We transferred all our belongings from the car, abandoning our rental car and got on the road. All of the people who had wanted to go to the airport with us (ten of them) all piled into the back of the truck laughing and having a good ole time. We were homeward bound. Everyone was very excited though a little sad but we made the best of it.

We arrived at the airport and began checking in. Because Bongo and Sister D were traveling as 'in transit' passengers through the United States we were separated once our bags were checked in and the ticketing was complete. The next time I saw them they were sitting in the First Class Section of the plane, drinking cold Red Strip beers.

"Yo family," I greeted them as I walked into the cabin of the plane. "What are you doing sitting here?" I asked.

"The Mon tol' we to take a seat, and asked what we wanted to drink. So here we stay."

"Great," I said.

So when the steward approached and asked me if I wanted the same thing, naturally I accepted.

"Sister D, Bongo Man, I don't think we're suppose to be sitting here," I continued. In fact, I knew full well that we weren't suppose to be sitting there.

"Well dis be the place dem tell we fer sit," Bongo replied.

So I just kicked back too, laughed and enjoyed my beer knowing that this would not last long. Sure enough as the rest of the people began to board the plane, a woman approached us and very sharply stated, "You're in my seat."

Just then the Steward appeared asking, "What is the problem?"

Again the woman said, "They're in my seat."

"Let me see your tickets please," the steward asked.

Well, I knew from that moment that the picnic was over.

"You belong in coach", he said. "Please move to that section."

"No problem," I answered.

"OK family, let's take our beers and move."

Boy, did I get a good laugh as I explained the situation to Bongo and Sister D, who had never been on an airplane before. They had only done what the steward had told them to do when he welcomed them aboard, which was to "take a seat" in the first seat they came to.

Coach was definitely different and Sister D being a rather large framed sister, the coach seats were rather tight for her. Luckily no one was sitting next to her, except Bongo, so she had two seats. What a way to begin our journey home...First Class.

The first stop in our journey was Miami, Florida where we were to change planes to continue our flight to New York. Sister D was feeling apprehensive and was chain smoking. A customs officer met us as we cleared Customs to escort us to our connecting flight.

"Do we have to take another plane?" she asked sorrowfully.

The customs officer laughed and answered, assuring Sister D that everything was fine and that she would enjoy the flight. She looked at Bongo and I and shrugged her shoulder.

That's easy for you to say, the look on her face said as she lit another cigarette.

Our next flight was smooth and when we arrived in New York at John F. Kennedy International Airport there was another customs officer to meet us and escort us to British Airways. He was a very friendly brother and became quite excited when we told him that we were returning home to Afrika to live. We laughed and talked and he did everything possible to help Sister D relax.

All of us were so relieved to be in motion that the seven-hour layover before our departure to London did not phase us. I never even looked at the New York City skyline as we transferred to the British Airlines Departure Terminal. I still had visions of that nightmare I had in Jamaica of being Lot's wife and turning into a pillar of salt. When we arrived at the departure terminal Nana was there with our good friend and brother Gene who stayed with us until departure time. Everything had been taken care of except the disposal of our van or so I thought. Then I asked Nana about the van.

"Oh, I gave it to Gene." he replied nonchalantly,

Everything had indeed been taken care of. After nearly one year of facing and defeating obstacles and resisting a rising paranoia of being trapped forever in the United States and the Caribbean, we were making our Exodus "forward" across the "Middle Passage," the watery graveyard of our ancestors, to our Ancestral Homeland, Afrika.

Home! This was no vacation...this was forever. From that day forward our address would be Ghana, West Afrika.

CHAPTER EIGHT

WE MADE IT HOME

Yes, I was home...again.

When we finally returned in October 1991, our friend and brother Kwadjo was most gracious. He met us at the airport with our car, which we had previously purchased from him in 1990, when we originally relocated to Ghana. He drove us to his home in Cape Coast.

When we inquired about the color of the car being changed, he said that it had begun to rust and he wanted it to look nice for our return. Our best Ghanaian *friend,* all around good guy and man about town, had painted our green Mercedes Benz another color without our consent.

He had also removed the license plates and been using our car as a rent-a-car service. It was seen by some other friends of ours being driven all over town by some white folks. The truth of the matter we would soon learn, was that by painting it white, no one would recognize it (or so he thought), for it was originally painted a distinct bluish green, with the license plate number 7777, One Africa. But what could we do? The damage was already done. The car had been re-painted.

We generally stayed with Kwadjo and his family, who hosted us during our previous visits to Ghana, as we were preparing our exodus from the United States. He was also known to our original group, from our first visit in 1987 and thought he was a *cool* guy. So did we!

Coming home again was joyous and we were all so happy; Sister D, Bongo Shorty, Nana and I. A dream come true! What we had talked about, prayed about and dreamed about for more than 15 years had finally materialized.

This was "Mother" Afrika and we were finally back in her bosom. Mother Africa; Black ... Ebony ... smoking ... rich ... green ... friendly ... historical ... and mysterious. And we were right in the center of the earth: Ghana, West Afrika was finally our real home.

The first thing I did when we arrived in Cape Coast was to visit the Cape Coast Castle Dungeons. Feeling the cooling breeze and ruminating about the past I recalled my first visit to Ghana in August 1987. When I entered the Women's Dungeons after having flown across the watery graveyard of my ancestors, I had become even more aware of being on a spiritual journey – I had become another "destiny soul seeker." Spiritually I had been awakened and I knew that I would never be the same again - ever.

The spirit of the land and the spirit of my ancestors took hold of me as I re-entered the Cape Coast Castle Dungeons – They were there waiting for me. Pulling off my shoes, I slowly and quietly walked on that sacred and historic ground to better commune with them. Touching the rough, cold and damp stones of the dungeon walls and looking up at the cavernous ceilings, I felt the darkness closing in around me as I once again pulled up nightmares of being enslaved and dehumanized by strange looking, dirty pink men.

I remembered my ancestors. Smelling their musty, sweating bodies and feeling them – hands touching me, caressing me, quieting the anguished flow of my hot tears: warmly and strongly welcoming me home but forcing me once again to remember how it must have been for them, taken from these shores in the holds of strange, ominous looking vessels. Slave ships that rolled and pitched and swayed on the vast waters of the Gulf of Guinea that waited to "swallow them up quick" into the Belly of the Beast: floating houses of horror. Thousands upon thousands of Afrikan men, women and children stacked side by side and on top of one another in 24-inch spaces, maybe 5 to 6 feet in length, destined for unknown lands, never to see Afrika again.

I thought of the millions of our Afrikan Ancestors who passed through these same "DOORS OF NO RETURN": forced to undergo the inhuman conditions of disease, filth, torture and unrivaled cruelties. Some of them committing suicide, in transit, preferring death to facing the unknown. Others, sick or so weakened from near starvation resulting from months of forced overland travel and weeks of cramped imprisonment with little food and water were thrown over board to the sharks, with the rebellious who continued to resist up to the end.

But then, after over 500 hundred years of enslavement in a strange place, I, their daughter, my husband and my brethren & sistren, one of their many children, had been blessed to return home.

And what had we left behind? Everything: our family, children, grand-children, life long friends...and the stress of living in the hellish condition of many Afrikans born in the United States and often being a *"paycheck away from being homeless."* For protection from the outside world we lived behind multi-locked doors with bars and gates at the windows, and fearful of being in the streets of the South Bronx after dark. Places where none but the brave or foolish dare trod. Now we were free of that, we were home.

But the return home also came with certain conditions, certain expectations from my ancestors. I had been given the task of being one of the "Gatekeepers" for the DOOR OF NO RETURN; to be there to welcome home those brothers and sisters that would be returning in their numbers. Once again thanking God and my ancestors, I slowly walked out of the Women's Dungeon into the daylight. Realizing the awesome task that I had been given I prayed to be able to handle it.

Everyone was excited those first few weeks. But for some reason Sister D was feeling more than a little uncomfortable being in Kwadjo's house. She didn't like the vibes she was picking up from our host and doubted his sincerity. Additionally, she didn't feel welcome in his home.

"Relax, we told her, everything is fine," we assured her continuously.

But she didn't feel better until we had moved her and Bongo into our little village of Iture, where Nana had been made the Sofohen in 1990.

Sister D or Mama D as she was now called, was happier living in the village with Bongo. But I missed them very much and wanted to be where they were. We hadn't come this far together to be separated in our homeland. Nana and I would go out often and spend the night with them, but it wasn't the same. The living conditions were very close, the mosquitoes were fierce and giving us a fit. Though not too happily, we were managing. We were also on the look out for a larger place.

Nana and I were still staying at Kwadjo's house, making arrangements for the construction of our new house, which was also being handled by our brother Kwadjo. Even though the relationship was getting a little strained. Still, we managed.

It was hard to believe. We had been in Ghana for a month and it was time to go to the Immigration Authorities in Accra to extend our Visa: one of many extensions that we would be required to have in order to stay in the land of our ancestors. Utter nonsense, but we complied.

We set out early that morning about 6:00 a.m. Everyone was in a jovial mood. This was Bongo and Mama D's first trip to the capital.

About 20 miles outside of Cape Coast we ran out of gas. We had traded cars with brother Kwadjo, who had loaned us his car to go to Accra, however, he neglected to put gas in the car and the tank was empty. But Nana said he faulted himself, he looked at the wrong gauge and should not have assumed that Kwadjo had gassed up his ride, (even though Nana had gassed up our Benz before giving it to him). But all things being equal the car ran out of gas in front of a filling station so all was not lost, I thought. When we rolled into the station, a man waved at us. Not understanding what he was saying, Nana got out of the car and went to speak with him. Nana didn't speak the language, so I asked the young man who was moving with us to go with Nana and translate so that there would be no misunderstandings. After some discussion Nana and Tommy, our escort, returned to the gas pump.

The gas pump was one of those old fashion, gallon glass jars, where you could see the gas as it fills up from one gallon bottle to another, and the number of gallons being pumped in was counted by the attendant using stones, which he put one aside each time the bottle filled up.

This was definitely different from the way it was done in the United States. In all we took in six gallons of gas.

I suggested to Nana that 'we might as well fill up,' but he refused stating that he wanted to get the balance in town at a well-known place like a Mobile or Shell Station.

"Six gallons of Taylor's Gas would suffice," he said.

Anxious to get to Accra early we started out again.

One mile down the road the car began to belch out black smoke, jump and sputter. Nana immediately pulled over and we all jumped out of the car. Black smoke billowed out of the tail pipe and the car would go no further.

"What's wrong?" I asked Nana.

But before he could answer, Tommy spoke up.

"I think it's the gas. We used Diesel fuel, because they were out of Petrol."

"What?" Screamed Nana, "Diesel fuel? Are you mad? Didn't I tell you Petrol?"

Well, that was not exactly true. What Nana meant and what Nana said were two different things. Nana had used the term "gasoline," which does not mean the same thing in Ghana as it does in the United States. Gasoline translates to Gasoil and Gasoil translates to Diesel Fuel, which was not meant for our car. We were stuck! But what really ran our blood pressure up was when Tommy admitted, that he thought the car did not take Diesel Fuel, but said nothing as they pumped six gallons of Diesel Fuel into our gas tank.

Since Tommy had created the problem we sent him back to the gas station to get a large plastic container and a hose to draw out the "Gasoil."

In the meantime, some brothers stopped to assist us. Tommy returned with the container. It didn't work ... there was a screen separating the gas tank from the gas pipe, which kept out the trash ... and us. Nana was pacing up and down, mad as forty Mad Hatters. And as much as I disliked cigarette smoking, I tried to find him a cigarette, to hopefully calm his nerves. No luck ... no stores ... and no one around us smoked or had a cigarette.

In the meantime, a real cool brother went down the road and found some rope to tow our car to the next service station, eight miles away. A taxicab arrived and attempted to pull our car but no luck ... as soon as we got rolling the towrope broke. Finally the ingenuity of our Ghanaian helper got it fixed and off we went, again. A half a mile down the road the towrope broke again. We fixed it and two miles down the road it broke again. A real *comedy of errors*. When we broke down this time, the same brother that had helped us the first time reappeared, and just in time. He again helped us to secure the car again and we prepared to leave again but not before I stopped at a roadside kiosk (store) to secure cigarettes and a drink to soothe the *raging* Nana.

We finally made it to the 'fitter's shop,' which is what Ghanaians call the auto repair shop or mechanic. The fitter also could not drain the gas tank without removing the tank from the car. Once removed, the gas was drained, the tank washed out and re-installed. Next the carburetor had to be cleaned. However, the fitter had trouble getting the gas tank back in the car.

If that wasn't enough drama for one day, suddenly out of nowhere the wind started kicking up and dark clouds rolled in from the east and the heavens opened up. Showers of blessings! The rain lasted only a short time, while the work on the car was quickly completed. Nana and the fitter took a test run and all was well, again.

Nana asked the fitter for the cost of the job, which we thought was going to be monstrous, for the amount of work that he had done and the time involved.

He thought for a minute and finally replied, "Three thousand five hundred cedis."

"Are you sure?" I asked.

I didn't see how it could only cost us the equivalent of eight US dollars, for all that work. Tommy, our guide started shouting at the fitter, "It is toooo much money, you are cheating the people."

"Calm down," we told him. "It's all right: we want to pay him what he is asking. Ain't no way in New York City we could have anything done to our car for that kind of money."

Besides we had just come home and we had it like that. We had a little extra cash and it really wasn't a lot of money to us. Plus we were extremely grateful. Tommy still didn't like it but what could he do. Finally, he just thanked the fitter, in Fante, on our behalf and we were on our way again.

It was now after 1:00 p.m. We had been on the road trying to get to Accra since 6:00 a.m. In addition to going to Immigration, we had also come to town to do some shopping for my birthday party. The trip to the Immigration Office was another adventure of sorts. Even though we had been given a visa for three months, it was still necessary to:

(1) Fill out multi-copies of an Immigration form (no carbon copies allowed).

(2) Take new Passport size photos (in black & white only).

(3) Submit a letter from Nana Mbra, the Omanhen of the Oguaa Traditional Area in support of our wanting to stay in the country and

(4) Wait for approval of our request.

We ran around like chickens with their heads cut off trying to accomplish everything before the office closed.

"Why is all of this necessary?" we questioned the Immigration Officer. "Our visa is valid for three months."

"It doesn't matter," he said, "this is our policy and you are foreigners."

"*Ouch!*" I said to myself.

Just the term *foreigners* was enough to make the hairs stand up on the back of our necks.

"We're Afrikan people just like you," we said. "So how could we be foreigners in Afrika, the land of your ancestors?"

"There's nothing I can do about that," he continued, "if you want to stay in Ghana this is what you will have to do."

There was no such thing as Dual Citizenship. Not too happy with his answer, we completed our tasks and by five o'clock we were finally finished, at least for the moment. Whew! It had been some day. We did the rest of our shopping and returned to Cape Coast.

It had been a real struggle, but I had made it home to Ghana in time to turn 50 in my ancestral homeland. On November 7, 1991, I turned a half a century old: a precious gift from The Creator.

That was one of the most memorable days of my life.... It was *my* day. Sister Malkia, a dear friend and jazzy elder sister and Queen Mother from Detroit, was the Managing Director of the Oyster Bay Hotel. She gave me a night's reservation with dinner and drinks as a birthday present. I had met her during one of my visits to Ghana and we had become close friends. In fact, she, Nana and I were the only Afrikans born in the United States that lived in the Cape Coast/Elmina areas. So naturally we gravitated to one another.

That day we were all very happy, cracking jokes, laughing and talking with everyone we met. Trying to speak the language. I even tried cooking Ghanaian food.

Plus we had just given our friend Kwadjo, five thousand US dollars to begin construction on our new house in Iture. We spoke to the lawyer and he was drawing up the papers spelling our terms of agreement with Kwadjo. He advised us to proceed with the project. Plus Kojo was anxious to get started. If I said we were excited, I'd be grossly misrepresenting how we felt. We were going to have our own home, in our ancestral homeland. Dreams did in fact come true.

That afternoon Mama D., Bongo Shorty, Nana and I hung out in our village, Iture. We had a little birthday party with the children. They sang Fante songs and we taught them songs from America and the Caribbean. Someone cooked Fufu, a local dish made with cassava and ripe plantain, which was pounded in a mortar until it became a dough-like substance and was served with light soup. Other refreshments (chips and candy) were served, nothing big and the adults drank Apoteshi, the local hooch (or kill me quick) as they called it and we had a good ole time.

Life in the village was so simple but it was hard. There were no cars running up and down the place and children could play freely but many of them didn't go to school because their parents didn't have money for school fees. There was also no electricity and people used kerosene lanterns and didn't seem to mind. There was no running water in individual homes. You had to go to the standpipe in the middle of the village, where you paid to retrieve water. The cooking was done on a wood fire for there was no gas stove and most people slept on mats on the floor instead of foam rubber mattresses. The children rose early in the morning and searched for firewood before going to school. Yet, the people laughed so easily in spite of their troubles and sparse living conditions. Boy, were we spoiled living in the States. These wonderful people made this day a very memorable one. I looked forward to being able to do something that could help them in some way.

Around nine o'clock that evening Nana and I left for my honeymoon, birthday present at Oyster Bay Hotel. It had been a perfect day and now we headed for a perfect night. My honey and I made sweet and gentle, but passionate love that evening that floated me away on a cloud of bliss. Sweet memories of our past together and a promising outlook for our future warmed my body like a blanket, as we cuddled up and drifted off to sleep. The next sound I heard was the thunder of the crashing waves on the shore and the sweet music of birds outside our window. The night had faded and a new day had come.

I went outside to greet the morning, watching the long boats sailing by with their multi-colored flags from many nations flying in the wind. Boats powered by 40 Horse Power motors, and others powered by eight strong, Black Afrikans, moving their boats along with good, strong, precise strides as they sang, chanted and rowed.

I reminisced about my first trip to Ghana in 1987, when I stood in this exact spot: a look at that day and a look at today, on that same Atlantic coastline our ancestors were taken from. The Elmina Castle Dungeons and Fort St. Jago loomed in the distance. I felt the pain of yesterday, the pain of the dark and damp dungeons of living hell for our people, a New World for many and death for so many others.

As I stood there, absorbed by those memories, I cried. Feeling the pain of yesterday and the joy of today, I gave thanks once again to The Creator and our ancestors for making it possible for me to be standing there and for the joy of coming home to "Mother."

After breakfast Nana and I went back to Kwadjo's house, where we were still staying until we found a place.

Other arrangements were under way for my "Big Fifty" birthday bash. Everyone was excited. I was particularly ecstatic, as I had vowed with the help of The Creator that I would be back in Ghana permanently and in time to celebrate my fiftieth birthday and here I was. Nana and Kwadjo gave me the greatest party in celebration of my half a century observation. We were expecting a few people according to our host, who knew everybody. And holding to his word by midnight the house was over run with people, most of whom I did not know. There must have been over 50 people at the party and we danced and laughed, ate and drank until daylight. I didn't know half of the people at the party but it didn't make a difference to me. I had a fantastic time. I finally went to bed, people were still there but I could no longer hang and went to bed exhausted but happy.

Following the birthday party, our days were busy and we spent quite a bit of time in the village with Mama D and Bongo. And we continued to look for another place to stay.

Two weeks after my birthday we had the ground-breaking ceremony for our new home in Afrika. The Queen Mother from our village, Iture, and many of the people from the village were present for this most auspicious occasion. Libations were poured by the Fetish Priestess and traditional prayers offered up for our safe return and our new beginning. Photographs of our parents were buried in the foundation of our new home. It wouldn't be long now. Work had officially begun. All of us were excited about our new house. We even built a small hut on our land where we used to hang out while the construction of our house was going on.

More and more, even I was beginning to feel uncomfortable about staying in Kwadjo's house, as certain things about the brother were being revealed to us. One day a man from a community development agency came to the house to see us. He said that he had been in touch with Kwadjo, who told him that we were his partners. Kwadjo had borrowed six million cedis and had defaulted on the loan and now they wanted us to re-pay it.

"We don't know anything about any loan," Nana told the man. "Nor did we know that Kwadjo borrowed any money against the business. We're not paying that."

Next we found out that the company had been registered but our names had been omitted. We were told that our names would now be put on the papers, now that we were here because it had been impossible to do without us.

"Just a minute," Nana told Kwadjo, "You expect us to put our names to something that has a six million cedi default and you never discussed any loan with us. No way my man, it don't work like that."

I had spent another sleepless night, brought on by the shock (for want of a better word) of the actions being taken by Kwadjo. With the passing of time, less and less, did I want to be referred to by him, and some others, as *Sister*!

But some of our dilemma I must blame on ourselves for we were caught up in the excitement of returning home. Our romanticized notion of Afrika, clouded our vision, as did our acceptance by a brother who was so willing to help us and to share his home with us. He portrayed himself as our good friend and we were trusting and taking him at his word. We forgot for a moment that business is business and friendship is friendship. And those business matters should have been spelled out in writing, in advance, before the release of our hard-earned cash. But this was now hind-sight and we were being burned ... again. The original contract had not been signed.

"Why is it being delayed by the lawyer," we asked Kwadjo. "You already have funds that we've given you without a signed contract."

Kwadjo re-assured us, "no other money will be necessary until the house was completed." But shortly thereafter, Kwadjo came and told us, "I will need additional money to continue construction on your house."

"What happened?", we asked him.

"Oh, the prices have gone up and your money that you have given to me did not reach. I am using the money to build your house."

He was right; it was our house, so his argument did have some merit. Nana and I discussed it further and although reluctantly, we agreed to give him the additional $5,000.00 to continue the work. Money was tight everywhere and we were anxious to be in our own place, which was being promised by mid-February and we were still trusting. But the alarm light began flashing as I remembered that we still had not signed the contract and every time we approached him to sign it, he didn't have time, he was very busy with the house, and had many things to do.

"Don't worry Sister Vienna, don't worry Nana, I will do it. Not to worry."

And as if we didn't have enough on our plate, next Bongo and Mama D. got sick with Malaria and Nana then got sick. Mama D. continued to be sick but Bongo and Nana got well. I also fell sick for a week with a severe attack of Malaria. I thought I was going to die. It certainly felt that way. I had a high fever and chills: my body ached all over. I had no appetite and spent most of my time sleeping and when I wasn't sleeping I was puking my guts out. I didn't ever remember feeling so bad, except when I had the Swine Flu. Not being able to stand it any further, I literally crawled into the doctor's office, only to be greeted by the bright, smiling face of the doctor. As Nana explained my symptoms the doctor instructed him to put me into the bed.

Once settled he said,

"Welcome, you are officially home. You have malaria. But you'll be just fine after the medication begins its work. Go home and get some rest."

When I was feeling better Nana and I presented the contract to Kwadjo again. By now the light was flashing faster and faster in my mind for I had met and spoken to a man who knew us and had asked, "Is everything in order, have you gotten your contract signed? This is very important," he warned, "for contractors and friends acting as contractors have been known to take your money and leave your project unfinished."

Feeling sick to my stomach I immediately began to pray fervently, "Lord, please keep our brother's heart righteous and let us get this contract signed immediately."

I rushed home and told Nana of the conversation that I had with this brother.

By now Nana had reached the end of his patience.

"Oh, no problem," Kwadjo said again, when we approached him for the fourth or fifth time, "we'll go to the Commissioner of Oaths in the morning."

The next morning he rushed out of the house,

"I'll be back by 11:00 o'clock," he said.

We waited and waited, papers in hand. Kwadjo didn't come back until after 3:00 p.m. When he came in, he was talking about the money we had already given him.

"Nana, the $10,000.00 that you and IMAH gave me is almost gone. It wasn't enough. I'm going to lose money in doing this job for you and another 1.6 million cedis above the balance due of Six Thousand Five Hundred Dollars is going to be necessary. Can you give me the balance of the money, before the house is completed or the contract signed?"

We must have really looked like *jerks*.

"Of course not," we lamented.

To which he responded, "Well, I will go as far as I can with what you've given me and unless you give me the balance of the money the house will not be finished."

We argued and argued but to no avail. He then called his lawyer who gave us an appointment for all of us to come in together. I was livid.

This "Nigger" (and as much as I hated the term, I used it loose-ly), was ripping us off or should I say had "ripped" us off.

"Where was the trust?" I cried to Nana. "What about brother-hood, love, honesty and all that stuff we had reasoned about togeth-er?"

It was a crock of crap and we had been taken for a good, expen-sive ride. If I had a gun I would have killed that man.

Fuck him, I thought, *and his lawyer.*

But, I also realized that this kind of attitude was going to get us nowhere.

We agreed to go to the lawyer. When we arrived at the lawyer's office, Kwadjo tried to make it sound as though he were helping us.

"I was trying to do them a favor by agreeing to build their house so cheaply in the first place," he told his lawyer. Now it is going to cost me money, my own money," shaking his head and trying to look sorry. "Because things have gone up I want to change the orig-inal agreement and I want them to pay all now, before I will finish the house."

"No way," we said.

But before we could continue, his lawyer wanted to know, "What are their protections should you default on your agreement," the lawyer said looking at Kwadjo; trying to sound like he was on our side.

"I'll put up my trucks and the deed to my house (which was not his we ultimately found out). I only want to finish the job (of rip-ping us off) for them and go on to my next project," he continued.

The lawyer seemed to be in perfect sympathy with him.

"Well," he said, "he is trying for you."

It sure as hell did not sound that way to us. We told him and his lawyer that we would discuss it with our family and get back to him in a few days with our decision. In the meantime with heavy hearts and lighter pockets, we left him with his lawyer and returned to his house.

We had to decide the best way to proceed in the best interest of our investment. We also sought the advice of another lawyer. After explaining our problem to him, he assured us that everything was going to be all right. In fact, he was going to set up a meeting between Kwadjo and another upstanding member in the communi-ty, who would make certain that our brother Kwadjo kept his part of the bargain.

The meeting went off, and assurances were again given. Then our lawyer advised us to give Kwadjo the balance of the money so he could finish our house, minus a few of the things that we were suppose to get like terrazzo floors, red tile roof, and stone facing on the house. Everything else was to remain the same.

Were we supposed to be pleased? Whose side was he on anyway? This was a real rip off to say the least. But we went along with it. What else could we do? The amended contract was signed and witnessed by two chiefs, who acted as witnesses for both sides, Kwadjo, his lawyer and us. We had paid in full for our house and now we had to wait and pray.

We immediately began to move our possessions out of Kwadjo's house, taking them to our village and keeping them in another friend's house. We finally got everything out and settled into that little room in the village with Bongo and Mama D. At least we were all together. I had to admit to Mama D. that she had been right. She recognized what we could not see... the vibe was not right, but we had not paid serious heed.

And as if we did not have enough on our plate, shortly after we moved in Bongo took sick again and had to be admitted to Central Hospital for an emergency hernia operation. I came down with Malaria again and had to be hospitalized also.

"Nana can leave you with us for a couple of days," the Doctor advised, acting like he was glad to see me again.

I really didn't want to stay but as bad as I was feeling, I would have stayed in the middle of the jungle with Cheetah if it would make me feel better. The following day Mama D. was admitted to the same hospital. In this case "misery" was not enjoying company. The doctor joked and said she was in sympathy with me. Sympathy or not mama D and I both felt like hell.

Thank God Nana stayed well. But brother, was he ever busy, running up and down between two hospitals, bringing food for us because meals were not provided by the hospital. Other than a cup of tea and a piece of bread that was all you received. The hospital didn't even supply the medication. Your family was responsible for buying it and bringing it to the hospital. Nana had to do it all.

In the meantime, just before Christmas (or Xmas as it is called here) an uncompleted house in the village became available for our use. On Xmas eve, Nana brought Mama D. and I home from the hospital. On our way to the village we stopped at the hospital to visit Bongo, only to find him fully dressed and standing at the front door of the hospital, ready to go home.

"Did the doctor release you?" we asked him, happy to see him up and around.

"Me naw need no doctor fer tell I n I when I can go, I fine Star and I wan go home," he said, "I released Iself."

The doctor walked up while we were standing there and asked if Bongo had been discharged and we all started laughing.

"Thank you for everything, doctor," Bongo said. "But I discharged Iself."

The doctor himself started to laugh and offered no argument to that, only remarking that, "Mr. Morrison, you're a remarkable patient. I wish all my patients were like you."

For Bongo had gotten up the day after his surgery and been visiting the other patients offering them words of encouragement and singing inspirational songs to them. With no further ado, the doctor officially discharged Bongo and we all went to our new home in Iture.

It was a three bedroom house. It had windows and doors but needed screens for the windows. There was running water but no toilet, so we used buckets. We agreed to take the house and make a few repairs, dig a cesspool and paint the inside of the house, in exchange for rent. Not having any furniture, we hung our hammocks in our respective bedrooms and there we stayed until our house was finished. Or at least that was the plan.

The peace, quiet and serenity of village living, surrounded by lush green trees and foliage, set into motion the healing of wounded souls.

But returning home ain't easy!

On our return we found that we had a new set of challenges to face, that of the 'returnee' or 'pioneer;' language barriers, differences in culture, sicknesses like malaria, mysentery, bilharzia (worms) and the lack of conveniences that we took for granted in the United States. We had to re-acclimate ourselves to the differences in the seasons, the go-slow attitude of our people (much like the Southern states in America).

But the hardest of all was the perception by many Ghanaians of us as *Obruni* (white man or foreigner). But even with all of this, it was still a blessing and a challenge to be home.

On Christmas day, some new friends that we had met, brother Daveed and his Ghanaian wife Sister Milka who had been living in Ghana for several years and Mamalena and Majuwa, two sisters who had relocated from Detroit, surprised us with a visit to celebrate our first Kwanzaa together. They had come to spend a few days.

"We don't have any real accommodations," we told them. "The best we can offer you are some sleeping bags on the floor."

That was fine with them.

"We're with family and family is as family does," Brother Daveed cracked, making everyone laugh. He's a real comedian.

Nana and Bongo agreed to give the sisters the hammocks and the guys crashed on the floor. We had a wonderful time, eating and drinking and dancing and laughing and cutting up like only we can do. And we spoke of plans for our respective futures. It was great being with folks who had made the same move. We weren't the only ones who had lost their minds (as we had been told by folks in america when we said we were going to Afrika to live) and we had so much in common. In fact it was the best Kwanzaa we had ever celebrated in the true sense of *Unity and Collective Work and Responsibility.* Several days later our friends returned to Accra.

With the holiday season behind us it was time to get back down to the business at hand. Getting our house built. Our present residence was for a six-month period and the owner would return to Ghana at that time.

It was good to be home. And I meant that in every sense of the word. We lived in a small village, shopped at the local market and bartered for items like everyone else. I always dressed in my traditional garments. But folks still looked at me curiously. I was a constant reminder to them that I was not a tourist but a returned Afrikan Descendant, a distant family member, desirous of living among them, at home.

However, there were those who insisted that I would always look like a tourist. When I inquired as to the reason they felt that way, one sister pointed to my locks and said, "we don't wear our hair that way in Ghana. Most women wear their hair like this," pointing to her own hair, which was permed. "If you want to be a beautiful Afrikan woman, you have to get a kit."

"A what?" I asked.

"A Kit," she repeated. Then it dawned on me.

"A Jerry Curl Kit?" I asked. Would I really look less like a tourist if I Jerri Curled or permed my hair?"

"Oh yes, then you would be more like us."

"Thanks, but no thanks," I said to her. "This is mine with no help from anyone other than the Creator."

"It is OK *me nua Besia* (my sister)," she laughed. "Akwaaba, you are welcome home."

Me dase paa, (thank you very much) I responded and everyone standing nearby started laughing. It wasn't ridicule, but I guess I did sound a little funny to them. After all, my intonation still had that New York twang.

What was even more amazing, was little children who could barely walk or talk called me *Obruni* (foreigner/white man), from their mother's back, where they were being carried. I was constantly reminding people that I was *Bibini* (an Afrikan /Black person).

"But you sound like the white man," they'd say.

"Well, what do you expect, I have been in the white man's country too long," I responded.

And they would just laugh again and call me sister. It was still good to be home.

Another person approached me for some "wee" (marijuana).

"What makes you think I have wee?" I asked her.

"Everyone knows that Rasta smokes wee," she said.

"Oh really, and who told you I am a Rasta?"

"You have Rasta hair, so you are Rasta," she replied with a very serious face.

Case closed........

NTESIE or MATE MASIE
(I have heard and kept it)

The symbol teaches the importance of imbibing all forms of information prudently in order to acquire wisdom and knowledge. It stresses the importance of keeping secrets and also advises people to ponder over issues before taking decisions. It however warns against gossiping and rumour mongering.

CHAPTER NINE

REALITY SETS IN

Every day we would go to the work site and wait. The workers would come but not brother Kwadjo. When he did come very little work went on and then he just stopped coming altogether.

Nana would go to town tracking him down and he always had an excuse. And our lawyer wasn't much help.

He just kept saying, "not to worry!"

"Do something," we demanded. "You're our lawyer. Aren't you supposed to be looking out for our interest?"

Finally, after threatening a lawsuit, the lawyer got Kwadjo to come to our "unfinished" house, which was not being completed per our agreement. After listening to a lot of bullshit conversation that was being spoken by both of them, Kwadjo told our lawyer, "I'm doing the best I can. Everything is very high and they are always questioning and complaining about how I do things."

We had been questioning because people who knew the job, were trying to help us for they knew that he was cheating us and they would never say anything to him being fearful of his wrath and/or the loss of their job but they could quietly advise us on the 'Q T', which they did. And we were grateful, for we needed all the help we could get.

"Well, I understand that the cost of materials is going higher each day, but you must try hard for them," the lawyer croaked. "They will soon have to give up the house they are staying in."

"They are my sister and brother," Kwadjo crooned.

With a snide smile on his face, not looking at Nana or I as he spoke and the lawyer kept nodding his head up and down like one of those kiwi dolls, that people use to have in the back windows of their cars.

"If a person can't look you in the face when they talk to you, don't trust them," my mother used to say.

With those words ringing in my ears, I knew we would not get anymore from Kwadjo than we currently had and our 'Jack Leg' lawyer wasn't going to help us much either.

I got so mad, that I told them both off.

"Don't call me sister," I told them, "neither of you know the meaning of sisterhood, brotherhood or righteousness." Turning to our lawyer, I continued. "And one day that Bible that you're always preaching from will burn up in your hand and you will both get your just rewards for what you've done."

Nana signaled to me to be quiet but I was too fed up. Tears flowing I continued to blast them.

"How could you both be so callous and greedy? You can both, go straight to hell!" I said as I started to turn away, leaving Nana in discussion with them.

"You're both wicked men and will burn in hell for what you've done to us."

With that I stormed off to have a good cry all by myself.

Another friend that we met in town a few days later had the temerity to ask us,

"What kind of lucky charm are you using on Kwadjo that he has not ripped you off?"

Seething, I responded through clenched teeth, "You should have asked that question a few weeks ago. There isn't and never was any good luck charm."

It was now clearly out in the open and I understood beyond a shadow of a doubt that our good brother Kwadjo, big man about town was nothing more than a petty thief and con artist and our lawyer wasn't much better. Well, so much for the help of a brother when coming home. This brother had helped himself.

From that point on we were totally on our own. Between Nana, Bongo Shorty, Mama D. and I, we were determined to finish building 'our' house, ourselves. We were the perfect contractor's team, a retired New York City firefighter, an ex-human resource administrator, a fisherman/Boat builder and an artist. We were good to go.

When we took over the construction and moved into the house it had no windows, no doors, no ceilings, no floors, no running water in the house, no electricity, no sinks or toilet seats. The roof in the master bedroom was incomplete and the stars were our covers. If it rained we'd just sleep in another part of the house.

I felt quietly excited. Two of the most beautiful stars had risen from the southeastern side of the ocean, part of the Dragons Tail, yet another miracle of The Creator. As I sat and reflected I thought about the many Ghanaians who think that we're crazy for leaving America to come here and suffer – and rich because we were able to leave. We took basically the same kind of chance coming to Afrika as they would take in coming to America. In fact, they would have a better chance in America. I feel safer here. We didn't come here to alienate anyone or cause problems. We just came home.

Our experiences with brother Kwadjo was a learning experience (a costly one) but one of many experiences that we would have in the repatriation process. The man is a real beast with a capital "B." Lord, give me strength! I still had a hard time believing that he had treated us in such a negative and ugly manner. We had lived in his home, with his family; staying with him before we finally came to settle (at his invitation). We didn't stay, rent free either; we paid our way. His daughter carries my name and he was one of the people that offered the most encouragement, valuable assistance, time, and energy, while he was setting us up.

When we first found out that we could build a house, a real house, for about ten thousand U.S. dollars, we were ecstatic and immediately put the process into motion by the time we were forced to return to the United States in November 1990 to bury my mom. By the time we returned to Ghana again in 1991, the price of the house was sixteen thousand five hundred dollars according to brother Kwadjo. Still, it was not a bad price for a four bedroom, two bathroom (or water closet as they call it in Ghana) house on the oceanfront. Not bad at all!

But we got suckered, real good from a non-caring, greedy Afrikan con man who would have taken our place if we had given him more chances. As it was he chopped fifteen feet of our property but more about that at another time. How unfortunate that man must live this way. I'm still trying to pray for those who spitefully use me. Oh well!

The following day Nana went to the Carpenter to get the doors but he refused to give them to us, claiming that Kojo had not paid him all his money.

"That's not our problem," we said. "It's up to you to get your cash from Kwadjo but we have already paid and paid plenty for nothing."

Nana then went to the Police where he also got no satisfaction. He spoke to a person who said he was the Police Chief, who finally got the Carpenter to bring the doors to the Police Station. He then wanted Nana to drive him over to Kwadjo's house (because they didn't have a police car) so he could bring him in for questioning. Needless to say, he wasn't home and did not respond to any of the messages left for him. After several days Nana returned to the Police Station and met the same person again.

"What's happening with my doors," asked Nana.

"Nothing," came the reply, from the Police Officer.

Nana was furious.

"What kind of justice is this," he continued. "Doesn't anyone take these things seriously?"

But the officer, not in the least bit ruffled, asked Nana in a most condescending tone,

"Would you like to visit your doors?" (Like he was there to visit a friend).

"Hell no." said Nana as he stormed out of the Police Station and got into his car.

As Nana was starting up the car, the Policeman walked up and leaned into the window.

"Why don't you buy me a couple of beers?" He asked Nana.

"Get off my car," Nana shouted at him in frustration and proceeded to drive off.

But as he reached the gate he reconsidered and returned to the officer. Putting some money in this hand, he told him, "Buy yourself a few beers."

After all, it wasn't his fault that things had gone the way they did. The officer then smiled at Nana saying, "Now you know how we do business in Ghana!"

The next day our doors were released from jail.

It was now July and the owner of the house that we were staying in was coming home from France and would need his place back. We had never met the owner, only the owner's brother, who was also his caretaker. In fact, we were a few months late in vacating the premises as we had anticipated moving back in February had everything gone according to our plans.

Bongo, Mama D, Nana and I reasoned over the situation we were in and decided to move into our uncompleted house immediately. After all, our uncompleted house was almost in the same condition as the place we had been staying in while we waited for the completion of our house.

The most significant difference was that this was our house. We owned it ... No rent ... No mortgage...and no windows, no doors, no ceiling or floors, no toilet or running water in the house but what there was of it, it was ours.

So we just put screens to the windows, installed the doors, hung up our hammocks in our bedrooms, bought a couple of 'Slop Jars' (buckets) to take the place of our toilet and moved into our first home in the "Mother" land.

That first night was very special. Mama D and I cooked this fabulous meal of fried fish, plantain, rice and peas, while Nana and Bongo played the drums with Bongo firing up his repeater (drum). We chanted and sang songs of redemption and praise, while thanking The Almighty Creator for returning us safely home and putting us into our own space. That entire night a cricket sang, blending in perfectly with our drumming, singing and chanting: as though reaffirming our blessings.

I couldn't have been happier. We had learned a lot of lessons and we were about to go into the business of building a house...ours. There was much to do. We were officially our own contractors.

I awoke the next morning looking at the sky. Good thing it wasn't April-July, the rainy season, for the roof of our bedroom was still uncompleted and the sun's rays were shining in my face. I glanced over at Nana who was still sleeping and eased out of my hammock and went to stand on the verandah. It was a perfect morning. A slight breeze was blowing.

"Welcome to our place," I practiced saying. "Welcome to One Afrika's home. We're still in the process of building but just sit down anywhere." I laughed to myself. "Yes," I shouted, forgetting that the rest of the house was still sleeping. "Hot damn in the morning, I's in my own place ... Thank ya, thank ya, thank ya Lord."

While I was acting the fool, Mama D. walked up. She had been awake for a while herself and was also enjoying being in her own space.

"Well," she said, "we got plenty work to do but we'll get it done."

The first few weeks were spent sorting things out and assessing what had to be done, how to do it and who to get to do those things that we couldn't do ourselves, like concreting the floors, building the windows, installing the electricity, etc. Most of our money was gone, but we were still in fairly good shape and Nana's monthly pension check would carry us through.

When the word got around that we had moved into our uncompleted house, many of the workers started coming around again. They were looking for work and knew we needed to complete our house. But our biggest problem was that we could not pay an entire crew for we had gotten none of our money back from "brother" Kwadjo. We were going to have to finish this house a little bit at a time.

Our first undertaking was to complete the roof in our bedroom. We had to buy additional roofing sheets and get someone to finish the job. In the meantime, Mama D fired the painters who claimed to know what they were doing but had already used two buckets of paint and had not completely painted one room. They had succeeded in getting more paint on themselves than they had on the walls. Mama D looked at the mess they had made and immediately relieved them of their job.

"Ya call yaself painters?" she wanted to know.

They just looked at us kind of funny and said nothing.

"Well it's all right, we naw be needing ya again. Just put down the brushes. Me ah clean dem myselves. Me can paint, Mon ya know," she said.

"Yes Mon," Bongo chimed in as he joined us. "Mama D can out-paint most men I know. We got plenty of work but we can do it weself."

We paid them, thanked them for the mess they had made and sent them on their way. Our next professional painter was Mama D She attacked the job of painting with a vengeance and within a week the entire house had been beautifully painted with a minimum of paint on the floors and less on Mama D, who also used a lot less paint. We were on a roll.

The mason finished concreting the floors in place of terrazzo and since our funds were limited we couldn't even buy tiles but it was all right. Things were going to get better. Besides, we were just happy to be in our own place. Each month when the pension check came we did a little more. By the time the mason had completed concreting the cesspool, the plumber was called in to hook up the plumbing.

We were ecstatic... we would now be surrendering our 'Slop Jars' for a 'show nuff' toilet. We tied a red ribbon around the commode and had a ribbon cutting ceremony in the toilet or the Water Closet as it is called in Ghana. And the eldest got to 'sit' first.

The water had been off in the area for most of the day and according to the water company, they were not prepared for expansion and the pipes which were originally used, when they laid the pipes were too small to accommodate the demand, but it would get better (so we were told). We would just have "to exercise patience." We had to wait a while longer to use the facilities but we weren't complaining for it would not be as long as it had been. We all retired early that night, having worked hard all day.

I woke up about one o'clock a.m. that morning and decided to go out on the verandah. As my feet touched the ground I was in water up to my ankles.

"Nana, wake up!" I shouted. "There's water everywhere."
Everyone jumped up at the sound of my shouting and they themselves started shouting. From the other side of the house we could hear Bongo and Mama D. There was water in their room also. When we got the lanterns turned up we saw that the entire house was flooded. Water was flowing out of the walls, from every pipe, the toilet, the shower. Water was everywhere. We found the shut off valve and stopped the onslaught of water. We were all asking the same question.

"What happened to cause such a flood?"
But we could only speculate that something was wrong with the pipes. At daylight Nana went in search of the plumber who had

done this job but could not find him. He was told that the plumber had traveled. When Nana returned home the mason said that he knew a good plumber and brought him to the house. When the new plumber saw the job, he said, "That first man did not know what he was doing. I don't believe he was a real plumber."

Where there should have been elbow pipes the man had burned the plastic PVC pipes and bent them, causing them to crack. Other pipes were not connected correctly and in some cases not at all. It was a big mess. We were furious. The first plumber could not be found so we went ahead with our new plumber who set everything right.

A few days later the old plumber finally showed up, having received word that we were looking for him.

"Don't worry, I'll fix everything." He told us smiling sheepishly.

"What," I said furiously, "you call yourself a plumber?"

But in the entire scheme of things, what else could we expect. The same person who had chopped our money had hired him. After much debating and begging for another chance to complete the job, he finally accepted the facts that (1) we knew that what he had done was not correct. (2) that much of the materials that we'd originally bought, was missing (3) many of our clothes and papers that were in boxes on the floor got wet and (4) the best thing for him to do was to go away before he was beaten!

This was just another adventure, in building our house and the returning home process.

Next we found someone to make our windows. Living on the oceanfront we chose to have wood louvers. It was also less expensive than glass and aluminum. The man came and measured the windows, assuring us they would be completed in a few weeks. We were required to give a 50% deposit to start the job. That was fine with us. As we did not suffer from brutal winters or extreme cold, not having windows in was no big thing. Except, someone always had to be at the house because we couldn't secure the place. With so much work to do, someone would always be around the place. Three weeks came and went but no windows. When we went in search of the person who was making our windows we were told that he had gone to the United States and had given someone else the job.

"No problem," we said. "But when will we get the windows?"

"Soon, soon," replied the brother, "I finish soon. The boys, they be work on it."

Two weeks later we went back and the windows were still not completed.

"All right, enough of this crap," Nana said, "If you can't do our windows, just give us our money back."

"But the money finished," the carpenter cried. "And I be tryin' for get the wood I need. You must give me small more deposit," he insisted.

By now both of us were furious. We had been here at least five times with no success.

"I won't give you another pesewa and you'd better finish my windows or I'm going to have you arrested. Do you understand? I don't care where the wood comes from. But it had better come fast or you are going to jail," Nana threatened.

I couldn't believe that we were having a repeat performance.

"Is this guy related to Kwadjo?" I joked lightly with Nana. "I know one thing, I'm beginning to lose my frikkin' patience."

Two weeks later the man came with the windows. Most of them did not fit and they had not been stained, as we had agreed upon. I was ready to scream.

"Oh you don' worry," the carpenter told us, "I be make it fit."

There were those words again "you don' worry." It was getting so that every time I heard those three words, a warning bell went off in my head.

He and his apprentices then proceeded to saw and hammer and nail, until all the windows were finally installed. Now, some of the windows were a little too small, where he had cut them too short.

"Lord, give me strength," I prayed.

"It be fine," he tried assuring me, "it be fine."

Seeing that I was getting nowhere, except frustrated, I paid him most of his balance, holding a small portion back until he brought the last window, which they had forgotten to make. Being your own Building Contractor was not going to be so easy. But finally, all the windows were installed and we painted them ourselves.

In the meantime we were without electricity. So we did everything by the light of day, using lanterns and candles at night, an otherwise real romantic setting. Most nights we sat out under the stars reasoning with each other and planning our next strategy in the completion of our house. The people in our village were always asking why we didn't have electricity.

"Oh, we'll get it one day," was our constant answer.

Then the village got electricity. Nana had previously worked with them toward obtaining lights for the village. And then they also got assistance from the government. So you know when the lights went on in the village and we still didn't have electricity, everyone thought it was terrible that Nana, the Safohen, from America, didn't have lights!

"In order of priority," said Nana, "in order of priority. Nothing before its time."

Well, it was time but we just didn't have the money. So we made do and did not complain. After all, what did we have to complain about? We were where we wanted to be, doing basically what we wanted to do ... we just didn't have lights. No, let me correct that. We had lights (lanterns & candles): we didn't have electricity. Since we also did not have a computer or a refrigerator, there was no real rush. Any typing I had to do was done on my daddy's forty-year old manual Royal Typewriter, which I inherited when my moms died. As for refrigeration, we cooked daily and ate what we cooked. Anything left over was breakfast the next morning. And so it was with our return home.

This kind of living was no stranger to me for I had traveled throughout South America and lived in similar situations. I had also lived in Jamaica, West Indies, off and on since 1972. Previously on vacation; from 1983 to 84 I lived with Bongo Shorty and Mama D. I had thought that I wanted to live in Jamaica permanently at one time but the pull to Afrika was too strong and none of us wanted to remain in Jamaica. But we had no electricity in our living area either (other than that of a roadside street light).

What was paramount was that we were home.

It was shortly thereafter that we met Dr. Robert E. Lee or Uncle Bobby as he is affectionately called. Uncle Bobby came to Ghana in 1957 at the invitation of his classmate Osageyfo Dr. Kwame Nkrumah, who had also attended Lincoln University. We were reflecting and sharing some of our return home drama with Uncle

Bobby. Ghanaians would call it "Akan Drama," a daily soap opera in different dialects.

"Listen young people," (he was 73 and we were mid-fifties) "if you're expecting someone to roll out the red carpet and celebrate your return...forget it! Celebrate your own return. I don't know where my family came from in Afrika, I just know that my ancestors are from here. We need to stop trying to be Fante, Ashanti, Ewe, Ga or whatever. We have our own tribe; that tribe of Afrikans born in America, in Europe, the Caribbean and other parts of the Diaspora. All descendants of those Afrikans sold into slavery and, those who remained behind."

That made so much more sense to me.

"I've been here since 1957 and I am still not fluent in a particular language/dialect but I manage and I'm still learning. Learn the language though, for sometimes I feel shut out when my friends start speaking in their own tongue, when they tire of speaking English, and I don't know what's going on."

Listening to Dr. Lee made us feel more hopeful.

Dr. Lee advised us not to take it personally, "folks here chop their own families and good, life long friends. So what of you, the new kids on the block? Take your feelings off your sleeve and be about the business of being home once more. What are your plans? What are you going to do now that you're here? And how are you going to do it? Maybe in thirty or forty years you can share some advise on returning home to those still seeking to come."

Many things had befallen Uncle Bobby in his return home; the loss of his wife, son and other loved ones. Discriminated against by the country of his birth and the boycott of his dental practice by 'other' Americans because he chose to take on Ghanaian citizenship and his strong position and commitment to being in Afrika.

Most of us would have called it quits and returned to America. But this man had maintained a sense of humor: a home, a business and he generously shared his knowledge and experiences with us. He gave us a real wake up call. Being home came with many tests of one's will, patience and sense of humor: from people picking our tomatoes without permission, to white folks with bibles coming to 'save the souls of the heathen.'

One evening around 7 o'clock the dogs began to bark furiously. Nana went out to the gate to see why the dogs were barking and lo and behold there was Professor Leonard Jeffries, our friend and renowned Afrikan-American Scholar Warrior in the struggle for Afrikan people, from New York with a group of brothers and sisters and elders from around the States and the Caribbean, who were on a pilgrimage to Ghana.

What a pleasant surprise! We laughed and joked while giving them a tour of our little unfinished palace.

"These are some brave souls living like they're living, here in the dark and all but determined to be home. They're Pioneers! I know some of you people would be fit to be tied if you didn't have lights," Prof remarked.

Everyone started laughing and agreeing. One of the elder sisters, Fannie Clark asked, "Well, why don't you have lights?"

"In order of priority," was the answer from Nana, "in order of priority."

"Well, what does that mean," sister Fannie continued.

"When we get money honey," Nana laughed.

"Well, I hope you will get them soon," she continued, "I don't know how long I could live without lights."

"These are pioneers," Dr. Jefferies said again, "a little strange but didn't I tell you they were pioneers?"

"Yah", I interjected, "pioneers with short money but living in a place where short money will go a long way. We're fine, really. We are just happy to have made it back home. This is our blessing from the Creator and we are not complaining."

Shortly thereafter the group left, with us promising to hook-up with them the following day at their hotel.

We spent several days with the group, emotionally filled days traveling with them as they made their pilgrimage to seven other dungeons, forts and castles along the West Coast of Ghana. This was definitely a pilgrimage and we made some lasting friendships. It was soon time for the group to return to the United States.

Sister Sybil Williams, Assistant to Dr. John Henrik Clarke Professor of Afrikan/Afrikan-American history, another renowned Elder Historian and Warrior Scholar, was part of that group and promised to keep us abreast of the news about the goings on in the

United States, which we thirsted for. We didn't often receive news about the community unless a group came through.

So in lieu of news from across the waters, we had to satisfy ourselves with *The Daily Graphic*, *The Times* and other Ghanaian newspapers. The hottest thing on the press those days was the upcoming presidential elections. We did not involve ourselves in the political workings of Ghana. We observed closely and kept our comments and opinions to ourselves. During the first Democratic election in Ghana in 1992, during the pre-election campaigning we were approached by numerous friends soliciting our financial support for their respective parties. But our answer was always the same,

"We do not involve ourselves in the politics of Ghana but pray for a peaceful election that will be of benefit to all the people. We have friends that are umbrellas, chickens, corn, elephants and coconuts (symbols, which represent the various political parties - NDC, NIP, NCP, NPP AND PNP), and we can't take sides. All of you are our family."

Most of them understood our position.

"As you are not citizens of this country, it is better that you maintain that position," one brother told us. "In this way you will not have trouble."

For the most part the election campaigning was not very violent, considering that Ghana was now a newly democratic republic. There were a few scattered incidents but I think that above all it had been rather quiet. However, the information that was filtering to the outside community by the international media and others who were not "pro Ghana," was that Ghana was not safe for visitors. In fact we didn't really have any problems and the kind of violence we did witness was mild, mild, mild in comparison to what we had lived through in the United States when we were trying to get the right to vote. Ghana was going from military to democratic rule.

It was during this time that I got a job working as a Consultant with a news reporter for WABC Channel 8 News out of Dallas, Texas, the sister station to Channel 7 out of New York. He had contacted us after being referred by someone we had met during one of his or her visits to Ghana. He was doing a feature on Ghana and needed someone on the ground to prepare an itinerary covering various aspects of Ghanaian society and culture and was also interested in meeting some other Afrikans-born-in-America who were living in Ghana.

However, the war broke out in Somalia and he was re-assigned by his network to cover it so our plans changed slightly. Instead of meeting him, I got a call asking me to 'wife sit' with his significant other, while he was off reporting the war. It was fine with me. I spoke with the Mrs. on the phone and we arranged that I would meet her at the airport. She gave me the following description: "I have real short brownish hair, fair in complexion and about six feet tall. I'll be wearing a black dress and probably towering over the crowd."

"Don't worry," I told her, "I'll have a placard with your name on it in the event that all else fails. See you at the airport."

I was now on duty. Sure enough when I saw the sister, I threw the placard away (for she stood heads above the crowd) and welcomed my sister to Ghana. Both of us were a little apprehensive – me about where I was going to stay and she about sharing her room with another, strange woman. After we discussed it, we decided to share a room. After all, it wouldn't be so bad. And it worked out fine.

With this being Bernestine's first time in Ghana, she was shocked, as many other Afrikan descendants are when they walk the streets of Ghana at the pictures of a 'white' Jesus. Ghana is a Christian country and this is a very sensitive issue, when there are those of us who contend that according to scripture 'Jesus' is an Afrikan.

Especially after being taught the truth in our study of ancient Black people, by some of our great Afrikan historians, Yosef A.A. Ben-Jochannan, Dr. John Henrik Clarke, Cheikh Anta Diop, Chancellor Williams, John Jackson, Ivan Van Sertima and others. They and other Afrikan scholars have done their homework well, and in the process sent many white historians and theologians back to school. In addition many of the people mentioned in the Bible were Afrikan and the descendants of some of them still reside there, for example, descendants of the ancient Cushites. Additional support is the biblical reference in the Bible, Revelations 1 Vs 13 - 15 which states:

And in the midst of the seven candlesticks one like unto the son of man, clothed with a garment down to the foot, and girt about the paps with a golden girdle. His head and hair were white like WOOL, as white as snow; and his eyes were a flame of fire; and his feet like unto fine BRASS, as if BURNT in a furnace.

"Who does that sound like? Whom is the Scripture/Bible referring to?" We often ask our brothers and sisters. "Isn't the Afrikan's skin tone like that of being burnt/blackened? Someone who looks like us, an Afrikan or like that picture that has been painted with blond hair and blue eyes."

And more often than not they will say, "It doesn't matter what color Jesus was."

"Well then, if that's the case, take that picture of white Jesus down. And give people some choices so that they can make up their own minds...let's also display some pictures of a Black Christ and his prophets...if, it doesn't make a difference."

My sister was having a real big dose of culture shock.

"It's unbelievable," she said. "I never thought I'd see this in Afrika."

"Neither did I, but like everything else, you get used to it. You may never agree but you do get used to it but you continue to teach the truth."

"Have you ever thought of going on a midnight raid and painting the faces brown," she laughed.

"It's been considered," I said, "but the thought of prison was a very strong determining factor in my decision to leave it as it is. Folks in this "very Christian" country would be royally pissed off if I touched their "white" Jesus. Besides I have other more important things to do with my time and jail is not among them."

We both got a good, hearty laugh. But it was and still is an issue for us.

We traveled around meeting other friends and we had a ball for the three days that we were together before her husband, Gary Reeves and his cameraman, Cliff Williams arrived from Somalia. She knew a whole lot more about Ghana from the inside and could tell them a few things.

He would be working on a documentary entitled *"Visions of Africa"* which was a three part film covering the war in Somalia; the recovery of Uganda; and the Republic of Ghana, going from military to democratic rule as well as other aspects of the country. It was a great opportunity and we were going to make *a nice piece of change* (money). And I must say that we put together a real sweet itinerary.

I had the opportunity to meet with President Jerry John Rawlings at Osu Castle. Upon introduction, he asked me, "Where's your husband?"

I was flabbergasted. I couldn't believe that the President of Ghana had remembered Nana – or for that matter had remembered us from that one casual meeting, in a crowd at the Bukatue Festival in Elmina. I was too impressed, especially since I had never personally met any president of any country, and an Afrikan president at that.

"He's in the village, ah, at home Mr. President, taking care of some other matters." I managed to get out, without looking too foolish.

"Greet my brother for me, please."

"Most definitely, Mr. President, most definitely," I responded, trying not to appear like I was in shock, which I was.

After the interview, we were driven by the President, to the military airfield, where the interview continued with Gary Reeves, the news reporter and President Rawlings.

After the interview, Mr. Tsikata, the cameraman and the reporter were preparing to go on a flight with the President who would be flying the plane. President Rawlings is an ace jet plane pilot.

As Bernestine and I stood on the side the men boarded the plane, without us. Speaking loudly enough for Mr. Tsikata to hear us, I said, "Is this a man's thing?"

To which Bernestine responded, "I didn't think so but it does look like they're leaving us!"

"Well, that's not fair," I continued, "I like to fly too, don't you?"

"You know it my sister," she responded.

As we stood lamenting and sulking a little bit over the fact that we were being left behind, Mr. Tsikita who had left our side was now speaking to the President. Suddenly the President laughed, looking in our direction, he smiled and beckoned to us. Bernestine and I looked quizzically at one another and walked towards the President and Mr. Tsikata.

As we approached the President spoke, "Of course you're welcome to join us. We're taking a spin around Accra and up to Akosombo Dam. Get on board."

Once inside that plane we were both wishing we had kept our mouths shut. But our feet were already firmly planted in our mouths. Neither of us had ever been in a "small" jet plane before. So we nestled back in those little seats and acted like we had been doing this all our lives.

As we flew over the city, the sky and the ground turned sideways and my stomach moved into my mouth. The President was still talking and conducting his interview and flying the plane at the same time. More than once I felt like asking, *"Shouldn't you be paying more attention to the road/sky?"*

But I restrained myself and thought about what a wonderful opportunity I was having and how lucky I was to be flying with the President of Ghana and ain't this great, while my stomach screamed at my brain, *"WHAT ARE WE DOING UP HERE?"*

Before long we were returned to the field. It had been a great flight but I was real glad to be back on the ground.

This was some assignment. I was in seventh heaven and was being paid for being there. We even went to the home of the First Lady, Nana Konadu Rawlings and met with her.

* * * * * * *

The days flew by as we proceeded with the filming. They also captured the commemorative ceremony "THRU THE DOOR OF NO RETURN - THE RETURN," that Nana, Bongo and I were conducting for returning Afrikan descendants in the Cape Coast Castle Dungeons. A group of students from New York University were in town and had requested the ceremony. That day the ceremony was very highly charged and very emotional, especially in the Women's Dungeon. The young sisters were so full, they had so much to release and they were so glad to be home.

143

One sister related that,

"For the first time in my life I know the true meaning of sister-hood," as rivers of water flowed from her eyes.

Sisters removed their shoes and knelt down, their foreheads touching the ground, softly weeping. Others let out tortured screams as the spirit took them over. And although I had taken many sisters through this ceremony before, each time was different, each time it hurt. But, that is my portion, as the "Keeper of the Gate." By then the brothers had arrived from the Men's Dungeon and patiently waited for us to finish so that we could go "THRU THE DOOR OF NO RETURN" together.

Our filming next took us to Kumasi to the village of Ntonso to see the Adinkra dyes made and the production of Adinkra cloth. Adinkra cloth is usually worn for mourning. Its black patterns are hand-printed on ordinary cotton material with stamps carved in pieces of calabash. We went on to Ahwiaa, the carving village famous for its wood carvers and sculptors.

We then visited Bonwire, the center of the Kente weaving industry, where we witnessed the colorful and intricate Kente Cloth being woven by some of the best weavers in the country.

In a total cultural context, kente is more than just a cloth. It is a visual representation of history, philosophy, ethics, oral literature, religious belief, social values and political thought. Originally its use was reserved for royalty and limited to special social and sacred functions. The Ashanti people developed Kente weaving in the 17th century. However, historical accounts trace the origin of Kente to early weaving traditions in ancient West Afrikan Kingdoms that flourished between 300 AD and 1600 AD, prior to the formation of the Ashanti Kingdom in the 17th century. With the increased production of Kente it became more accessible to those who could afford to buy it. There are many, many different designs, each with different meanings. Today, Kente is used for many different things (to make jewelry, hair bands, shoes, etc.). I don't agree with the way it has been mis-used and in many ways cheapened. It is a special clothe and should be maintained as such.

But what can we do? It's called progress. (For a complete and beautiful pictorial & historical map on Kente Cloth, see Bibliography for details).

We then traveled to Aburi, where we visited and conducted an interview with an elder friend of ours who was one hundred and twenty (120) years young: the eldest person in Aburi. Nana and I had met her while visiting her grandson, who was a wood carver. She'd had a problem with her foot that she kept wrapped in newspaper. After looking at her foot, which had an infection, I was able to convince her to let me have her looked at by a doctor, who was a friend of ours and who lived in the area. I promised to return from time to time to check on her and we became instant family. Other than her foot, which forced her to get around with the assistance of a walking stick, she was in excellent health, didn't wear glasses and couldn't accept the fact that the family would no longer allow her to go to the farm. She still cooked and cleaned for herself and other than an occasional ache or pain, she was fine. She remained within the family: she was their matriarch, no nursing home business there.

The family affectionately called her 'old lady, old lady,' to which she would respond with a broad smile on her face, "Plankkay," which means, "I'm fit and strong."

During the interview she poured libation for our safe journey, and shared some words of wisdom before sending us on our way.

The last leg of my assignment was the Inauguration of President Rawlings and Ghana becoming a Democratic Republic. It was an exciting time. There was pomp and circumstance to beat the band. The Presidential Guards, the military, schoolchildren and dignitaries from all over the world were there. It was a chance of a lifetime and I had a Press Card and free admission. It was great!

There was only one problem though! I was not there.

A few hours before the Inauguration I got knocked down by malaria and spent my time with my head in a bucket, throwing up my guts and feeling miserable. The closest I got to the Inauguration was in front of the television but my head hurt so bad I could barely see it.

So much for my Barbara Walter's assignment! A few days later they were all gone back to Texas and we were a little richer both financially and spiritually. We had interacted with some really great folks, established some lasting friendships and got a million dollars worth of a free coverage for our organization. Great!

NSOROMMA

Symbol of guardianship.

As a child of the supreme being I do not depend on myself, my illumination is only a reflection of him/her.

Top: *IMAHKÜS & Nana Okofo at the front gate of our home, One Africa House.* **Center Row:** *Bongo Shorty with his newly built boat, Bongo Shorty and Mama D (Daisy Melbourne); Nana being enstooled as Safohen of the village of Iture-Elmina.* **Bottom Row:** *Nana and IMAHKÜS in Harlem, New York two days before returning home to Ghana, in 1990.*

Top left: *Lucy Hagar-Grant, her grandmother, Elder Ekua Nsiah Minnah, age 110 & IMAHKÜS , Center: Bongo Shorty with Min. Clemson Brown visiting from New York.*

Top right: *IMAHKÜS, Nana Okofo & friend George leading the 6th Annual JUNE-TEENTH Day Celebration in Cape Coast – Ghana, West Africa.*

2nd Row: 3rd Row: *IMAHKÜS & Prof. Rosalind Jeffries at the Women's Dungeon, Nana Okofo with group of men & Prof. Leonard Jeffries in the Men's Dungeon of the Cape Coast Dungeons conducting "Thru The Door of No Return – The Return Commemorative Ceremonies.*

Bottom Row: *Nana Okofo, Jacob Eshun & IMAHKÜS with the children and staff of the Educational Sponsorhip Program.*

Top Row: *Our house in Iture, Ghana. 2nd Row – A white man in chains who came to our home to apologize for his ancestors' part in the Trans-Atlantic Arab European Slave Trade, standing in front of the Cape Coast Castle Dungeons with Bongo Shorty and Nana Okofo; Labourers working on our new home;* **3rd Row:** *Bro. Jacob Eshun, Nana Okofo, Bongo Shorty & Kwesi Acquah in front yard of our house; the wedding of Kamali & Justice (in the center) with Kohain Nathanyan HaLevi, Rabbi, the Maid of Honour, the Best Man, Nana Okofo and IMAHKÜS;* **Bottom Row:** *the condition of our unfinished house when we first moved in & our first watermelon harvest with IMAHKÜS, Cheryl (Adjoa) Sterling, Bongo Shorty, Nana Okofo & Mama D*

Top Row: *IMAHKÜS & The President of Ghana, His Excellency Flt. Lt. Jerry John Rawlings.* **2nd left:** *Kohain & Nana Okofo. Middle right: IMAHKÜS enjoying a laugh with Ghana's First Lady, Nana Konadu Agyemang Rawlings.* **Bottom right:** *Secretary General of the United Nations, Kofi Annan, IMAHKÜS, & her godson, Kwame HaLevi.*

CHAPTER TEN

OUAGADOUGOU BOUND

Back home again, and still floating from my "Barbara Walter's" assignment, I was coolin' out in my yard. The evening breeze was warm, the sky jet black...no moon tonight as I layback in my hammock enjoying the quiet of the evening.

I had been in town most of the day shopping, returning home hot and bone-tired. Nana had recently returned from Accra and was telling me about a filmmaker that he had met, a Rasta sistren from London, who had engaged him to drive her to The Afrikan Film Festival in Burkina Faso at Ouagadougou. She was renting a car and needed a good driver and Nana had agreed to take her. So typical of my husband: he was always there to lend a helping hand. As long as I've known him, which is more than thirty years, he's been that way. And most of his friends are sisters.

"IMAH you'll like the sister, she got a good head and a righteous heart, a beautiful and committed sister. When you meet her I want you to think about who she reminds you of," he said.

"Who?"

I wanted to know but he wouldn't tell me.

"Just wait and see for yourself," he continued and left it at that.

"Well you tell me about the sister, would you please tell me where Ouagadougou is? I've never heard of the place."

"I don't know much about it myself," Nana replied, "I just know it's north of Ghana."

Suddenly the dogs started barking and out of the darkness emerged this petite, majestic but humble sister, smiling brightly and calling out to Nana.

"JAH Rastafari, I told the I, I was coming forward, I just didn't think it would be so soon," she laughed. "My plans changed so I thought I would come down to the coast and meet the I's Queen," she continued.

"Sister Elmina, come in, come in," Nana responded happily, "I was just telling IMAH about our meeting and planned trip to the film festival. You see the power of the word? I just talked you up."

"Yeah girl, you're going to live a long time. Welcome home Seestah Lady," I greeted. "Welcome to the Half Way House (a pet name I had given to our place). Half way between where you're going and where you've been. Just make yourself comfortable."

I couldn't see her face very clearly, but there was a familiarity about her. The light from the lantern was not very bright, for we were still without electricity, but I could feel a special vibration, a sense of warmth and sincerity. I liked her immediately. I went and brought her water, which is the custom whenever someone visits your home. First you give them water to quench their thirst from the dusty road and then you ask if anyone is in pursuit of them. Once that is done you ask what is their mission.

"Can I get you anything else?" I asked.

"No, I'm fine," she said, "I just want to enjoy the peace and serenity of your place. I just love the sound of the water crashing against the shore. I've been dreaming of this place since Nana told me about it and Bongo Man and Mama D."

By this time I had surrendered the hammock to Sister Elmina. Chillin' out in the hammock we reasoned together for awhile. Bongo got out his repeater (drum) and we sang and made a joyful noise for hours. Bongo man was full of songs.

Sister Elmina had recently completed a documentary on the history and views of Rasta women *Omega Rising, Women of Rastafari*.

"My purpose in life is to make films - to document history from the people's point of view and unite all black women," she said.

The previous year she had visited the Elmina Castle Dungeons with her kingman (a Rasta term meaning husband), JAH Youth and son, Tau. On the way back to Accra their car had broken down near our house and they had spent the day nearby on a stretch of property that we owned.

"It's JAH's time - just imagine here I am one year later here with my family," said Elmina.

At that time we had not known one another but the spirit of the ancestors had finally brought us together. Before long Sister Elmina was fast asleep. Around midnight I woke her so that we could go to bed.

"I'm great company," she laughed, stretching.

"The I is safe at home, so can sleep," Bongo responded.

"Don't feel bad sister," I chipped in, "I do it all the time and it doesn't matter who it is either."

We both laughed as we retired for the night.

"First light, sister, first light family," said Elmina.

"First light," I responded, as I blew out the candle and climbed into bed (next light means in the morning).

When I awoke, daylight was just coming into the bedroom, the shadows of darkness, slowly lifting itself from everything in the room. I love this time of morning. It was so peaceful and beautiful, the singing and chirping of birds announcing the coming of a new day. I laid there for a while enjoying this special time before pulling myself quietly out of bed and going outside to my favorite spot on the rocks to say my prayers and wait for the sunrise. As I faced the East, saying my prayers, I thanked The Creator again for the blessing of being home and watched the light fog on the horizon begin to dissipate as the reddish orange ball of the sun slowly began to make its appearance. The new day had officially begun.

By the time I returned to the house everyone was up. Nana and Sister Elmina were making plans for their trip. Mama D and Bongo were making breakfast of fried fish and dumplings.

"Why don't you join us, it will be fun," said Sister Elmina.

"I really wish I could, but unfortunately I have some unfinished paperwork to take care of and you guys are leaving today. Plus my money situation is a little funny," I said.

"Oh, please try my sister," Sister Elmina responded, "You won't have to pay hotel accommodations or food, just get yourself there."

"Sounds great but I just can't do it this time," I said.

"That's what she says now," Nana interjected jokingly, "I know my wife and if that wandering bug bites her she will find a way to get there. The girl's got a severe case of wander lust."

"Oh, go way," I laughed, "you act like I have no control. Besides, I really can't make it, so you and Sister Elmina have a great time."

"Right! Tell that to someone who doesn't know you, sweetheart," Nana chided me. "Remember you're our family's official Wandering Jew."

We all laughed, but it was true.

As we talked I kept looking at Sister Elmina. In fact, I was staring and kind of distant in my conversation with her. She looked so familiar. Nana saw the way I was looking at her and said,

"Now, whom does she remind you of?"

I was kind of puzzled and it took a few more seconds before it struck like lightening. She looked like Shey, our daughter who had died of Lupus (Leukemia) back in 1980. They could have been sisters. I asked questions thinking that there might be some family connection, but there was none. But Shey had come back in Sister Elmina.

"We have another daughter," I said, hugging her with tears in my eyes.

She hugged me warmly in return and said that she knew there was something special about Nana, (and there was) and something special about our place. We all agreed on that account. Shortly after breakfast, Nana and Elmina were on their way back to Accra to pick up a car that someone was renting to her for the journey.

I had just sat down at my desk to work on my report, when our friend Gilda Shepard came by.

"What's up girl," she asked, "Are you going to Burkina Faso for the Film Festival or not? Adjoa and I are leaving this afternoon. We're supposed to meet a sister named Elmina, in Accra."

"Well, you just missed her," I said, "she and Nana just left for Accra and then they are leaving for Burkina Faso. You're toooo late, my seestah."

"Darn it," she said, "I could have rode into town with them. Well, aren't you going?"

"Girl friend, sister lady, I'll tell you the same thing I told them. I'm too busy, my money is too funny and I just don't have time," I reiterated.

"Well make time IMAHKUS, everyone is going to be there and the Festival only comes around every two years...and it's going to be fu-u-un (with emphasis on fun). You could go if you really wanted to," she prompted. "All you need is a visa to get into Burkina Faso and you can get a bus directly to Ouagadougou from Accra. Come on IMAHKUS, you'll be sorry that you let this one go by."

It did sound good but my mind was really set on what I had to do, which was complete my Annual Report for The Educational Sponsorship Program, which was already late going out to our sponsors. I thought about the reputation for traveling that I had with my family and friends. My mother always teased me saying,

"All anyone has to say to you is 'let's', and you're gone."

Well, I'd fool them this time.

"Have a good time my seestah, see you when you get back," I said rather regretfully. But she had started me to thinking. I finished up what I was working on, got dressed and went into Cape Coast.

I was at Barclays Bank when this brother came in. We laughed and talked while we waited on our transactions to be completed.

"Where's Nana Okofo?" he asked.

"On his way to Burkina Faso, to the Film Festival," I responded.

"Really. Without you?" He said. "That's where I'm headed. I'm leaving this afternoon. Aren't you going?" he wanted to know.

"Naw, I've got things to do here."

"I hear a lot of folks will be there: Spike Lee, Denzel Washington, Larry Fishburn and others. You ought to go. Have you ever been to a Film Festival?" He continued.

Here we go again, I thought to myself. *What is this, some kind of conspiracy?*

When I make up my mind to suppress my "wander lust" and hang around the house and work, plenty of temptations keep coming to tease me.

Well I wasn't budging.

"Sorry brother, not this time but you go and have a great time. Greet the folks for me and take good pictures," I said.

We parted and I finished my chores in town and returned home. But this time I couldn't keep my mind on my work. I kept thinking about the Film Festival.

The following morning I called an associate in Accra and was told that she had also gone to the Festival. Now I was really wishing I had gone. I sat down and started figuring out how much it would cost me to make this trip. By the time I finished borrowing from Peter, putting off Paul, finding a few dollars in my stash, I was ready to make the trip. The bus did not leave until Wednesday so I could still make part of the Festival.

But first, I had to go to Accra to the Immigration Office and retrieve my passport. When I arrived at Immigration they told me Nana had already been there and collected his passport. The Immigration authorities had been holding onto our passports for months. Each time we went to re-new our Residency Permit, it took months before we got the passports back and this had to be done every one to two years depending on how much time you were given. It was a real pain in the neck but because we were not citizens and there was no such thing as Dual Citizenship we were treated like any other foreigner, sometimes worse and there was nothing that we could do about it. Additionally, as a result of our Non Governmental Organization (NGO) status through the operation of our Educational Sponsorship Program, we had to go through this in order to remain in the country.

One day Nana had been reasoning with a brother about citizenship when the brother said, "There are Ghanaians that feel that you Diasporans who are returning *home* should give up your American citizenship."

"That isn't necessary." Nana explained to him. Those of us born in the United States received our American citizenship, not by choice. In the giving of American citizenship, when slavery was abolished in the United States, we lost the citizenship we had before going into slavery. The question is *where is the citizenship we had before being forced into American citizenship?* According to documented historical facts, the citizenship we Diasporans had before slavery had to do with being African.

"So when will some Afrikan country or the whole of Afrika re-institute my original status, as a citizen of "Mother" Afrika?" Nana asked the brother.

In fact as a result of the Afrikan Holocaust, The Trans-Atlantic Arab-European Slave Trade, we Afrikans born in the Diaspora represent a "Historically Unique Group" and have the right to return home. But at present there is not a single Afrikan nation other than Liberia that has a written policy concerning the return of the children of captivity, to the land of their ancestors but it is not Dual Citizenship and you must relinguish the citizenship of your birth. There is no agency, department or committee to address the needs, assist in the transition or help to re-acclimate us to our cultural customs and traditions that we have been too long separated from.

However, by the amazing grace and mercy of the Almighty God, the prophecy of scripture and the vision of our forefathers, there are remnants of us who have returned home in reality with our resources, experiences and most of all our commitments. We are those who act without guarantees or security but rather upon the vision of our forefathers and upon faith that one day very soon we will have Dual Citizenship.

Those of us who were born in the Diaspora, who seek to re-claim our Afrikan Citizenship, should be allowed to do so and retain our Diasporan citizenship. Not as an act of double mindedness but to be able to take advantage of what our ancestors have worked so hard to earn in the Diaspora and, to use those resources to help benefit the re-development of Afrika.

Such an example has already been set in Northern Afrika by the state of Israel, whose Parliament has established a "Law of Return," as well as a policy governing Dual Citizenship. This allows Jews from all over the world to be enfranchised and feel spiritually, morally, consciously and financially connected and responsible to the development, well-being and security of Israel. So what about us?

The brother agreed that this was an acceptable argument and did make sense.

After leaving Immigration, I went to the Embassy for Burkina Faso and paid $38.00 US for a visa to enter another Afrikan country, Burkina Faso, a francophone (French speaking) country. It pained me (as they say in Ghana) that I needed a visa to travel from one Afrikan country to another. It was hard to accept the fact that as an Afrikan, though born in the United States, that I needed a visa to travel in Afrika. It hurt like hell! It felt like being locked out of your own house.

I spent the night with a friend and arose early the next morning and went to the State Transport to wait for the 6:00 p.m. bus. They didn't start selling tickets until 3:00 p.m., but in order to get on the bus you had to begin lining up early. I was there before noon! As the time drew near I could see why you had to arrive early. There was a mass of people for the Burkina Faso bus and I didn't see how all those people were going to get on one bus.

When the ticket window opened people started pushing and shoving, everyone trying to get to the window at the same time. People from the back of the line jumped in the front, people were pushing and arguing. This was my first experience and I was still trying to be polite.

"Excuse me please, excuse me please but I was here first," I said to some people who had jumped in front of me.

"There's a line," I said to others who tried pushing in front of me.

But by being polite I seemed to be getting further and further away from the ticket window. So I started to press forward with the rest of the people. There was absolute chaos trying to get a ticket but I finally made it to the window, only to be told that the last ticket had just been sold (to the woman who had jumped in front of me) and there wouldn't be another bus until next week.

"What!" I hollered, "You can't do that! I have been in line since 12 o'clock."

Someone whose face I couldn't see mumbled from behind a window painted pea green, "Come back next week."

There was only a little opening, which served as the ticket window and was just big enough for you to slide your hand in to get your ticket. I shouted, "You can't do this!"

But I might as well have been talking to myself. The little opening was slammed shut, nearly catching my fingers. But, I wasn't alone, about 30 other people were also stranded.

"Dis is not right," people argued and fussed. "We demand a next bus be put on."

The Stationmaster said that would be possible if we had more people. At another section of the terminal, other passengers were having similar problems trying to get to Kumasi in the Ashanti Region.

"Why can't we combine those passengers?" I suggested, pulling on my administrative training, from the United States. "We're all going in the same direction and those travelling further can catch their connection in Kumasi."

"That's impossible," the Stationmaster argued, "we just don't do things like that."

"Even if it means that fifty people are going to be stranded," I wanted know. "Now that's impossible to understand," I fumed aloud at him. But his ear was closed.

And it did no good aahh tallll to talk.

A young brother that I had met during the confusion said that if we could just get to Kumasi, we would be able to pick up another bus going to Tamale and then on to Burkina Faso. Very simple! Right? Wrong!

I tried to speak with the Stationmaster again.

"Please sir, why not combine the passengers?" I suggested again.

He just shook his head, shrugged his shoulders and walked away.

Now what was that suppose to mean?

Most people said they would be happy to get as far as Kumasi. After wasting our time the Stationmaster finally came back and said it wasn't possible.

Folks were in an uproar, shouting and insulting the Stationmaster, until he walked away, again. Just then my newfound friend came up with this bright idea. He summoned the thirty odd people who were stranded and told them that there were enough of us to charter a bus to take us to Kumasi, that we should get taxis and all meet at the Kaneshie Station.

That sounded great to me, so the brother and I shared a cab with another couple and headed for the Kaneshie Bus Station. When we arrived at the station most of the people had gone for themselves and took whatever bus had seats, completely forgetting about us. I managed to buy the last ticket but that left my new friend by himself and since he had helped me I decided to sell my ticket to someone else and move with him.

Big mistake! It was another two hours before the next bus finally filled up going to Kumasi and by the time we arrived in Kumasi the bus that I was to connect with going to Tamale had just left. Talk about timing! There were no other buses that night but I was told I could get a Tro-tro (small buses and vans that are used by a large majority of the people, who don't have cars). People are packed like Sardines: five across and these vehicles are not always in the best condition.

Not to be deterred, off I went to the Tro-Tro yard – by myself. The brother I gave up my ticket for decided he was going to stay in Kumasi for a few days.

By the time I reached the Tro-Tro yard, I had just missed the Tro-Tro but another one was waiting to fill. I was the third passenger to arrive and based on what the driver told me we would be leaving small-small (in a short time). Little did I know that I would remain the third passenger, until five o'clock the next morning; I spent most of the night sleeping in the back seat of a beat-up mini van.

The area was lively though. It reminded me of Harlem, New York. After-hour shops were open and folks were selling everything; music was loudly playing; brothers were playing draft (played like checkers) and Ludo (a popular game played with dice and chips); folks were just hanging out in the streets and having a good ole time. So I just hung out, got a bite to eat and climbed back into my bed, in the back seat of the van. Still the third passenger to arrive and it was now two-thirty in the a.m.

But at about four-thirty, other passengers began to arrive and it looked like we might get an early start. By seven o'clock there were still three seats remaining and we were not budging until the last one had been filled. Then I came up with another brainstorm.

"Listen people," I said, "Why don't we buy the other three seats and at least we can get rolling and as we travel we can pick up people along the way, they will pay for their ticket and we can get our money back."

A brother who spoke English translated for me. There were only two other people in the Tro-Tro that thought it was a good idea. The rest of the folks said,

"No, no, no, we no can do et."

So we sat. Finally we had only one seat left; it was now eight a.m.

"All right," I told the driver, "Let's go. I'm buying the last seat."

But I don't think he understood me for he responded,

"No, no, we no go, one seat is der."

"Don't worry," I told him, "I am buying this seat for me."

He finally agreed and we were finally on our way to Tamale, which was a seven-hour ride away. Now I was everyone's friend because they were glad to be moving. It had been hot as hell sitting in that crowded mini van. Shortly thereafter, we picked up another passenger, but the driver did not want to give me the money.

"This is my seat, that you're selling," I argued, "So the money is for me."

But he wasn't having any of it. After arguing back and forth, (I didn't understand most of what he was saying but I did know that there were a few insults thrown in), a more reasonable passenger, acting once again as my translator, finally got the driver to understand that the money was in fact for me. He reluctantly gave me the money but he still didn't like it.

* * * * * * *

The ride to Tamale was uneventful. We stopped often along the way to eat, make pit stops, shop etc. The country was beautiful and spacious. The landscape reminds you that you are nearing the desert. The teeming villages began to disappear, opening up to dry plains, sparsely populated by the indigenous people living in clans and leading a rural lifestyle. The further north we drove, I noticed that the style of the building structure was also changing. The rectangular houses usually roofed with corrugated iron sheets familiar in the South gave way to a more authentic, traditional architecture: separate standing round mud huts with thatched roofs.

In the north a lot of different languages are spoken, (often changing from village to village). Here, Akan ceases, even though it is widely spoken and understood. In its place are different dialects and languages. Most of the languages are related and are classified under the Gur Language Group. The most prominent are Dagbani with its sister dialect Mamprusi, Gurma and Grusi.

With respect to religion the population is mostly Moslem as opposed to the predominately Christian South and the sight of Mosques become more frequent as churches become scarcer.

We finally arrived in Tamale, capital of the Northern Region and the biggest city in Northern Ghana. After driving through dry and dusty country it was a pleasant surprise to see tree-lined streets, teeming with busy people and bustling businesses. Most of the people were riding bicycles and motorcycles. It looked like an interesting place to hangout but I was on a mission and immediately got another Tro-Tro (with windows missing and seats falling apart), I continued on with the next leg of my journey.

Three hours later covered with red dust and feeling like a milk-shake, after having driven over some of the worst roads in the world (they made New York City pot holes look like small cracks in the sidewalk), I finally arrived in Bolgatanga. I negotiated with a driver who said that he could drive me directly to Burkina Faso but I thought he was asking too much money, so I took a car to Paga (a border town), where I cleared Ghana Customs and proceeded to the Border.

It was 5:30 p.m. when I arrived at the border. The Border Guard was polishing his boots and talking with a sister, totally ignoring me.

"Excuse me," I said, "Is this where I cross the border?" while holding out my passport.

He slowly continued to polish his boots and ignore me. I waited before speaking again.

"Parlez-vous anglais? Qui. I said in my very limited, broken french; trying to remain calm.

He finally looked up and giving me a very dirty look.

"Qui, but the border, she is closed."

"What do you mean closed?" I stuttered.

"Et es six o'clock and the border, she will no open 'til tomorrow," he continued.

"But that's crazy," I told him. "I have been standing here since five-thirty watching you polish your damn boots. I was here before the border closed. You can't do this," I said excitedly, my voice beginning to rise. "I have to get to Burkina Faso today."

"Well, der es nuthin' I can do, the border she is closed!"

"I want to speak to someone in charge," I demanded.

"OK, OK, you talk to my Chiefy, what he will tell me, I will do. See him der?"

Strolling up the road dressed in Army fatigues came the Chiefy. As I rushed up to meet him, he nonchalantly looked at me. The expression on his face never changed as I explained my plight. I further explained that I had arrived in plenty of time but his man just didn't mind me.

162

"Oh, I'm sorry," he said calmly, in perfect English, "but the border is officially closed. You can come back tomorrow morning at six in the morning."

I was outdone, totally frustrated, tired, hungry and in the middle of nowhere. But I wasn't going to be outdone for long. I proceeded to make myself cry, screwing up my face and squeezing tears out.

"You can't do this to me, my husband is waiting for me in Burkina Faso, I don't have money for it is with him and he will worry when I do not come," I bawled. "I did everything I was suppose to do but your man was very mean to me."

I raised my voice and really began to wail, putting on my best Sarah Heartburn number.

"I must get to Burkina Faso today or my husband will beat me," I cried even harder.

"Oh Madam," said the Chief, looking distressed, "please, please, do not cry more, do not cry more. I will let you go. I will open the border for you. Please do not cry and scream so!"

With that he stormed up to the Border Guard.

"Why do you make the madam wait?" he shouted. "Stamp her passport and open the border for her to pass immediately."

By now I was sniffling and wiping my eyes and trying not to laugh. I had learned since being here in Afrika, that men do not like to see women cry, especially wailing the way I was doing. I humbly and quietly thanked the Chiefy and went on my way.

Hot dog, I'm on my way to Burkina Faso, I thought.

After crossing the border, I looked around for transport but I didn't see any taxis. The road was deserted except for some broken down wreck standing by the side of the road.

"Jew need taxi?" the man asked, with a heavy French accent.

"Yes," I replied.

"None will come today," he continued.

"What? How will I get to town?" (Thinking the town was Ouagadougou). I'm going to Ouagadougou," I said.

"When the border closes all the taxis go town," the man continued, "no come back 'til tomorrow but I take jew."

"How far is it?" I asked.

Looking at that hunk of junk that was passing for an automobile,

I was scared to get in it. The car looked like an accident going to happen but I was even more scared of being on that road for it was fast getting dark.

"I go," said the man. "You give me dollars I take you town. No dollars, no ride town," he continued in broken English.

"But I don't have dollars," I told him.

By now he was cranking up his chinchinum (wreck), preparing to leave me in the middle of nowhere.

The heck with him, I thought to myself. *I'll just walk to town.*

"How far is town?" I asked.

"Go there," he said pointing straight ahead, down a never-ending road.

With night looking me squarely in the face, I knew that I wasn't about to walk.

"All right," I said, getting into his wreck, "let's go but I give you cedis."

He wasn't too happy about it but he finally accepted after I agreed to add a five-dollar bill. The car coughed, black smoke filled the car as it shuttered and shook. You could see the ground through the floorboard as we drove along for miles. I didn't see any houses or lights. Except for the one headlight on his jalopy, there was no other light to be seen. Half an hour later, we pulled into a small town.

"You pay now," the man demanded.

"Is this Ouagadougou?" I wanted to know.

"You pay now," he demanded again.

"OK, OK already, here's your money, but do you know where I can find this hotel?" I asked, getting out of the car.

"I don' know," he said, "talk wit somebody."

Off he rode into the night, leaving me standing in the middle of the road.

It didn't look like a whole lot was happening in this town considering a major Film Festival was being held here. *But I had just arrived and things would get better,* I thought. My other dilemma was that everyone spoke French, which further complicated my problem. After *Parle Vous Englais and Qui,* I was finished in that department. I finally met someone who could speak a little English and didn't mind helping me. I asked about the hotel and directions on how to get there.

"Es no Ouagadougou," he said, "Ouagadougou et es far."

"No, no," I continued. "The man told me this was the place, he brought me from the border and I paid him to come to Ouagadouguo."

"Es no Ouagadougou," he said again, very patiently. "You must take Bush Taxi, to go there."

"You gotta be kiddin'! And what the hell is a Bush Taxi?" I asked sharply, refusing to believe that I was not in Ouagadougou.

Here I was in God-only-knows-where, unable to speak the language: dirty, hungry and thirsty, looking for something called a *Bush Taxi*. It was getting late. It was now ten o'clock. It wasn't the man's fault but there was no else to take my frustration out on. However, the young man was very understanding and offered to help me find a Bush Taxi that would take me to my destination.

"The taxi will take seven people," he said, "and you will get there in small time."

We went to the place where the taxi would load and I was the first in line. An open vehicle with boards on either side pulled up. Down the middle were wooden slats that served as seats. There were no windows but the sides of the vehicle were open all around.

This couldn't be the taxi, I thought wearily to myself, and then out loud.

"Is this the taxi?" I asked in disbelief, dreading the answer.

This was it and it would be going directly to Ouagadougou after it loaded...and load it did. People got on board with everything you could imagine. And they had plenty, from bags, to boxes, from children, to chickens and goats, etc. The brother who had brought me to this Bush Taxi had said seven people to a car but there were already twelve people in the car and the driver was still cruising around town looking for more passengers. Didn't anyone tell the truth or tell it like it really was? I was smashed up against the far end of the taxi (so much for being first in line), almost hanging out of the back of the vehicle. At last, with about 17 adults, bags, boxes and babies and God-only-knows what else we started out for Ouagadougou. The young man who befriended me in town was a Godsend, for he spoke a little English and helped me to understand what people were saying.

It was as dark as a million midnights: you couldn't see your hand in front of your face or anybody else's face for that matter, and the stars twinkled like Christmas tree lights.

The road was dusty and the tires kicked-up plenty, covering everything as we sped away into the night. It was impossible to hide from the dust in this open truck. When we first started out everyone was talking and laughing but as the road became worse and we got bounced around and choked by the dust, conversation died down. The passengers held tight to whatever they could grab hold of and covered their heads, trying to keep the dust from their faces. Peeking out into the darkness, once again, I had no idea where I was. When I asked the young man where we were, he told me,

"No Man's Land, a stretch of land between Ghana and Burkina Faso, that was claimed by neither country."

So you can imagine my surprise when we were stopped at a road-block in the middle of nowhere. This was the military and they stopped all vehicles coming in from Ghana, checking the goods being brought into Burkina Faso. They made everyone get out of the vehicle and had them unload the car so that everything could be checked.

They must be kidding, I thought to myself, *we'll be here all night,* for there was plenty to check.

Most of the passengers were women from Burkina Faso who had been shopping in Ghana for things to bring back for selling and they had plenty of stuff. The Bush Taxi had been packed tight with things tied to the top and along the sides of the vehicle.

Sensing that this was going to be a long drawn out affair, I took my *lappa* (two yards of cloth), and made myself as comfortable as possible lying on the ground next to a lady with a baby. Other than the glow of the light from the flashlights of the border guards/soldiers and a lone lantern, the entire place was pitch black.

Watching the stars, I drifted off to sleep only to be awakened abruptly by the roar of a truck engine, bearing down on us. Screaming and scrambling, we jumped out of the way of the oncoming truck. Shaking like a leaf as it roared past us, I realized that when I lay down beside the lady with the baby, that we had been lying in the middle of the road. The truck stopped briefly at the barricade and then drove off into the night. I watched the red lights of the truck growing smaller, thinking that I should have tried to get a lift with them, for we seemed a long way from getting back on the road soon.

One of the sisters who had been shopping could not find her receipts and the soldiers were not letting her back into the taxi with her goods. They told her that she had to return to Ghana, get her receipts and come back before they would release her goods. But she and those other sisters were not having any of that. They were all arguing with the soldiers in French. They knew that if they left their goods, they would never see them again – and they were not leaving their sister or her goods with the guards. So they just sat down in the road and refused to move. These were strong and determined sisters. They had gone to Ghana together and they were going to return home together, and with all their goods. Some of the other passengers began pleading with the soldiers to let them through, after all.

"You can't hold up all the people," they said.

Occasionally, the sisters picked up the argument themselves. Finally, after being there in the middle of "No Man's Land," for more than an hour, a deal was struck between the sisters and the guards. Everything was re-packed on the Bush Taxi and once again we were on our way. The sisters fussed and talked about how wicked the soldiers were and how they always wanted to take their things and get money from them.

When we finally arrived in Ouagadougou it was after two o'clock in the morning. I was exhausted. The Bush Taxi stopped next to a brand new Mercedes Benz bus parked along the side of the road. As the women got out of the taxi, they started unloading and transferring things to the bus. When I asked the brother what was going on, he explained, "They are called *Mercedes Benz Mamas.*"

Although it would have been easier and better to drive their bus into Ghana to do their shopping, they do not because they have to pay a bigger tax and dash plenty when the border guards see their bus."

"They will rob us," one of the sisters said; "they take plenty of our things because they say we are rich," chimed in another of the sisters.

167

These were some serious, no nonsense, hard working, business-women and they knew how to maneuver. Unfortunately for me they were not going in my direction, so we said good-bye and I proceeded on my way to find the hotel that my people were staying in.

The young man who had been so helpful invited me to come home with him. He lived with his parents and said that I could sleep in his room, with him.

"No thanks," I said, "I don't think so. Just direct me to the hotel and I'll be fine."

However, he was insisting that it would be better if I went home with him, refusing to take *no* for an answer. I just walked away, leaving him standing in the street, more than a little pissed off. But I really didn't care. A taxi was passing so I hailed him and went directly to the hotel.

But when I arrived, the lobby was deserted and I was told that many of "my people" were at the disco, however Nana and Elmina were not registered at the hotel. The desk clerk suggested I check the disco, so off I went in search of Nana and Elmina. Leaving the hotel, I met a young woman and asked directions. She offered to take me to the disco and as we walked I told her that I was looking for my husband and my daughter. We searched through the disco with no success.

"Oh well," I told her, "I'll just camp out in the lobby until morning."

As we were walking back to the hotel she asked, "Es your husband the elder Rasta Man with long white Dred Locks, traveling with his daughters? One that has Dred Locks hanging down to the ground?"

"That's them," I replied excitedly. "Do you know where they are staying?"

"No," she said, "but they will come in the morning. They come every day to see me. I am called Fayola (Fah-YOH-lah), it means 'good fortune walks with honor.' I come from Nigeria. You can come to my house and sleep and we will come back in the morning. I am selling at the Festival."

It did not sound like a bad idea to me for I was hot, sticky and exhausted, hungry and in desperate need of a bath. My deodorant was failing me miserably. A twenty-one (21) hour trip had taken me 38 hours to reach Ougadougou from Ghana. I gladly accepted the invitation.

Fayola said, "Come, we will drive to my house, et es not far."

Not far, I thought as I followed her into the parking lot.

Not far to Afrikans could be an hour's ride away but by this time I would have followed Tarzan into the jungle. Once in the parking lot I got the surprise of my life, the sister did not have a car but a small Motor Scooter. I hesitated not sure I wanted to ride.

"Why don't I follow you in a taxi," I suggested.

"Oh no, et es all right you can ride behind me," she said smiling at my uncertainty.

Reluctantly, I climbed on behind her.

With me holding on for dear life, we sped off into the night towards her house. As we zipped around curves on unpaved roads, with no streetlights in most areas, my heart was in my mouth. I couldn't see much of anything. But it looked like we were driving through a series of little villages. But Fayohla was a good driver and I managed to settle down and enjoy the ride. In 15 minutes we were pulling up in front of her house. The dog started barking and a light came on behind a large white gate. The watchman let us in. She had a quaint little place, very comfortable, nicely decorated with bamboo furniture and colorful Afrikan materials. Round straw mats adorned the floors and the place was very warm and welcoming. As tired as I was, a tree house would have also looked welcoming.

Fayohla showed me to the room that I would be sleeping in and gave me a towel and some soap. Looking in a mirror for the first time since I had begun my journey, I screamed, I couldn't believe what a mess I was. No wonder the people at the disco looked at me so strangely. I was covered with red dirt. In fact, red dirt was in my hair, my eyelashes were red, my face had a dusty reddish tint to it, and red dirt covered everything. I looked like I had been rolling around in the dirt and I felt like it too. I quickly stripped off my clothes and jumped into the shower. Twenty minutes later I was looking and feeling better. I didn't think the water would ever run clear. The more I washed the redder the water became. I stepped out of the shower and began drying myself only to find that I still had that red dirt on me. Back in the shower I went and washed until the water became clear. I had never in my life been so dirty. Now all I wanted was the bed. When I got back to my room, Fayohla had prepared a bite to eat and a hot cup of tea for me.

The girl is a mind reader, I thought to myself, (for I had just been thinking about something to eat). I sat on the side of the bed and fell asleep eating.

When I awoke that morning the sun was bright in the sky and remnants of my last night's meal was still in my mouth. It's a wonder I didn't choke to death in my sleep. The smell of freshly brewed coffee drifted into my room. It took me a few minutes to get myself together and figure out where I was. Making my way to the bathroom, I passed Fayohla, who was in the kitchen.

"Good morning sister," she said. "I hope you had a good sleep. I looked at you earlier but did not want to wake you. You were sleeping very good."

"What time is it?" I asked.

"Ten o'clock, she replied. By the time you get dressed, breakfast will be ready."

Fifteen minutes later, we were having breakfast, while she told me about herself. I had seen pictures of her and a big white man, with a heavy beard in the room that I had slept in.

"He es my husband," she said smiling broadly. "He work for mining company in the bush and come home once in a month. He es really from California," she continued, "where he live with his other wife. When he go back to America, he take me with him," she beamed happily.

"Really," I replied, "is that what he said?"

"Oh yes, Jim love me and want me to go to United States with him. That es what he tell me all the time," she continued.

"How long have you been married to him?" I asked.

"Two years," she responded, "when he come to Burkina Faso."

"Well, I wish you the best, my sister," I said, "and I hope that you really get to go to the United States."

I seriously had my doubts. But she seemed happy and who was I to rain on her parade. She had befriended me and taken me into her home and I wasn't about to hurt her feelings.

"You will meet him," she continued. "He will come in one, maybe two days."

Great! I thought.

She spoke like I was going to be at her place for a while.

After breakfast we left for the hotel and the Festival area.

Ouagadougou, the capital of Burkina Faso was nice but very dusty and hot. It lies on the fringe of the Sahara Desert. I was told that soil erosion does not exist in Burkina Faso. It is as though the creeping Sahara Desert, which creeps about four miles per year, has skipped over Burkina Faso to Northern/Eastern Ghana. In Burkina brush fires and destroying of the land by cutting down trees and burning is a violation of the law and perpetrators are dealt with harshly. In Ghana this is not the case and consequently Ghana is suffering and must plant more trees.

Ouagadougou does not give you the impression that it is the capital of Burkina Faso. It has a lot of large expanded villages and suburbs. It looks more like a rural area. Everyone rides around on scooters, the primary mode of transportation. The people were very friendly but looked at me strangely, calling me "Rasta, Rasta," because of my locks. But still I felt quite comfortable and, I was happy not to be chasing Tro-Tro's.

When I arrived at the hotel, the first person I ran into was our young daughter (as we called her) and friend Adjoa.

"So you made it," she laughed, "wait until Nana sees you."

"Girl friend," I told her, "you would not believe what I have been through to get here."

"Well," she continued, "he said he wouldn't be surprised if you showed up and here you are. He's around here someplace. He and Sister Elmina are moving together."

She then introduced me to the other people at the table and continued on with her interview.

Sister Adjoa was a young sister that we had met in New York when we were preparing to re-locate. She was a schoolteacher and had been at an orientation session in 1990 at City College in New York that Nana and I had been invited to, to discuss our re-location plans to Ghana. After we had met her a few times she decided that she was also going to Ghana, to continue her education at the University of Ghana at Legon. So we were quite surprised when we met her on the same plane that was bringing us to Ghana. It was a real re-union, for we had not seen her for months. We had become fast friends and extended family, spending time at one another's houses between Cape Coast and Medina.

As I was telling the people (actors, actresses, film people who were attending the festival) who were gathered around the pool about my adventure getting to Burkina Faso, I had them in stitches, laughing about my trip.

"Well, I hope the Festival is all that you expect it to be," said one sister.

"You've been through a little bit of hell to get here," she said, as the others fell out laughing.

Just then Nana and Sister Elmina walked into the area. At first he didn't see me and was making his way towards us, waving and talking to people as he came. He was almost to the table, when he saw me, his eyes lit up.

"Didn't I tell you she was coming?" He laughingly said to Sister Elmina, "I know my wife, and after two people, who had arrived from Ghana told me she wasn't coming, I knew the 'Wander Lust Bug' had bitten her and it wouldn't be long before she showed up."

Everyone laughed as we embraced.

I told them where I was staying and all about their friend who had taken me in. I was happy that my sense of adventure had driven me to come. I met a lot of interesting and creative sisters, who were film writers, directors and actresses. I was looking forward to seeing *Daughters of the Dust*, a dynamite film made by an Afrikan-American sister. There were plenty of films to be viewed and seminars for theatrical folks. So I took in a lot of movies and enjoyed the festival.

There were great things to buy but all I could do was *eyeball* shop. They had some great leather works, large orange and brown leather cushions, with rugs to match, beautiful, odd and colorful looking jewelry as well as fantastically designed Batiks. I managed to squeeze out a Batik for the house. But even though I had very little money it did not prevent me from having a great time.

Nana and Sister Elmina were staying in a small hotel on the outskirts of town with some other folks, who like me had limited funds or were unable to secure a room at the film Festival hotel site, which was really fine with them considering the cost. We hung out, all day and into the night.

When I saw Fayohla again she invited me back to her place and also invited Nana and Sister Elmina. The following day Sister

Elmina went off with some other friends of hers and Nana and I stayed with Fayohla. Her husband had come home from the bush. He and Nana hit it off quite well. They got into the sports thing and left us to handle the kitchen.

That night we all went to see this film entitled *Sankofa*. It had not been entered into any of the competitions but we had heard from friends that it was a '*don't miss*' flick. When we arrived, the theater was packed. As the film started I was happy to see that it did not have French sub-titles.

I had gone to see the *Malcolm X* film for the first time earlier that day and it was dubbed in French. People were laughing in places that were not funny and the entire theme of the film was misunderstood. I walked out. I didn't see anything funny and I couldn't speak French.

But *Sankofa* was different. It was powerful and it was in English. It took us from the Cape Coast Castle Dungeons and across the waters to the Caribbean and into the bowels of hell called slavery. As I watched the film I was afraid, I became angry, no incensed: I cried, I cheered and when the lights came on most of the white people who had been in the audience had left the theater. I guess they were afraid that we *natives* would rise up out of our chairs and kick some ass. Who knows, and "Frankly Scarlet" I didn't give a damn, I really did not care. The people, who were supposed to be there when the lights went on, were there.

Sister Sherikiana Ania, a humble, small framed, determined Afrikan born in America sister had co-produced the film, and was there representing her husband, Haile Gerima, an Ethiopian born film director, living in Washington, DC who was the producer of the film.

As she spoke, I liked her immediately. She spoke of the obstacles and roadblocks that had been put in their way, to prevent the making of the film. She also spoke of their determination, the will of God and the cooperative spirits of the people involved in the making of the movie. She introduced and praised the actors and actresses from the movie. Everyone who remained was touched by what they had seen and heard.

Later that evening, after the movie, I walked down the dark streets of Burkina Faso with her, talking. Against all odds and with little money, taking them years, they had managed to finish this picture. It was the stark, hard truth and White folks and Conservative Negroes did not want it out there. It made *Roots* look tame in comparison and I loved and respected them for what they had done.

We enjoyed several more days and then we were on our way back to Ghana, together this time and on the State Transport, Ghana's version of the Greyhound Bus in America.

CHAPTER ELEVEN

TESTING THE WATERS

The morning broke beautifully and as usual we had company. Our spiritual daughter, Sister Elmina was visiting from Accra. We had established a very close mother-daughter relationship. We had recently returned (on March 1st) from FESPACO, the Film Festival held in Ouagadougou.

We arose early and went down to the waterfront, onto the rocks. Finding a comfortable position, amongst the rocks, which had formed into natural seats, we sat back, relaxed and talked of our future in the "Mother" land. Sister Elmina was going to make films about Afrikan woman from various parts of Afrika and I along with Nana Okofo would be working to expand *The Educational Sponsorship Program*, an Extended Afrikan Family relationship and not for profit program, which we introduced into our village, when we moved to Ghana.

The sponsorship program seeks Afrikans-born-in America and other places in the Diaspora to sponsor the education of Ghanaian children. It was initially started to assist the children in our village, with their education through sponsorship from brothers and sisters in the Diaspora, while fostering the concept of the Extended Afrikan Family. It was also our way of helping to give something back to our community. But our focus was gradually changing as we were being introduced to other children from the Cape Coast and Elmina areas.

We also had a company called "One Africa Productions" that was being nurtured by the people in Cape Coast. The name One, Africa was given to us by the children in 1992, shortly after we had returned home.

One day I did my P'NUT BUTTER the Clown number for the Fairweather School in Cape Coast. At first, I thought my act was going to be a disaster, when I showed up at the school and all the children, including teachers ran from me screaming and locking themselves in the school. When no one would let me in, I just sat on the steps, a sad looking clown, with my chin in my hands. Several little boys inched their way close to me, hesitating but curious. They wanted to touch my big red nose. After a while we were having great fun and the others seeing that there was no danger, all began to come out but not before I had pulled back my wig, taken off my nose and let them hear my true voice.

"Oh Sister Vienna," one of the teachers said, "oh, we were so scared, we did not know it was you. We are sorry-o."

After that, the party was on. Other children, who did not attend the school, living up on a hill behind the school, saw the balloons and the clown and raced down the hill to join the party. But they were not allowed to enter the school grounds. There must have been over 100 children outside, trying to come over the wall to the party but the school headmistress was having none of it. She already had over 75 of her own children to deal with. But Nana Okofo came to the rescue, the "Pied Piper" of the diaper set, as I always call him. A child's best friend!

He was having a ball with them. He reasoned with the masses of children on the wall.

"Listen up," he said, "you can watch the party from the wall, if you behave."

And the children started cheering.

"We are One Afrikan people and we must act like proud Afrikans," he continued. "I want all of you to repeat after me."

"One Afrika! One Afrika! One Afrika!"

And sure enough, all the children started chanting, until they got a real rhythm going, both in the school and on the wall.

"One Afrika! One Afrika! One Afrika!"

They chanted, swayed and rocked. They rocked the house big time, with a couple of hundred children between the ages of three and ten chanting, "One Afrika! One Afrika!"

We had a ball.

Several days later we met some of the children in the street. Greeting us they said, "Hello, One Afrika!"

Well, this continued for a while until even the adults began to call us "One Afrika." In fact people were calling us One Afrika so often, I began to wonder if they knew our real names. One day I stopped a young man in the street and asked him,

"Do you know my name?"

And he smiled very broadly and said, "Yes. Mrs. One Afrika."

So, if you ever get to Ghana and you want to find us, don't ask for the Robinson's, (our name before we changed it in 1993) or Ben and Vienna, you may never find us. But ask any taxi driver or child at the Cape Coast or Elmina Castle Dungeons for "One Afrika" and they will either bring or direct you to us. And that's how we are known today for most people think our name is "One Afrika" and that's all right.

Under the name of One Africa we have organized other programs such as the Annual "JUNETEENTH" Celebrations, which commemorates the "Last Day of Slavery" and the "First Day of Freedom" for enslaved Afrikans in the United States and celebrated for the first time in Ghana, in 1992.

We also conduct special commemorative ceremonies entitled *Thru the Door of No Return* - The Return in the Cape Coast and Elmina Castle Dungeons for our brothers and sisters when they return home to Ghana. It's a time to give thanks, and prayers as well as praise to The Almighty Creator and our ancestors for bringing us safely home to mother. It also helps to facilitate the healing process that most of us as Afrikans born in the Americas will begin to go through upon our return.

And we also have our *Deep-Sea Fishing Project*. Brother Bongo Shorty built our first 30-foot fishing boat, by hand, with no electrical tools. Our maiden voyage carried twenty-one brothers & sisters between the Cape Coast and Elmina Castle Dungeons.

So sitting there that day, we had plans-a-plenty between us: and we were enjoying watching the huge waves crashing against the rocks. Occasionally the waves would break near us but there was plenty of room between the sea and us so we felt we were in no danger. Sister Elmina decided to return to the house and had left her seat and climbed higher up on the rocks above me. A thought flashed in my mind as she moved away from me that I'd better move my position too. So I began to climb up to where Sister Elmina was standing.

At that moment I turned around towards the sea and saw this monstrous wave behind me. As I tried to run out of the way, the wave crashed on the rocks above me, snatching me off my perch. I was covered by water, thrown against the rocks and dragged forcefully towards the sea. The lappa (cloth) that was around my waist was ripped from my body as I was tossed and dragged across the jagged rocks. I was fighting to get a grip on the rocks as I felt myself being pulled out to sea. It was as though many hands were pulling at me. I was screaming and crying by the time the water finally subsided and I was able to scramble to safety – badly bruised, naked and scared stiff. My gold bracelet had also been ripped from my wrist and I was fortunate that I had not been wearing my glasses. What a terrifying experience that was.

The following year a Fisherman who had crashed his boat in front of our house, found my bracelet in the sea and returned it to me.

* * * * * * *

Sister Elmina was jumping up and down, screaming, "IMAH! IMAH," while reaching frantically for me.

Scrambling towards me she grabbed my outstretched hands.

"Are you all right?" She cried, as she helped me to my feet. "I don't believe what I just saw," she continued and neither did I.

I thanked The Creator and the Ancestors for giving me back my life but I had learned a very valuable lesson that day. This ocean was nothing to play with or take lightly. The tormented souls of many ancestors lined the bottom of these waters, a constant reminder of the horrors and torment that our people suffered as a result of slavery. These were angry waters and you could be gone in a flash.

Just then, our sister-friend, Professor Gilda Shepherd walked up. Seeing our excited state, she was immediately concerned, for I must have been quite a sight standing there "butt" naked as the day I was born, bruised, bleeding and hysterical.

"What the hell happened?" queried Gilda.

But without waiting for an answer, she rushed up to the house and returned with another lappa for me to cover myself with. Everyone was talking at once by now.

"Are you all right IMAH, are you sure you're all right?" Sister Elmina asked again, excitedly.

Still shook up, I squeaked out a, "Yes."

Once we realized that I was in fact all right we settled down on the rocks above and reasoned a little before returning to the house. I had enough of the sea to last me a good while.

Sister Gilda had come on a mission. She had brought a youngster for us to meet and evaluate for possible admission to our Educational Sponsorship Program. Gilda had been telling me about this thirteen-year-old youngster and preparing me for his visit. She said that based on his medical problem, he would not be easy to look at and she didn't want to shock us. He had a huge, grotesque tumor growing out of his mouth.

Three times the tumor was surgically removed in Ghana and once again in London, England in 1991. However, the tumor grew back, larger than ever before, the size of a grapefruit. This abnormal growth medically termed Fibrous Dysphasia caused difficulty in breathing and prevented Prince from eating properly. People stared at him in disbelief. But due to a lack of funds and available medical expertise he was unable to get the proper care in Ghana that he required. According to the medical experts in Ghana, they had done all that they could do and any further medical treatment would have to be sought outside of Ghana.

Young Prince talked of taking his life, for his day-to-day existence had become unbearable. His mother Maurice Mensah had been asked to remove him from school "for his own safety," the Headmistress said. Prince is the only child in the family with this disorder. Often in Ghana people believe that evil spirits are responsible for illnesses and other psychological and physical disorders. They will often seek help from a Fetish Priest, more commonly known as a traditional spiritualist, which is what Prince's grandmother suggested they do. However, his mother, a Christian, chose to rely on medical science for his treatment.

The youngster and his family were almost without hope when

they were introduced to *The Educational Sponsorship Program*..the family was extremely poor and Prince was suffering terribly, each passing day was pure hell for him. He was one of six sons. His mother was an unemployed, single parent. His father had deserted the family several years ago.

Professor Shepherd, who referred him to our program, had tried to prepare us for meeting Prince. She had described his physical appearance, explaining that, "He is not easy to look at but he's a brave little boy."

Even with that fore warning it was still a shock the first time I saw him with this large, bloody mass protruding out of his mouth. However, the thing that I remembered most about our first meeting, were his eyes. They were smiling. Through all his pain and suffering he still smiled.

After the introductions were made, we sat down to discuss the problems that would confront us, and the best way to tackle it. There was clearly no time to waste. After the interview with Prince and his mother we agreed to enroll him in the program. Although the program itself did not have the financial resources to provide for the major medical care that young Prince required, we saw a desperate need and decided to seek help elsewhere.

Photos were taken of Prince and letters written to people in the United States we thought could help. However, the responses seemed to be taking forever and Prince's condition was rapidly deteriorating. But a miracle was about to take place.

Minister Louis Farrakhan of the Nation of Islam and his entourage were visiting Ghana in March of 1993, in fact they were in Cape Coast, Prince's hometown. Although we were not personal friends of the Minister, when news reached us that he was attending a reception at the Regional Minister's residence, we didn't hesitate to reach out to him. We were more familiar with his International Representative, Brother Akbar who was based in Accra. We brought the appeal letter with us, and photos of Prince. One look at the picture of Prince with that grotesque tumor growing out of his mouth, Minister Farrakhan responded, "Bring the boy here so that our doctors can examine him."

Nana and I left immediately and quickly drove to Prince's house to get him. But by the time we returned with young Prince and his mother, the doctors and Minister Farrakhan had left.

They hade gone to the Cape Coast Castle Dungeons, the policeman on duty at the residence told us.

We rushed to Cape Coast Castle Dungeons, but again, we had just missed Minister Farrakhan and his party by a few minutes.

"Where have they gone to?" I asked the receptionist at the castle. "He's on his way back to the United States," she responded.

We finally had the help that we needed within our grasp but we kept missing our benefactor. But we were determined to get assistance for Prince. Our funds were low and time was fast moving against us. Our car was not in good condition and Nana said we would be taking a big risk in trying to drive to Accra, so he borrowed the money and chartered a taxi for us. Prince, his mother, Professor Shepherd and I set out for the two and a half-hour ride to Accra. The car seemed to be crawling along.

"Can't you go any faster?" I nervously asked the driver. "This is too important, please drive faster," I pleaded.

The driver complied and soon we were going so fast that I had to ask him to slow down. I wanted us to get there but I also wanted us to arrive in one piece. The road between Cape Coast and Accra is terrible with large potholes and craters along the route. Too many accidents occur on that road to suit my taste. We finally arrived safely in Accra and went directly to Brother Akbar Muhammad's house, who was accompanying the Minister: no one was home. We called the hotel where the party was staying. The person answering said, "They've checked out," and hung up before I could question him further.

We didn't have any time to waste. With prayers on our lips and determination in our hearts, we headed for Kotoka International Airport, our last hope of catching the Minister in Ghana. We finally arrived at the airport with not a moment to spare and this time the Almighty God and our ancestors shined their light on us. As we rushed up the stairs to the doors of the VIP waiting room, a security guard blocked our entry.

"Where are you going? You can't come in here," he said.

"Please," I begged, "this is very important. We must catch Minister Farrakhan, who is waiting to hear from us."

"You wait here, I will check," he said.

As he turned his back, I was like a shadow in his shoes, moving right along with him. As he approached the group I rushed out from behind him, as the Minister and his party were preparing to walk through the gates to board the plane for their return trip to the United States: 10 minutes to flight time.

"Wait a minute," the guard shouted.

But I wasn't hearing anything of what he was saying, for we had finally connected and they were all together, Minister Louis Farrakhan, Ghana's President Jerry John Rawlings, Dr. Alim A. Muhammad, Minister of Health for the Nation of Islam and Dr. Barbara Justice of New York City. Without hesitation the doctors took Prince aside and examined him. The Minister laid hands on him and prayed. Turning to me and the family he said, "If, you can get the boy to America we'll get help for him."

And President Rawlings agreed to assist us in those efforts.

"Thank you so much," I cried. "Thank you so very much."

As I watched Prince, smiling with his eyes, struggling to say, "Thank you," to everyone, I felt a sense of relief.

The flight was called again and they turned and continued through the departure gate. We stood and watched them walk away. Our hearts were full and we were thankful and grateful to God for the blessing that had been bestowed upon us.

We left the airport to begin our journey back to Cape Coast. Tired but joyful, weary but hopeful this determined family returned to Cape Coast to prepare for Phase II of our challenge. After dropping off Prince, his mother and Professor Shepherd at their homes, I headed for mine. It was after 3:00 a.m. in the morning.

Nana had not seen me since he put us in the taxi that afternoon for Accra. He was sleeping when I arrived, but I woke him up and brought him up to date on the day's activities. He was happy at the outcome.

"I knew you could do it IMAH, I had every confidence in you," he continued laughingly. "I can just see my baby busting into the VIP lounge and confronting the President of the country. You African American women are so bold...and pushy," he kidded.

He listened intently as I related the entire adventure. I was so excited.

"Well, we did it, we're going to America," I said.

"That's wonderful," he said looking very serious, "but didn't the

Minister say, "If," you get Prince to America that he would help you? Well how do you plan to get there?" he asked.

He was right! We had no money to buy airline tickets.

"We-l-l-l-l," I said, "back to my daddy's trusty, rusty typewriter."

This time I would be writing to all the airlines in Ghana that went to the United States. With love, will and determination as our driving force, we couldn't fail. Besides, a young boy's life was depending on us and with the help of the ancestors we would get through. After all, two families, one from the United States and one from Ghana, had re-connected: both descendants of those ancestors who had been separated from each other for over 400 years as a result of the Trans-Atlantic European Slave Trade. We were blessed to be together again and determined to succeed.

It took a couple of days to complete all the letters on my dad's 40 year-old Manual Royal Typewriter. But once completed, Nana and I set out to Accra again, this time to hand deliver the letters and make face to face appeals to all of the airlines that went in the direction of the United States. The first day the going was slow. Either the sales manager was not in or they said they would have to get back to us. KLM said that they would give us one ticket for Prince.

"But what about his mother and I," I asked.

"Sorry." they said, "We can only give you one ticket."

"Would you send your sick child to a strange country without one of his parents?" I asked the sales manager. "Get real," I told him as I tried to get him to see my point. But that white man would not budge from his position. I thanked them and told them that I would get back to them. British Airlines, another major airline said that they could give us a 30 percent discount on the tickets.

"But madam," I said, "I've told you that we have NO money. Your discount will not help us, as 30 percent of nothing is still nothing."

"Sorry," she replied. "But that's the company policy, that's the best we can do for you."

"Is there someone else that I can speak to?" I asked.

"No, there isn't! I'm in charge," she said "and there's nothing else we can do."

"Thank you," I said, trying not to cry or show any anger or frustration. I returned to the car, giving Nana the latest report.

"Don't worry," he told me. "Don't go into that negative channel, just keep praying and being positive, we'll get through."

Nana always managed to see the best in any situation and in any person. Me, I'd be ready to grab someone in the throat. We then set out for Ghana Airways Office. When we arrived, the sales manager was not available but we were referred to Mr. Sam Bannerman-Bruce, the Public Relations Officer. He remembered Prince from a couple of years before, when Ghana Airways had helped to get him to London for a previous operation.

"I'm so sorry to see that his problem has reoccurred," he said. "We'll do all that we can to assist you but we can only get you as far as London, for we do not fly to the United States. You'll have to find someone else to get you there."

"Well, that's a start!" I cried joyfully.

What a blessing we received that day for Ghana Airways donated three tickets from Ghana to London for Prince, his mother and myself.

"Once you have secured your tickets for the second leg of your journey, get back to us so that we can coordinate your departure date," Mr. Bannerman said. *"Nyame N'adom*, you'll get through!"

(Nyame N'adom is an Akan expression that means "By the grace of God.")

After further research, we found that American Airlines, though they did not fly out of Ghana, did have an office in Accra and flew out of London to the United States, so we went to see them. Again we received another blessing. American Airlines agreed to help us. Our departure date was set for 4 July, now all we needed was the final approval and confirmation. But we still endured more bureaucratic and technical delay before we finally got our tickets in hand, through no fault of the staff who couldn't have been more cheerful and helpful during this time.

Additionally, we were still waiting for the medical reports to come from London, the location of the last hospital that treated him for this disorder. The doctors in the United States needed these reports to be able to properly evaluate Prince's case. They also attempted to get the records from the hospital but had still gotten no response.

"What else can we do? What else can we do?"

It was then that we learned that our daughter and friend, Adjoa Sterling, was going to London for a brief visit before continuing on to the United States. We went to see her.

We asked her if she would hand deliver a request to the hospital in London for Prince's medical record, and wait for the medical records and deliver them to the doctors in the United States?

We were desperate, and Prince was getting worse.

"Sure, but you've got to get the request to me quickly for I'm leaving tomorrow night," she said.

She stayed in London four extra days. It took that long with the hassling, going and coming, long waits, uncooperative attitudes, and fighting the bureaucracy for Prince's medical records, before she finally got through.

In the meantime, we worked on securing visas for Prince and his mother. It was then that we found out that Prince's passport had expired. We had to get another one issued but only after quite a bit of running around, being sent from first one office then another, and if that were not bad enough, the people at the American Embassy gave us an even worse time. They did not want to give a visa to Prince and his mother. I had Prince; the letters from the doctor's, proof of airline tickets, and still the woman (another white woman) gave us a hard time.

"What is your problem?" I asked her. "Why are you being so difficult?"

"What assurances does the U.S. government have that they will come back to Ghana?" she snippily asked.

"Mrs. Mensah has four other children here," I said.

"That doesn't mean anything," she said. "Visa denied."

"What?" I nearly screamed. "Are you a mad person?"

But she wouldn't budge. She just stood behind that glass with a very smug, mean look on her face.

"What is your problem?" I asked the clerk again, who had had an extremely nasty attitude during our entire interview.

"How can you be so cruel? Look at the boy. He is in desperate need of emergency medical care. Everything is in place. The doctors are waiting, the tickets have been secured and it is only the visa, which you can issue, that is standing in our way. Why are you doing this?" I asked her again.

"We have our policy," she said with smug authority.

"If that glass wasn't separating us I'd ring your neck like you do a chicken. I've stood here and taken your snide, rude remarks for as long as I'm going to and I'm going to get that damn visa in spite of you!"

Some of the clerks at the Visa Section of the American Consulate are notorious for giving Ghanaians a hard time when they are trying to secure a Visa to leave the country.

But the Creator knows all things and with teeth tightly clenched and my head throbbing, I left the Embassy fuming, with Prince and his mother. Nana was cool throughout.

"Calm down. We'll work it out," he assured me.

"How can I calm down? Everything is a go. Our reservations are for tomorrow and this chick is just being difficult."

We contacted Brother Akbar who is the International Representative for the Nation of Islam in Ghana and explained the situation to him. He could also not believe that we had been turned down for the visa. Not wasting any time or words he went directly to the Ambassador.

The following day I was back at the American Embassy, in front of the same person. Boy, was she ever pissed off. We arrived at 2:30 p.m. per the directions of the United States Ambassador, but before the visa was issued I had to sign a sworn statement that would guarantee the return of Prince and his mother to Ghana. Finally, the visa was reluctantly given but not before that witch made us wait until every person in that crowded room had been dealt with. It was after 5:00 p.m. when we finally got through. It was time to go to the airport.

On July 4th at 11:00 p.m. we took off for London en route to the United States. We landed in London early the following morning. As we worked our way through Customs and our connecting flight to the United States, people stared, jumped back in startled amazement and pointed at Prince as we walked by. I felt so bad for him and found myself on numerous occasions shielding him from the staring eyes of people, some that were more than a little curious and were down right mean. But Prince seemed to be oblivious to the taunts and stares. He just held his head high, shoulders and back straight and acted like those people weren't even there.

When we arrived at the American Airlines Check-in Counter I explained our situation to the attendant and asked for special consideration, for this was in fact a medical emergency. She was very kind and did not appear shocked at Prince's appearance. As she checked us in she talked with Prince, asking him his age and making small talk, she then turned us over to the Flight Attendant who made things very comfortable for Prince for the duration of his travel to the United States. The pilot came out to meet him. They gave him games and toys to play with and just before we arrived in New York, they gave him a pin, with airplane wings on it. As we left the plane the crew and flight attendants wished him luck and said they looked forward to seeing him when he returned to Ghana, after his surgery.

GYE NYAME

Symbol of the supremacy of God.

"Except God, I fear none".
It is God that makes this possible.

CHAPTER TWELVE

MIRACLE OF MIRACLES

We arrived at John F. Kennedy International Airport in New York and were met at the airport by a Public Relations Representative of American Airlines, who secured a private waiting room for us during our three-hour layover in New York before departing for Washington, DC. We were also met by the Nation of Islam Security, a good brother who stayed with us until we boarded our connecting flight to Washington DC; he was wonderful — acting as a 'buffer' between Prince and people who gawked and acted foolish and impolite. When our flight was called, the brother accompanied us to the door of the aircraft.

Our flight to Washington was approximately one hour and we were met at the airport by Dr. Alim Muhammad, the Medical Director for the Nation of Islam, other members of the NOI, and the press and taken to Howard Inn Hotel, where we would be staying until after Prince's surgery.

Dr. Etienne Massac, Chief of Plastic Surgery was another miracle.

When Prince Edmonds plight was brought to his attention, by his former teacher and medical colleague Dr. Alim A. Muhammad, he immediately responded and sought the assistance of Howard University Hospital in Washington, DC.

Dr. Massac had previously visited the Ivory Coast of West Afrika where he successfully restored the face of a youngster who had been severely burned. And being the very humble leader that he is, he pulled together a "Dream Team" of dedicated, skilled and compassionate physicians who were to perform the surgery for the removal of this massive tumor.

Prince was scheduled for evaluation from all the services that would be involved in his surgery. A lot of this was frightening for him. Here he was for the first time in this big city and in this big, modern hospital with so many strangers probing and examining him. Every day there were tests and some days Prince fought against going.

When you asked what he'd prefer to be doing, he'd respond, "Look at television."

This was a big thing for him and at times he would lock himself in his room, turn up the volume and pretend he didn't hear us calling to him. We were having a rough time.

A very special person, Brother Arthur X, befriended Prince, escorting him everywhere. He became his father, friend and brother. One night Prince had waited up until 11:30 p.m. for Brother Arthur who had promised to take him out for ice cream. Prince refused to take off his clothes or go to bed and finally fell asleep in his clothes. At 12:15 a.m. in the early morning, Brother Arthur showed up. He had been delayed at work. As soon as Prince heard his voice he was out of bed in a flash.

Not to be deterred, brother Arthur said, "A promise is a promise and Prince and I are going out on the town."

And off they went. When it was time for visits to the hospital, Brother Arthur X was there. One day at the hospital, one of the physicians who had been called in to observe an examination began to discuss Prince's case as though he were not even there. As he continued to talk Prince was becoming more and more agitated. Having walked in on the discussion and seeing the situation, I asked the doctor to please step outside.

"Dr.," I asked, "where is your sensitivity, you're talking about Prince like he isn't even there."

"Well," he responded, "he doesn't speak English."

"You're wrong," I said. "He speaks and understands English quite well thank you. You should not make assumptions."

But the damage was already done and when we returned to the room, Prince had disappeared. We looked all over the hospital for him but no one had seen him. Brother Arthur finally found him, terrified and hiding in the basement of the hospital, in the Boiler Room. Another time he just walked out of the hospital and came back to the hotel, which was a block away from the hospital. When I answered the knock on the door, there he stood.

"What are you doing here?" I asked. "Aren't you supposed to be at the hospital?"

"I'm finished," he replied sadly, and went into his room and turned on the television.

I didn't question him further and returned to my room. Shortly thereafter the phone rang, when I answered an excited voice asked, "Have you seen Prince, we can't find him anywhere?"

"He's here, what's the problem?" I responded.

Just then there was an urgent knock at the door, it was Brother Arthur, one of the doctors and a security officer from the hospital. Prince had run away from the hospital and they were frantically looking for him. By this time, Prince was laying down in his room, sleeping.

He had been so frightened. This was the fifth operation he was undergoing: three times he had surgery in Ghana, one in England and now in the United States. We decided not to awaken him and assured the doctor that we would bring him back to the hospital in the morning.

When Prince awoke we all talked to him and Brother Arthur assured him that he would not leave him and that he would be there for him until everything was finished and he returned to Ghana. That seemed to allay some of Prince's fears and the following day Brother Arthur was there to take Prince back to the hospital. He was admitted and the surgery scheduled for the following morning. And true to his word, Brother Arthur never left his side, staying with him until he was rolled into the Operating Room.

The hands of the Almighty God, were on Prince in the Operating Room of Howard University Hospital that day and was manifested through a dedicated team of physicians and support staff who offered their skill, love and compassion to relieve his suffering and transform his face.

The surgical team came from throughout Howard University Hospital, requiring the expertise of many medical disciplines. They surgery took more than fourteen hours to complete, while music from our "Mother" land Ghana played during surgery to provide a familiar atmosphere for Prince during his surgery, although he was asleep during most of it, the sound of the music could still filter through to his subconscious.

As the surgeons and physicians working in the Operating Room took short, periodic breaks; food was prepared and provided for them by the sisters from The Nation of Islam.

The surgery required removing the largest part of the tumor located in the lower jaw. It was the largest tumor of its kind removed at Howard University Hospital. Tumors were also removed from his upper jaw, nose and skull. Plastic surgery was necessary to re-shape and re-mold both his upper and lower jaw. The tumor had destroyed most of the bridge of his nose, which necessitated borrowing a piece of bone from his hip to re-build his nose. The surgeons also re-molded his forehead because it was slightly oversized causing his hairline to recede. But the miracle had been accomplished.

Tired but joyful the surgical "Dream Team" finally emerged from the Operating Room with the news that the surgery had been a success and our young Prince Edmond was on the road to recovery.

It truly was a *"One Afrika"* surgical *"Dream Team"* of brothers and sisters who had come from different countries in Afrika and the Diaspora.

Plastic Surgery: Dr. Etienne A. Massac, Jr., *Virgin Islands*; Dr. Robert H. Dennis, II, *Liberia*; Dr. Monica Joyner and Dr. Joan Coker, *Afrikan-Americans*; **Oral Surgery:** Dr. Dana Jackson, O.M.F.S.; Dr. Marcus Daniel, O.M.F.S.; Dr. Fred Campbell, DDS, *Afrikan-Americans;* **Otolaryngology (ENT):** Dr. Ernest Myers and Neal Brickhouse, *Afrikan-Americans*; Dr. Arthur Mcunu, South Afrika; **Anesthesiology:** Dr. Baffour Osei, Ghana, *West Afrika*; Dr. Barbara Roberts, *Jamaica, West Indies*; Dr. Cheryl Burruss and Dr. John Sampson, *Afrikan-Americans*; Dr. Haile Mezghebe, *Eritrea, Ethiopia;* **Operating Room Nurses:** Janice Basharan, Helen Toms, Frankie Robinson, Claudette Rigby, Megen Houston and Albert Pearson, *Afrikan-Americans;* and **Medical Videographer:** Robert Brown, *Afrikan-American.*

They truly represented a united, *"One Afrika"* Dream Team, in the true spirit of oneness. These physicians donated their medical expertise, skill and money to give a youngster from Ghana, West Afrika a new and brighter future.

With the surgery now behind us, the recuperation period began and according to Dr. Massac, it would be six weeks or more before Prince could return to Ghana.

When Dr. Massac was asked to summarize some of the factors that might prohibit Afrikan countries from providing the kind of surgery performed on Prince, he stated,

> "Since there is such a shortage of doctors in Ghana and Afrika as a whole and a vast number of people, the ratio of people to the numbers of doctors could prevent this from happening. Howard University is unique in that sense, because there is a concentration of highly trained and skilled Black physicians in one location. The high degree of medical expertise is what this operation required. Additionally, there are factors involving follow-up care, working relationships and kindred spirits. All that we've done was pull this together to give the youngster the care I think will make everyone proud. Any doctor in the world with the medical expertise could do the job, however the brotherhood and sisterhood of being Afrikan adds a bit more."

The miracle continued, because neither the family nor The Educational Sponsorship Program was able to pay for the many other expenses incurred for this undertaking. However, once again the brothers and sisters of The Nation of Islam, Muhammad's Mosque No. 4, under the direction of Dr. Alim Muhammad, Director of The Abundant Life Clinic, coordinated the fund raising efforts to maintain the family during our stay in the United States. They saw to our every need, not a stone was left unturned. Housing and food were provided and we were made very comfortable.

Donations came in from churches, organizations and concerned community residents in and out of the Washington, DC area. A group of *"underprivileged, inner city"* (the term used by the person making the presentation) youth from a Summer Work Training Program donated $800.00 of their earnings to Prince and prepared four huge greeting cards which all of them signed. A taxi driver was taking me to the hospital one day recognized my face from a picture he had seen in the newspaper and refused to accept the fare when we reached my destination.

"It's the least I can do for the little Prince," he said.

Sharon Pratt-Kelly, Mayor of Washington, DC also pledged her support to Prince and his family in securing funds and provisions for our stay until Prince was ready to travel.

Dr. Alim Muhammad best-described love, as "H-E-L-P" and that is what the brothers and sisters of The Nation of Islam and the Afrikan-American community so abundantly demonstrated. Their love continued to manifest itself in the good deeds they performed.

"Care and concern for a youngster go beyond mere sympathy and is akin to welcoming a long, lost relative," Brother Simeon Booker, Editor of *The Final Call* newspaper remarked.

Most of the people we interacted with truly demonstrated what we are supposed to be about as Afrikan people.

Everyday I woke up thanking The Almighty Creator and thinking, *It can't get any better than this,* but it did.

There was also a farewell reception held for Prince in Minister Farrakhan's downtown suite in Washington, DC. With Prince sitting by his side, The Minister remarked to the members of Muhammad Mosque No. 4, whom had been our primary host family, organizers and facilitators during our stay in Washington, "You have proven and shown the love of the Honorable Elijah Muhammad that he has placed in our hearts for our people."

He then thanked Allah/God for the medical team who performed the surgery.

"I don't know how much more I can do but sing the praises of Howard University Hospital. Many of our own people don't even trust our own doctors for heart and liver transplants. That's the kind of (mental) sickness we must destroy." Dr. Etienne Massac, who had accompanied Prince to the reception responded by saying,"This effort shows our innate skills and abilities to demonstrate that we as Afrikan people can build bridges and help someone in need."

During the brief but emotionally filled meeting, Minister Farrakhan further remarked, "Because of young Prince's life experiences, he will grow to be a king to lead our people to great heights. He will be an example of courage and strength to the world."

A great comforter to Prince had been Brother Arthur 2X, who was a constant companion and father figure who helped Prince over

194

the many emotional and traumatic hurdles that he had to overcome. At times he was the only person that could calm his fears and get Prince to cooperate with his doctors. During the reception Min. Farrakhan rewarded Brother Arthur's expression of love by bestowing upon him the name Muhammed Abdul Salaam.

Prince and his mom returned home to Ghana, the first week in September. Brother Muhammad escorted us to the airport on the day of departure and gave Prince an even bigger surprise, when he entered the airplane with him, escorting him from Washington, DC to New York and staying with him until his departure for Ghana. Other brothers, sisters and children of the Nation of Islam, as well as personal friends of mine and Nana also came to the airport to see him off.

We had been blessed beyond expectation. I continuously thanked the Creator for the manifold blessings that had been bestowed upon us: for the precious gifts of love, compassion, unity and fellowship and for a little Prince who had drawn us together, to help bridge the gap between the Afrikan-American community and our Afrikan brothers and sisters on the continent.

Additional funds were donated and given to Prince's mother for the construction of a small house, school supplies, clothing and many other things for Prince and his brothers were also given by our brothers and sisters in the Afrikan-Amerikan community. It had been a long and difficult task but the job had been done.

With Prince on his way back to Ghana, I stayed in New York for a few additional weeks to visit with my family and friends whom I had not seen for years.

NOTE: I am happy to report that as of this writing, Prince is still doing quite well. The tumor has not returned. He has completed Senior Secondary School (High School) and is currently pursuing his career in Accounting and Business Management. However, further Plastic Surgery will be necessary to rebuild his facial structure.

Additionally, to date eleven (11) other children in The Educational Sponsorship Program have completed Senior Secondary School and have either gone on further to pursue their education, are self employed or have secured employment in the trades that they had undertaken during their course of study.

This has been possible due to the unselfish love and contributions of the following sponsors from America:

Mr. & Mrs. George and Hazel Miller (2 children)

Mrs. Elaine Turner

Sister Pauline Williams (2 children)

Dr. Mark Fields

Dr. & Mrs. Yubie Metcalf (2 children)

Brother Adelabu Oshiyemi

Brother Eric Ruffin

Sister Mildred O. Saunders

Sister Mabel Haddock

Top left: Prince Edmond Ostibu, age 5, Top right: Prince Edmond Ostibu, age 13, before 5th surgery to remove tumor, Center left: Maurice Mensah, Prince's mother, IMAHKÜS, Prince Edmond, NOI Minister A. Akbar Muhammad and Dr. Etienne Massac outside Howard University Hospital before the surgery. Prince Edmond, age 21. Bottom: The surgical Dream Team in the Operating Room,

197

BESE SAKA
(Bunch of cola nuts)

Symbol of power and affluence.

CHAPTER THIRTEEN

HOME ONCE MORE

After spending a month in New York, it was October and time for me to return home. It had started raining and getting cold and I was in no way prepared for the weather nor did I want to prepare for it. I was missing Ghana and Nana toooooooooooo much (as they say here in Ghana) and like a pouting child, too long away from its mother, I wanted to go home! Within one week I had re-confirmed my reservations and was on my way back to Ghana.

It is difficult to describe the feeling that came over me as my plane landed at Kotoka International Airport in Accra. One was the feeling of relief...and joy but it went deeper than that. I was like a baby returning to the bosom of my mother. As I stepped out of the plane, the evening heat rushed on me, warming my body...a little muggy but wonderful. I could hardly wait to see Nana. I got a real surprise when someone met me at the plane and escorted me through the VIP Lounge. I was a little puzzled. As I came through the doors, there was Nana, all smiles and boy did he look good to me. I literally jumped into his arms. Laughingly, I asked,

"What is this? How come I was brought through the VIP Lounge?"

"You're a very important person," was his response as he hugged me again.

Nana was always full of surprises and this was no different. He always did the unexpected. A reporter from one of the national newspapers was also there to welcome me home: God, did that sound good to my ears...home...home in Ghana. The reporter also wanted to interview me regarding my trip to the United States and the success of Prince's surgery. Once the interview was completed and the bags gathered we set out for home... home to Elmina and my family. It had been a long three months. I was even happy to see the soldiers at the Check Points along the way and they didn't seem so intimidating to me this time. I fell asleep during the ride home and when I awoke I didn't have a clue as to where I was. We were riding along side a long wall, when suddenly we stopped and turned into this gate.

A little late to be visiting someone, I thought. "Where are we Nana?" I asked.

"Home," he replied.

"Home?" I asked again, still half asleep.

I didn't recognize anything. As we drove up into the yard, there were Mama D. and Bongo Shorty standing on the porch, waving and laughing and shouting. The car had not stopped before I jumped out. Two seconds later we were all hugging and kissing but I still couldn't seem to get a grip on where I was.

The roof had been under construction, with scaffolds surrounding the house when I left in July and the building had been unpainted. It was now white, with the colors of Ethiopia (green, gold and red) painted around the crown of the house. The roadside entrance of the house had been painted green. As I entered the kitchen I couldn't believe it was the same place for they had built cabinets and also painted the kitchen. I ran back outside like an excited child. I couldn't get over the place. It had been completely transformed in my absence.

Under the twinkling stars (and satellites) of the dark night, I felt like I was in heaven. The place was enclosed...and we had a gate around our compound, which was another surprise...a big surprise. The family had really been working. I was too excited to sleep. We stayed up until dawn, talking and enjoying the warmth and love of each other.

The following morning I explored the compound, I was still most impressed with our fence wall. We now had real privacy.

There were always people who walked through our open yard. Where food was growing they'd pick it. Since the water pipe was in clear view they would help themselves to water...all day. The children stopped for water going to school and on their way back home...one by one, about thirty-five children. If we were on the porch, each one would speak to each of us individually.

"Good morning Nana, good morning Auntie IMAH, good morning Mr. Bongo, good morning Mama D."

This happened everyday, 35 - 40 times, twice a day, with little girls curtseying and little boy's saluting, as they greeted us. Every person who passed our house said, "Mornin' mornin', ete sen (how are you?" and you'd respond until you finally fled back into the house...to hide!

One time we were growing watermelons. We took pictures eating our first, home grown watermelons: everyone was cheesin'. We were so proud of ourselves. We had a nice little watermelon crop, although it was not ready for harvesting. It's a good thing we took pictures. One day while we were away from the house someone came through our yard and broke open all of the watermelons and destroyed the tomato crop. It was such a waste for all they had to do was wait for the harvest and we would share.

By now I was really beginning to appreciate why almost everyone in Ghana had a fence wall (hedges, concrete or coconut boughs), which was not uncommon in the city, towns or villages. Why couldn't Nana see it? People lived in enclosed family compounds. But Nana had been adamant.

"No fence wall, I didn't come to Afrika to live behind concrete walls... no fence wall and that's that."

Mama D. and Bongo still tried to convince him.

"Tis not a home, tis a yard, til gate go pon de place," they'd say. Still no gate!

Another time I came out of the house to find a woman with a basket full of my tomatoes that she had picked from our yard.

"What do you think you're doing?" I asked.

"Ya ca' git mo!" she replied. (You can get more!)

"No, you can get more... from the market."

I told her as I took the tomatoes out of her hands. The look on her face was one of total surprise. But, it was a wide-open space, so I shared the tomatoes with her and told her not to take anything else out of my yard again, without first asking permission.

And if that wasn't enough, I never dreamed that I would come home to Afrika and get "white folks" for neighbors, white missionaries to be exact, who had come to bring Jesus to the people and save the souls of the heathen.

"God, oh God," I shouted to the heavens, "is this a test? Have I offended you in some ways? Mother, Father, Are you listening to me? Is this a test?"

I would be standing on our bedroom porch and there they were looking in my face. They'd wave and I'd stick out my tongue!

So after all of the experiences we'd had (and I've not cited all of them) I was tooooo happy to find a fence wall up around our place, when I returned from the United States.

"It is now a home," said Bongo, and I agreed with that, one hundred percent.

I also had quite a few visitors stopping in to welcome me home. It felt good too.

One evening while sitting in the yard reasoning with Mr. Kwame, the laundry man we'd contracted, he commented on our cat, whom we called "Mas' Tom," a big reddish colored Tom Cat that we'd had since it was a kitten.

"Cat meat e sweet-o," said Mr. Kwame, "make good chop-chop."

"What did you say?" I asked him, not sure of his meaning.

"Cat meat e make good chop, good for eating," he continued. "I like it toooo much."

He said with this big, mouth-watering grin on his face.

"You eat cat?" I asked in surprise.

"Oh yes, madam." he continued.

"Well that's not our practice, Mr. Kwame. We do not eat cats and if anything happens to our cat I will hold you personally responsible."

He just laughed. "Oh madam," he continued, "et es fine. Plenty people in the village dem eat cat and some eat dog."

The thought of eating cats and dogs was turning my stomach.

"Can we change the subject? I asked. You just remember what I said and do not touch our cat."

Lo and behold, several days later "Mas' Tom" was nowhere to be found. The last time that we'd seen him, he was sitting on the wall doing tricks and licking his paws. We looked all over the place for him with no success but we figured he'd eventually show up.

A few days later, as I was on my way to the market, I had to pass by Mr. Kwame's yard. There sat Mr. Kwame and a couple of his cronies, around a pot of red stew, small white bones littered the ground in front of them.

Our cat! I thought to myself.

Mr. Kwame looked very sheepishly at me, mumbled good morning and lowered his head.

"Mr. Kwame have you seen our cat?"

"Oh no, madam, I-I um I no see de cat. I, I don' know your cat," he stuttered, looking at the ground.

Still, I didn't believe him but what else could I do? I knew in my heart of hearts that they were eating Mas Tom. About two weeks later it was confirmed, as I overheard the mason who was working in our yard and Ama a sister who had come to do the laundry (for Mr. Kwame had not come back again, talking in Fante about how Mr. Kwame had trapped and eaten IMAH's cat.

I was too through.

"I heard what you said," I told them; "I heard you say that Mr. Kwame had eaten my cat. You wait until I get my hands around his neck."

"Oh please Madam," Ama pleaded, "please don't tell Mr. Kwame that we told you, for he will vex with us. He told us not to speak of it with you. I don' know you can hear the Fante. Please Madam, I beg!"

I finally agreed not to mention their names but I wasn't finished with Mr. Kwame yet. But as it were, he never came back and each time I saw him, he would duck and dodge me.

So I just let it rest and chalked it up to another series of events in the process of returning home. It took some getting used to though. But when I thought about it, didn't we eat chicken and cows, and goats and raccoon, etc. And, it was a different culture here. No wonder you never see a lot of dogs and cats wandering around. We must have looked like a real life version of *Animal Farm*, with all our dogs, cats and monkey running around the place.

We all managed to get a good laugh out of the whole thing and I continued to be pleasantly and sometimes not so pleasantly surprised in my return home from the United States.

I also got an unpleasant shock, when Mama D informed me that she was returning to Jamaica. She had only been waiting for me to return home. She had had enough of the malaria, was having a difficult time with the language and the culture, plus she was missing her family too much. As had been our agreement, if anyone felt that they could not hang, they had a year to return home. That's why we had bought round trip tickets.

But we ran into a little problem because our tickets had expired and Mama D had stayed three years. So we cashed in all of our tickets for their face value and used them to help pay for her return ticket.

We were sad about her decision but could not convince her to change her mind. Then there was the issue of she and Bongo because they had come together. But Bongo was steadfast in his commitment to stay in Ghana.

"Mi naw come forward to go back, if mi can' do it here, where me fer do it? If mi go anywhere it must be Ithiopia (Ethiopia). Maybe a trip back to Jamaica is what the I need at this time D," Bongo commented.

It was a sad day in our house as Mama D packed her bags and prepared to leave. I cried like a little baby because I was really going to miss my sister and I prayed that one day, some how, that she would be able to return home to Ghana. Unfortunately, we did not have the money to be able to make it happen again, ourselves. At least, not at this time!

Two weeks later, she was gone.

* * * * * * *

Bongo Shorty (also called Bongo Man) had been plenty busy in my absence. He had built a fifteen (15) foot craft, carved out of a piece of driftwood that had been on the beach in front of our place for more than ten years, according to some of the fisherman from our village. It was a fine boat.

"Bongo Man, the I has really been busy-o. I know that you said you could build boats but this is the first time I've seen one that you've built. It's wonderful. When can I go for a sail?"

"Anytime you're ready Mistress," as he often called me, "anytime the I is ready."

"Is tomorrow too soon?"

I asked like a little child.

"Not at all," he said. "I'll get a couple of the boys from the village and we'll take a trip up the Sweet River."

The Sweet River which stretches inland for about sixty to seventy miles consists of waters from three other rivers; the Kakum, Nkontro and Suruwi rivers which flow from the River Pra. These waters flow into the Sweet River, which links with the sea at our village, Iture.

History has it that this river was so named by the British in the 1700's because although the river linked with the sea, the water was still drinkable and said to be sweet. This same body of water is still used today which is equally historic and significant in our return for it is no coincidence that we have returned to a village more than 400 years old and whose ancestors were involved in building Elmina Castle Dungeons. Additionally, our home is located geographically on the coast between the Cape Coast and Elmina Castle Dungeons.

Early the following morning, Nana, Bongo Man, Brother Jacob and a few other brothers set sail up the Sweet River.

We didn't have an outboard motor so several of the young men rowed. We went past small villages, waving a people who greeted us from the shore. This was really a great little craft.

As we drifted slowly up river there were beautiful black and white birds dipping into the water, red, blue and turquoise colored birds flying overhead and perching in the trees. This was new for me for as often as I passed this river opening I had never been on it. It was a glorious day, the sun was bright...and hot but it felt wonderful.

We returned home that evening. I was black as tar after being in the sun in that open boat all day. And I really needed the sun. After three months in America, I had lost my golden Afrikan glow.

Bongo was also quite excited about the trip for it had been a long time since he had been on the water – and he had not been to sea since we arrived in 1991. But now he was on a roll.

The following morning he was up early. I could hear banging in the distance. When I went outside there was Bongo, making a couple of wooden horses. Stacks of wood stood nearby. My brother was busy.

"One Love and good mornin-O, Bongo Man!" I called out.

"One Love and good mornin' Mistress," he answered smiling.

"What's up?" I asked.

"Me gettin' an early start pon the next boat. Me-ah build a thirty-foot craft to do deep-sea fishing. I built that last boat out of a fallen tree but that's too much work and is too heavy for my suit. But a planking boat made with WaWa wood is very light and sturdy," he explained.

For the next couple of days Bongo was busy-busy, but I was a little concerned because it was blazing hot in the sun and the coconut trees did not afford enough shade. He was diligently working and not thinking about the sun, while I on the other hand was afraid he'd get heat stroke.

Later that afternoon, Bongo, Nana and I were reasoning and decided that they would build a workshop so that Bongo could work more comfortably. Nana was the Materials Manager, Bongo Man was the Boat Builder and I was the Administrator.

People came from near and far when they heard about the boat Bongo was building. Everyone knew and respected Bongo but many couldn't believe that he was building a boat out of WaWa wood, they thought the wood was too light and they didn't build them that way in Ghana. Plus he was building it by himself, without any assistance and without electrical tools. When he originally started a few people came around and offered to help but it was hard work and they didn't last long.

Additionally, it was a little frustrating for Bongo because of the language barrier. If he asked for the hammer he got the saw, if he asked for the nails, he got the screws. After a really frustrating day with a young brother who said he was an experienced carpenter, but really only came to eat and talk, Bongo hit the ceiling.

"Me naw wan' no help again, me can' take it no more. Me can' take the talkin' when dem suppose to be workin' and when dem suppose to work dem naw come. When dem come dey leave early cause someone sick or dead and dem wan' me fer give dem money. Chaw," he said with a sigh.

"Well what do you want to do man?" Nana asked. "You need some help."

"Me naw need help like dat," he continued.

"Just let me know what you need and I'll see if we can't get it," Nana responded.

"I wan' different size "G" clamps, a brace, a tool belt and a hacksaw. That will hold me fer now," Bongo responded.

So like the good Materials Manager that he is, Nana went shopping for the things that Bongo needed. Now with the workshop constructed and all of his tools in hand he was good to go. People called him the "One Man Contractor."

He was really amazing. Watching him work was a treat in itself. He would clamp the wood on one end, line it up properly, walk to the other end and clamp that side, get the saw and cut the plank to the desired size and never missed a beat. When people would come to watch him he would make it very plain.

"Mi naw want no loud talkin' and laughin' while mi a do my work. If you can' stay quiet, go through the gate," he'd say and would never miss a beat.

It took about seven months to complete the boat. He worked every day from sun-up to when done and because we had no electricity, everything was done without power tools, using plenty of elbow grease. Even the sanding of the boat was done by hand.

When it was time to put on the finishing touches, Nana went to Côte d'Ivoire for the fiberglass that was needed for the boat bottom. Again Bongo did it himself.

When Bongo was finished, we had a beautiful thirty-foot fishing boat with a small cabin. Brother Wailer, who moved with us for a time, lent his hands to assist in painting the craft and doing other odd jobs.

But Bongo is the man! He is our "One Man Contractor."

HYE WONHYE

Symbol of imperishability and endurance.

Symbolizing the ability to withstand pain
and other hardships.
That which cannot be burned!

CHAPTER FOURTEEN

IS THE BLACK MAN'S HISTORY BEING "WHITE WASHED?"

In the eloquent words of our Elder and Patriarch Dr. Robert E. Lee, who repatriated to Ghana in 1957 at the invitation of Osageyfo Dr. Kwame Nkrumah, "a return to the slave forts for blacks in the Diaspora is a necessary act of self-realization, for the spirits of the Diaspora are somehow tied to those historic structures."

I had been back in Ghana for a few weeks, when I decided to visit the Cape Coast Castle Dungeons. It had been a long time since I had been there to commune with the spirits of my ancestors. I needed to feel their spirit and let them know I was home, once more.

As I drove up the road towards the Castle, the scaffolds and the work going on at the Castle struck me. A massive piece of reconstruction was going on. It had not been this way when I left for the United States three months before.

As I entered the castle reception area, old friends greeted me.

"What's happening around here?" I asked. "Who's responsible for this?"

"It's not right what dey doin' here, One Afrika," one of the employees at the castle said. "The White people dey take over and do all dis."

"But who is in charge?" I wanted to know.

The name of someone called Nate at CEDECOM (Central Region Development Commission) was given to me but before I went to see him I wanted to visit the Elmina Castle Dungeons.

What I saw there really made me sick. Similar work was going on. I went to the Men's Dungeon but the door was closed so I pushed it open. I was surprised and stunned as I walked inside and looked around.

What happened to the Men's Dungeon? I asked myself. The room had been freshly painted yellow. I went back outside to look at the sign again and it did say, "Men's Dungeon." I was too upset. I again spoke to the Tour Guide and some of the workers, who really could not give me any answers. I was fuming when I left the Elmina Castle Dungeons. Tears ran down my cheeks and I could not stop trembling. Part of it was anger, the other sadness and a sense of hopelessness. Pulling myself together, I went to see this White man at CEDECOM, whom I had been told, was heading up part of this project. When I walked into his office, his attitude was very nonchalant. He took what I was saying very lightly and acted like he didn't believe me when I told him that the Men's Dungeon in the Elmina Castle had been painted. I wasn't going to stand there and argue with him.

"Just go and see for yourself," I told him, "I know what I saw."

According to him no one was supposed to be working in the dungeons.

"Well, I can see that you are not very aware of what's going on with your project or the activities that are going on in the castles/dungeons," I said, "nor do you seem to care."

"I bet you wouldn't be so nonchalant if foreigners were planting flowers and making hotel rooms out of the ovens in Auschtwitz, would you?" I demanded.

By now he had turned beet red in the face and was fumbling on his desk for something, anything.

"Thank you for bringing this to my attention," he mumbled sheepishly, "I'll check it out and get back to you."

I got up and stormed out slamming the door behind me. I was livid.

When I got home, I told Nana about my visit and asked him if he knew what this was all about. But he knew about as much as I did.

A few days later I got a call from CEDECOM to come into the office. The same White man greeted me.

"Please sit down," he began, with this sick grin on this face. "Well, I've been to the Elmina Castle and the Men's Dungeon hasn't been white washed, it's been yellow washed. Heh, heh, heh."

When he realized that his feeble attempt at a joke had angered me all the more, he began apologizing.

"So what are you going to do about it," I wanted to know.

He fumbled around in embarrassment some more and said that he was looking into the matter and would make certain that it did not happen again.

I was not impressed. It was like closing the door to the barn after the cow had escaped. Again, I left his office steaming.

Somebody had to listen, somebody had to care. And, somebody had to do something because the Black man's history was truly being white washed.

When I got home I immediately went to my typewriter and furiously began to write the following article entitled:

The Black Man's History is Being White Washed.

How many millions of Afrikan men, women and children have passed through the dark, damp dungeons of the Cape Coast and Elmina Castle Dungeons? Driven and prodded along through long, dark tunnels that led Afrikans to the "Belly of the Beast," into dark, stinking hell holes of strange looking ships, which would take our ancestors away from "Mother" Afrika in chains and shackles to unknown lands separating families from the love and warmth of their communities.

It was a Holocaust that had brought total confusion and desolation to Afrikan people and shame to others. The Afrikan Holocaust (The Arab-European Slave Trade) was real and must not be forgotten by anyone.

Are flowers being planted in the ovens at Auschwitz where an alleged 6 million Jews perished? Have the Death Chambers been brightly painted to somehow camouflage or silence the cries and screams of people who were brutally tortured and murdered? Think about that and then think about the Cape Coast and Elmina Castle Dungeons on the Gold Coast of West Afrika, where you can still hear and feel the presence of our Afrikan Ancestors when you enter the dark dungeons and tunnels. But will this be true when they finish renovating the Castles and painting the insides of the Dungeons? Restore, preserve, renovate, maintain? That is exactly what is being done and right up under our very noses.

If I sound in a panic...I am. Concerned? Definitely. Seeking collective help and responsibility to prevent an action that cannot be reversed or can it? But we must do something before it's too late.

I sit here daily, on my verandah in the wake of the Elmina Castle Dungeons, a descendent of those ancestors who passed THRU THE DOOR OF NO RETURN, an observer to the 'White Wash' of our Afrikan history.

I had recently returned from the United States after spending three months there. In that short span of time the Elmina and Cape Coast Castle Dungeons were going through a major 'phase' of renovation, not preservation, but the renovation and destroying of an important monument of the Afrikan Holocaust that befell our people over 500 years ago: a Holocaust inflicted upon a people the magnitude and denigration not heard of before on any other people, except the Afrikan and the world should never be allowed to forget, lest it happen again.

When I visited the Cape Coast Castle/Dungeons in 1987, it was my first trip to the continent of "Mother" Afrika. As I stood transfixed in the Women's Dungeon, I could feel and smell the presence of our ancestors. From the dark, damp corners of that hell-hole I heard whimpering and crying of tormented mothers and sisters being held in inhuman bondage, never knowing what each new day (which is difficult to discern in the dungeons) would bring.

Strange white men that kept coming to look at them, feeling them, examining their private parts as if they were some kind of animals. Removing them for their own sick pleasures, while they awaited the Devil Ships that would take them into a 500 year long hell. Sisters were dying all around...the breast milk for another child ceasing to flow.

As I stood in the center of that dungeon I felt tightness at the base of my scalp as though someone had grabbed me by the back of my neck, causing me to fall to my knees. Shortly thereafter, as I knelt crying and terrified, a warmth slowly crept across my shoulders, the fear that had previously wretched my gut was replaced by a feeling of serenity and calm I had never experienced before. Many hands caressed me, stilling my fears, wiping my tears and welcoming me home to "Mother" Afrika and Ghana, in one of the many dungeons along the West Coast of Afrika, where it all began for Afrikans born in the United States and the Diaspora.

And here I was today witnessing the 'white wash' of Afrikan history. But I could not sit in idleness and watch this happen without sounding an alarm and praying that Afrikan-Americans and other Afrikans of the Diaspora will hear, wake-up and get involved before it's too late, if it's not too late already.

That project underway in Ghana was called The Monuments & Cultural Heritage Conservation (Cape Coast Castle). The Donors were the United States Agency for International Development (USAID), the United Nations Development Programme (UNDP) and Shell (Ghana) Ltd. The implementing agency was the Ghana Museums and Monuments Board and the collaborating agencies were the International Council on Monuments and Sites (U.S. Chapter) and The Smithsonian Institute. The project was implemented under the auspices of the Central Region Development Commission (CEDECOM) in partnership with the Midwestern Universities Consortium for International Activities (USA). These agencies were the organizations charged with 'preserving' the history of the Afrikan Holocaust. Where was our input, both financial and otherwise? Where was our voice?

Webster's New Collegiate Dictionary defines preservation and renovation as follows:

PRESERVATION: to keep, guard, observe, more at conserve; to keep safe from injury, harm or destruction; protect, intact or free from decay; maintain, to keep up and reserve for and preserve for future use. Something regarded as reserved for certain persons.

RENOVATE: to make new, to restore to life, vigor or activity; to restore to a better state as by cleaning, repairing or *"REBUILD-ING."* To make *"EXTENSIVE"* changes in, *"RE-BUILD."*

At Cape Coast Castle/Dungeons, in Palaver Hall, where foreigners bartered and sold us; where documents were signed to seal our fate and that would ultimately begin the creation of other tribes of Afrikans (Afrikan-Americans, Afrikan-Jamaicans, etc.) carried away in the loins of the enslaved; in those hallowed halls windows have been removed and replaced with new glass windows. The outer walls of the Castle/Dungeons were gradually being chipped away and replaced with fresh cement, mortar and paint.

One day as I approached the Cape Coast Castle/Dungeons with a few brothers and sisters who were visiting from Philadelphia, one sister remarked upon seeing the castle,"Oh what a beautiful building!"

I was shocked, my entire being vibrated and the fear that was in my gut in 1987 returned, hitting me hard. My God, the dirty deeds of our Oppressors are being prettied-up. When I explained where we were, the sister's first question was,

"Why are they re-building and beautifying the Castle/Dungeons?"

Good question! For in the Elmina Castle/Dungeons similar reconstruction (renovation) was also going on. The Governor's Quarters overlooking the courtyard of the Women's Dungeon, with its secret doorway leading up to his apartment had been completely renovated. The Portuguese Church with its secret peep holes through which strange men came and secretly observed us before making a purchase and the Confessional used by the Priests to hear confessions (certainly not ours) had also been renovated. Gone were the old wooden shutters and heavy old doors, replaced by nicely painted gray doors and windows with glass panes.

But what struck me the hardest was entering the Men's Dungeon and finding that it had been painted a bright yellow. Gone was the musty, lingering smell of time and of Black male bodies, the lingering feel of the spirit of those ancestors who had been forcibly removed from their "Mother" land and taken away to the Americas and the Caribbean. I came out of that room stunned and looked again at the sign, this time in total disbelief, for it did say "Men's Dungeon."

But by its new look, feel and smell, it could have been just another freshly painted room in our house or another hotel room. A Horror House, now being given special architectural treatment while creating a false, superficial and artificial appearance. The Cape Coast and Elmina Castle/Dungeons are hallowed grounds and should be left undisturbed: otherwise you are tampering with history. The crashing thunder of the ocean waves breaking against the damp dungeon walls and the eerie darkness take visitors back in time to the nightmares of the Trans-Atlantic Arab European Slave Trade.

This is a staggering and traumatic experience, but very important in our re-connection with our roots. Numerous groups of Afrikan-American and other Afrikans of the Diaspora come through the Cape Coast and Elmina Castle/Dungeons when they visit Ghana and they talk of the importance of the preservation and maintenance of our history and these monuments. However, I do not think that what I see happening today is what we had in mind.

Dr. Robert E. Lee (Uncle Bobby as he is affectionately called) also had plans to preserve our history. He and other Afrikan Descendants of the African Descendants Association Foundation attempted to preserve Fort Amsterdam at Abandze, which was built in 1631 by the Dutch. It is one of the forty-six forts, castles and Dungeons to be built along the Gold Coast of Afrika by European powers that ruled the waterways.

These Afrikan descendants wanted to turn Fort Amsterdam into a Mecca for the thousands of African Descendants who were coming to Afrika in search of their identity, which was denied them in the United States.

Their dream was to set up an exclusive museum-library complex for old scrolls, writings, diaries, and paintings, drawings and artifacts that would unlock additional truths about the Afrikan's past. But through lack of financial support and dis-unity the project became dormant.

Are we like small smudges on a piece of paper that can simply be removed with an eraser? Isn't the Afrikan's history after centuries of toil, struggle and suffering worthy of being held up before the eyes of the world in honesty and truth? Are we not like our ancient forefathers whom Pharaoh sought to destroy? Who is our Moses? Isaac Hayes? I think not...for there are many Moses' amongst our people and we must band together in the preservation and further development and defining of our history and its impact upon the world *by any means necessary.*

I was writing to somebody about the white wash at that time and when I showed my completed article to Nana he read it through and said that he thought it was pretty good.

"Girl you should have seen yourself when you came in the door from the Castle Dungeons, that day," he laughed. You were madder than a wet hen. You gettum baby. However, I only have one comment and that deals with your title. You're making a statement. You're saying that, "the black man's history is being white washed!" So you say! That's your opinion. I think you should change the title ever so slightly and ask a question. *Is the Black Man's History Being White Washed?* Somebody has got to answer that question and will probably be looking for an answer for a long time to come."

"Wise council Nana, it does make good sense," I replied.

That's another reason that Nana and I are good together, we help to balance one another. I'm that Scorpion fire and he's that peaceful dreamer part of Sagittarian.

The article has appeared in quite a few newspapers, magazines and periodicals.

I even won a one-year's subscription to New African Magazine, out of London, when my article was accepted as "prize letter of the month," for submitting the most original and stimulating contribution to their mailbag, that month. The article has wound up on the desk of a couple of congressmen and others folks in government in the United States and Ghana. Isaac Hayes came and promised to raise 30 million dollars to preserve our history.

Needless to say the "renovation" of the Cape Coast and Elmina Castle/Dungeons has been completed and is now being "maintained."

And what we have today is one of the Male Dungeons painted yellow and being used as a storage area, the sign has been removed and the wall painted over; the other Male Dungeon was turned into a Gift Shop.

The Portuguese Church is now a museum and the Women's Dungeon Courtyard and surrounding area has been painted a blinding white.

The area where enslaved women were forcibly dragged, to be cleaned up, before being taken up through the trap door of the Governors apartment has been sealed off and life goes on as usual.

This whole thing smells like a statement that was made at a Slave Route Conference that was held by the World Tourism Organization (WTO) and the United Nations Educational, Scientific and Cultural

216

Organization (UNESCO) in 1995, under the theme *Development of a Cultural Tourism Programme for Africa.*

> *"The Executioner always kills twice,*
> *the second time by silence."*

Are we as Afrikan Descendants of those ancestors going to sit around and *silently* wait to be killed a second time?

Are we going to allow the last vestiges/evidence of those ancestors disappear silently?

Tell me brothers and sisters. Tell me, you "preservers" of our history, **"HAS THE BLACK MAN'S HISTORY BEEN WHITE WASHED?"**

As one European (white) observer who was doing a research paper on tourism commented, "The project has been given over to a blue ribbon list of international aid agencies and is controlled by their staff and hired consultants of whom I am one".

The United States is mentioned three times. The government of Ghana is not mentioned except through two of its agencies, which are themselves dependent upon USAID and the United Nations money.

So who "owns" the castles? Who has the power to represent one of Ghana's greatest monuments?"

A promising note:

Years after the completion of that renovation project in the castle/dungeons, the workers continue in their fruitless efforts to keep the castle/dungeons nicely painted. But the spirit of the ancestors is real and strong, for as much as they paint they can't keep the paint on the wall looking white for any length of time. The stone gray cement continues to break through the white wash. It is always looking like an unfinished job or building in need of a paint job.

When will they wake up and realize that the castle/dungeons do not need painting: in fact it should never have been painted in the first place. The best thing that has come out of this is more jobs for the people but they would have gotten them anyway, even if the project had been handled differently.

The struggle continues...

Cape Coast Castle dungeon during "Renovation" project.

Sign board showing the name of the project and its donors, implementing agency & collaborating agencies.

Outside view of Elmina Castle dungeons being white washed.

Note the sign over the "locked door of the male slave dungeon at Elmina Castle dungeons.

Note the space where the "male slave Dungeon" sign was removed and never replaced after dungeon was painted bright yellow.

CHAPTER FIFTEEN

LIFE GOES ON

I have heard more stories from folks here, about everything. Some of it is really sad but even in its sadness sometimes there is laughter. One of the sisters that lived in the village visited us quite often and when she wasn't busy breaking rocks she did our laundry. I'm not going to lie, doing laundry by hand is hard, especially for me having been raised in a washing machine society. I never washed sheets by hand; my light things like lingerie, yes. All that other stuff went to the machine, so for me this was quite an adjustment. Plus local folks around us felt that "Nana's" wife, rich foreigner from America, shouldn't wash her own clothes but should have a laundry person. So twice a month the sister came in and washed and did odd jobs around our place.

Life in the village is hard. There's no industry, no work. To make ends meet, which is basic survival, food for the stomach, many of the women break rocks. The men called "Rockmen" dig out large pieces of rock/boulders from the ground or the sea front (at least they did until the Department of Ecology stopped them because they were destroying the natural sea defense wall). They had been doing this for years as their primary source of income. The big stones were given to the women, who sat in the hot sun, all day, breaking the stones into small pieces, which were put in piles and sold by the Head Pan or Tipper Truck load full for use in construction. It could take many days for one person to break up enough stones to fill a truck.

This is the story that Sister brought from the village one morning.

Ama was tired...and hungry. It had been a long, hard day breaking rocks in the hot sun. When she closed at the end of the day she waited with the other women to be paid by the person they were breaking rocks for. When the man arrived with his truck and they had loaded the stones, the man said,

"I will need another load for tomorrow."

Good, Ama thought to herself, *for she desperately needed the money.*

But she was not prepared for his next words.

"I pay all tomorrow," he said.

"Master, you say you pay today," said Ama. "I no have money and my small boys no get food."

The man became angry and shouted in her face. "I come tomorrow, you wait." And got into his truck and drove away.

This happened quite often. A person would put in a day's work or a month's work and when it was time to get paid they had to wait and sometimes did not get paid at all.

Ama was crushed. Now what would she do? The children had come to her several times during the day begging for food and she'd promised them that they would eat tonight.

Dog tired, she dragged herself home. The children would be waiting...and hungry.

What I do? She thought. *What I will do?*

When she arrived home little Kwaku age 7 and Kwabena age 4 were anxiously waiting. Her heart ached. Looking forlornly at her children she decided that she could not let them go to bed hungry again tonight.

"Kwabena, go to sister Naana's shop and tell her to send twenty cedis of sugar and a half cup of Gari, (Gari is made from oven dried Cassava and looks like Hominy Grits and swells up when water is put on it). I be pay her tomorrow."

It wasn't much but at least the children would not be hungry tonight. Kwabena was happy to be going to the store. He was a small thin boy but he was feeling like a big boy now, for he was going to the store for his mother. Off he ran to sister Naana's.

A half an hour passed and Kwabena had still not returned. Becoming concerned Ama told Kwesi to go and find Kwabena.

Within ten minutes Kwesi returned without Kwabena. Sister Naana said that Kwabena had been to the store, picked up the Gari and sugar and went home over forty-five minutes ago.

Now Ama was really upset and called her sister to help her find Kwabena. Stopping everyone she saw, she asked, "Have you seen Kwabena?" And the answer was always the same, "No!"

Where could he be? She wondered. This was a small village...almost impossible to get lost but Kwabena could not be found. As they were walking towards the river, Kwabena's best friend Kofi appeared.

"Have you not seen Kwabena?" Ama asked.

The little boy looked a little sheepish and mumbled something that Ama could not make out.

"Where is Kwabena?" she asked again, her voice raising. This time with a little more force as she grabbed his arm. Kofi started to cry and pointed in the direction of the river.

"Show me where is Kwabena," she demanded.

The little boy reluctantly led her to where Kwabena was. There he sat, propped up against a coconut tree, barely moving, his little stomach swollen so tight that it shinned. His eyes had rolled back in his head. Ama snatched him up in a panic.

"What is wrong with him?" She shouted. "What is wrong with him?"

By now little Kofi was crying even harder.

"I didn' do nuffin," he cried. "Kwabena give it for me."

"Give you what?" Ama asked him.

"The gari, the gari," stuttered the little boy.

There on the ground lay the empty Gari and sugar bags and the remains of the food in a large calabash.

Kwabena lay limp in his mother's arms. She rushed home with him in a panic, not knowing what to do. When she arrived at the house her grandmother was there. Taking one look at Kwabena, she took him from Ama, telling her to quickly get an enema pump and water. They would have to pump his stomach immediately.

Several hours later, after pushing and pumping his swollen stomach Kwabena began to come around. Ama was so relieved that he was going to be all right. After Kwabena had dozed off to sleep she went outside and sat under the almond tree with her grand-mother and sister. She started to cry.

"Now what I will do," she said, "Kwesi is still hungry, I have debt with Sister Naana because Kwabena bought a cup of sugar and gari, et es more than I can spend."

And more than Ama would make in a day.

Ama had come to see Nana, Bongo and I that morning with her problem. It was a pitiful story but it was hard to keep a straight face as she related the incident. Ama was a natural comedian and we couldn't stop laughing as she related the story to us.

"Seestah, I will keel your Kwabena when he is better," she said. My money es no der and des boy chop all de food and I have to take it back from his stomach fer waste. Instead of buying 20 cedis of Gari and 20 cedis of sugar as I tell him, Kwabena take two cups at six hundred cedis. Sister Naana be looking for her money and et no der and we be still hungry," she continued, as she patted her stom-ach and rolled her eyes to the sky. *"Ah kumazon, Ah kumazon,"* (which means, I'm hungry).

Although Ama was laughing, she was also crying for she didn't have it. By American standards it was really no money (approxi-mately 45 cents) but for Ama it was plenty.

While Sister Ama continued to converse with Nana, I went into the house and returned with enough money for her to pay her bill with Sister Naana and to buy food for her and the children. She thanked us saying, "When de boy be wake I be send him to you fer cane him good. If you fer cane him, he no be do des thing no more."

"Oh no, my seestah, not me. You will have to cane him yourself."

This was just another day in the life of village living. My peo-ple are oh so strong. How many of us from the other side would be able to withstand the pressures and the lack of conveniences? Not many, I'm afraid. Village life is simple but hard.

* * * * * * *

We had been living in our house for several years without elec-tricity. It wasn't that we didn't want electricity we just did not have the money, after we were ripped off during the initial construction of our house. In spite of this we were happy to be home and any time some one visited us and asked why we didn't have lights Nana's answer was always the same. "In order of priority, in order of priority. In the meantime we do everything by the light of day."

It really was not too big of a problem for we did not have a computer, I was still using my dad's old 45 year old Royal typewriter and because we had no refrigerator we ate what we cooked and if we didn't finish it at dinner, it usually became breakfast the next morning. When nighttime came around I was too tired to do anything else but "chill out" so candlelight and lanterns worked just fine.

One evening we got a visit from Professor Leonard Jefferies along with another group who were visiting Ghana as part of a Pilgrimage. I recognized a few of the people who had been part of the group from the previous year. As always it was great to meet brothers and sisters from America, to get an update on the happenings back in the 'hood.'

Sister Fannie, of New York, who had been at our home the previous year commented about the lack of lights.

During this visit with Dr. Jefferies' group she again asked, "You still don't have lights?"

I responded, "we still don't have electricity."

"But why?" She continued.

But before I could respond again, Dr. Jefferies interrupted.

"Didn't I tell y'all they were pioneers," he laughed, "living out here in the wilderness, without electricity!"

Everyone laughed but this sister was serious.

She continued her remarks by saying that she had been thinking about us living in the dark and that it was of great concern to her.

Nana repeated again, "In order of priority, in order of priority."

"Maybe your priorities are a little mixed up, you really do need electricity."

"We're fine," I assured her, thanking her for your concern.

"I still can't believe that you don't have electricity!" she stated again.

"No not yet, but in time," Nana continued. "The finances are just not available at this time."

"I know what you mean," she stated (with a serious look on her face) "when you said in order of priority."

"But we're doing fine," I assured her again.

We had a good visit, with them staying a while longer before going on their way. It was always a treat to get visitors.

Everyone started laughing. Before the group left Sister Fannie pulled me over to the side and asked how much would it cost to install our electricity?

My response to her was between seven and eight hundred dollars for it entailed re-wiring the entire house and buying all the fittings and equipment and hiring an electrician.

"Well if it's alright with you, when I get back to the United States, I'd like to send you and Nana the money to turn your lights on."

"Thank you so much for your concern, but don't worry about us, we're fine."

What a wonderful gesture, I thought to myself after she had gone. Nana, Bongo and I talked about her concern for us and we were touched deeply. If she sent the money we would be happy and if she didn't send it we would still be happy, for she had cared enough to ask.

Many times people would visit us and promise to do or send things and it just didn't happen but we understood. For when they arrived back in the United States the reality of things hit you smack in the face and all good intentions had to be re-directed to their day-to-day survival. Life in America for a large majority of us was not easy.

However, several weeks later we received a letter from Fannie. She sent a check for five hundred dollars with the hope that we could do something with that. We hollered and shouted, danced and sang. Sister Fannie said she was coming for PANAFEST and we invited her to stay with us.

"We naw want Mistress to come and we naw have lights," Bongo said.

We immediately engaged Tony, a brother and qualified electrician from our village, who helped us to purchase the equipment, rewired our house and installed all the lighting.

After being without lights for the past three years we had finally come out of the dark. On the 16th of December 1994 our home was ablaze with new light. All thanks and praise to Creator and the love and caring of our sister Fannie. Unfortunately, Sister Fannie didn't make it to PANAFEST but we got a surprise angel's visit from our daughter Sister Elmina who had come with a group who was participating in PANAFEST. She walked in the door, all smiles. Everyone was shouting,

"Irie Star, my little grand-daughter," called out Bongo Man, "tis good to see the "I" once more. Welcome home."

"Tis good to be here family," she replied, "it was cold and damp in London, I couldn't wait to get here."

She looked a little tired and had lost a little weight. She said that she had been suffering with asthma since we had seen her last and she was tired.

"Well you're in the right place, girl," I said. This is home and here you can retreat from the outside world."

"That's exactly what I need," she answered, "and as soon as this group is finished with PANAFEST and returns to London that's exactly what I'm going to do."

We spent part of the night laughing and talking and bringing one another up to date, finally retiring well after midnight. It was good to see her again.

The following morning she was off and running. But before she left, she had begun to do some video taping of Bongo.

"The "I" should take time," Bongo told her, "there's no place to go in such a hurry. Dem people dem can wait pon the Queen. The "I" need to take time. Tis only one life the "I" have Star," he continued.

But she assured Bongo that she was going to take care of herself and return home to us on the 5th of January after the group had returned home. But Bongo had seen something on her and tried to warn her but she insisted that she was fine.

It was a busy time, we had other visitors from the United States and people were dropping in because of PANAFEST. People were everywhere, sleeping in hammocks, on the floor, in the chair and the time just flew by. I saw Sister Elmina again in Accra during the closing ceremonies of PANAFEST and she told me again that she was coming home very soon. She wanted Nana and I to go to a party with her but I begged off because I was too tired and all I wanted was my bed. We said good night, promising to get together real soon. The following day Nana and I returned home to Cape Coast.

Several days later while I was sitting at my desk trying to catch up on some work, a friend of Sister Elmina's showed up.

"Agoo, Agoo," she called out.

"Amee," I responded. "It's good to see you. So Seestah Elmina has finally brought her tired little butt home," I continued, looking around for her.

But she just stood there looking at me very strangely, not saying anything. Finally she responded, "I came myself!"

"Oh really, all alone," I questioned, "and what do I owe the pleasure of this visit. Just what is your mission?" I said jokingly.

Again that strange look crossed her face. After a few moments she quietly responded, "Judah send me. Sister Elmina is dead!"

It was as though someone had knocked the breath out of me. I couldn't believe what I was hearing.

"What happened, how did this happen?" I asked excitedly. "Is this some kind of bad joke? If it is I don't think this crap is funny!"

"Is no joke," she said, "she die this morning in hospital! At Korle Bu!"

I broke down crying.

It was so unbelievable and to make it even more unbelievable she had died exactly fifteen years to the day that we had lost our daughter Shey fifteen years before.

She and Shey had also bore a striking resemblance. I was devastated. I finally got myself together enough to be able to tell Nana and Bongo. Bongo was not surprised, he just kept saying,

"She naw listen, she just would not listen and now she gone!"

Her funeral was held the following week in Accra but I couldn't bring myself to go. It was like I was still waiting for her to walk through the door. But she never appeared and life went on as usual.

A few weeks later, we got word from New York that a friend of ours, Minister Brown who had stayed with us during PANAFEST had gotten very ill when he returned to New York. In fact he had been seriously ill for weeks and the doctors couldn't seem to find out what his problem was. His wife was a nurse and she was frantic. He was running very high fevers and was growing weaker everyday. Each time she took him to the emergency, they sent him home with aspirin and antibiotics. One day his wife was at work after having been off for several days taking care of him, when one of her co-workers inquired about him.

"Girl, he's real sick and no one seems to know what his problem is. He recently returned from Ghana and hasn't been the same since."

"Ghana?" the co-worker asked, surprise in her voice.

"Yes," his wife, Viola replied.

"My sister just died of cerebral malaria in Ghana," her co-worker stated. "You go home and get him and bring him back here to the hospital immediately. I'll inform the supervisor and notify the Infectious Disease physician."

Viola brought Minister Brown into the hospital where he remained for several weeks. He was diagnosed with cerebral malaria.

God is so good and the spirit of the ancestors intervened. Sister Elmina and Minister Brown had both been visiting our place during the same period and had been talking about doing some projects together as they were in the same business. It was ironic and a blessing that the families of these two people would be in the same place at the same time and in time to save the life of the other.

There are so many stories to tell about living in Ghana, for there has been one adventure after another.

Like the first time Minister Brown visited our home in Elmina.

He had a panic attack. It was early in the morning when he cane running back into the house screaming.

"They're everywhere, they're everywhere," he shouted.

"Calm down my brother," I said, "what's the problem?"

"They're everywhere, all over the rocks in front of the house," he continued.

"Who?" I wanted to know.

"White people, white people, plenty of them and they all got Bibles. Come see for yourself."

I couldn't imagine. But what I saw when I got to the edge of the lawn was unsettling. There, on the rocks in front of our house, were at least twenty-five white women dressed in pink bonnets & long pink dresses looking like Rebecca of Sunny Brook Farms. It looked like an invasion and, they all had Bibles in their hands. There were also a few clean-shaven white (pink) men.

"Kiss my foot," I said aloud. "Where the hell did they come from and what did they want?"

And more were joining the group. They had come from the Mission House next door to our house. A couple of years before, a parcel of land we were trying to secure was sold to these White folks. They were Missionaries who had come to Afrika to save the souls of the heathen. – On the front of their house was a biblical quote - "At the name of Jesus, every knee shall bow."

"Lord, give me strength!" I said.

In the meantime Minister Brown was livid. "I don't believe this," he sputtered.

"Neither do I, my brother, neither do I."

Speaking aloud I asked the Creator, "Is this another test Mother? Is this another test Father? Have I done something wrong?"

We've been blessed with the opportunity to return to our Ancestral homeland, to escape – to the African side of the globe where my next door, neighbors are White folks? Something was wrong with this picture! But wrong or otherwise, like it or not, they are our neighbors. I stay in my yard and discourage them from interfering in our affairs. White folks don't want us around them in amerikkka yet they seem to be following us to Afrika. However, they see what we don't see and have been returning in their numbers to be a part of the re-colonization of Afrika and her children.

* * * * * * *

I was jumping for joy when my sister friend Kiniaya stopped by. We'd known each other for several years since our repatriation to Ghana; she had also repatriated from Philadelphia in 1993 with her Ghanaian husband, Brimah, who was a lecturer at the University of Cape Coast. Our relationship was like family, for there weren't many of us returnees living in the Cape Coast/Elmina area from America. In fact, there weren't many of us in Ghana for that matter. We were a support network for each other, re-charging one another's batteries when the difficulties of return and/or the re-acclimation process began to wear one of us down as it sometimes could do.

"Hey, girl friend," I said, jumping and dancing around like a child. "Got some good news, got some good cash baby," I continued. "Got a little money to do somethin' with".

"As Salaam Alaikum," she responded. "Well, I sure visioned you in my dream and you were real happy too. I didn't know what it was that was making you so happy, but it was a good dream."

"Well thanks for that one honey. You and your dreams are right on target...again," I laughed. "Well, I was just trying to figure out how I was going to spend this cash."

"Wait a minute now, Miss Thing, I'm not trying to tell you how to spend your money but let me help to put you back on the right track. First of all establish your priorities," she said.

"Priorities? Oh yeh...right, priorities!" I laughed. "Well, it's been established my seestah, I'm buying me something special...and pretty!"

"No, seriously IMAH," she continued. "What about your kitchen? Didn't you say that you needed to do something badly in there?"

Slowly easing back into reality, I walked to the kitchen door and peeked inside - she was right! My kitchen really did need some help. What I needed was a sink and running water. Over time I had just grown accustomed to washing the dishes in two large pans (one for wash and the other for rinse), and hauling water in from outside. I had completely forgotten about a much-needed sink.

"You got a point, Seestah K. I think I will look for that sink. This just might be enough money," I said. "Thanks for the wake up call." *Besides I really didn't need any more clothing...not really!*

The following day, our partner Kwaku went to Accra and came back with a beautiful, shinning, double sink. I was ecstatic and even more so when he told me that I had a balance (change) left over. *I just might get me something pretty after all.* We contacted the plumber and within two weeks we had a sink and running water in the kitchen.

We made a big ceremony out of the installation; tossing the dish-pans into the yard, turning the tap off and on like a mischievous child. "Water anyone?" I laughed.

Just then Sister Kiniaya appeared. "Agoo," she called out. "What's going on?" But before anyone could answer she spotted the sink and started singing and dancing & whooping...happy sounds that we Afrikans make when we're celebrating. She danced around the kitchen touching the sink, turning on the water and got into some real heavy African dance of thanks and appreciation.

Before it was over, she Mama D and I were all dancing, beating pots and pans and having a good ole time. Just another positive step in our progress. Who would have ever thought that the installation of a kitchen sink could evoke such joy and laughter?

"You go girl," Kiniyah said, breathing hard. We were all laughing and cutting up as we embraced one another. Nana, Bongo and Kwaku stood there, joining in the laughter.

"Yes, mistress," Bongo commented. "Me can see that the I is happy, happy, happy. JAH know, me happy too. All of we happy!"

"Well, we're making progress," Nana said. "Nothing before it's time."

And that's how it's been...a little at a time. We don't just go through each experience - we grow through it.

* * * * * * *

Today we got some great news. Kohain Nathanyah HaLevi, our friend, Priest and Rabbi had made the ultimate sacrifice and after seven (7) years and fourteen (14) trips across the watery graveyard of our ancestors repatriated home to Ghana. Not only had he returned home but we were neighbors and he was building his first home in Ghana, about 150 feet down the road from us.

Of our original group who made the first pilgrimage in 1987, only three (3) of us had returned home. This return, again, was not without pain and suffering in the midst of the blessing, within the joy of being home once more. Unfortunately, he had come alone.

And like those of us before him, he had left behind, family, friends, business and community. There were those who did not share his vision of returning home to one's ancestral homeland, and others who were tied so tightly to their everyday struggle of day-to-day survival in America that there was no room to be able to put aside something that would even allow for their exodus. The most that they could hope for was a vacation and that was not without years of saving to make the trip. Sadly, because travel to Africa is so expensive, it, would not even allow for the entire family to visit together.

The struggle continues...

CHAPTER SIXTEEN

KNOCK, KNOCK

Having been born in the Western Hemisphere there are so many things not a part of my life as an Afrikan in America. So much of my culture was lost to me. So in my return home I was overjoyed as I was introduced to other facets of the Ghanaian/Afrikan culture revealed to me. One of them was the marriage proposal and ceremony called "knocking."

The first time I heard that expression I laughed, and thought back to the cave man days of the barbarian knocking his mate in the head and carrying her off to his cave dwelling. Well, at least that's the picture that had been painted for us growing up in the United States. But I was in for a pleasant surprise. I had attended at least one wedding since my return home but it was a very western style ceremony, although it was a lovely wedding, I must admit I was a little disappointed.

While visiting friends in Accra, our friend Cliff informed me that he wanted to be married.

"IMAHKUS, I met this wonderful sister and we want to get married. This is my first time and I have to take my family to meet her family. You know I don't have any family here. Would you and Delores, (another friend of ours), go with me, and act as my family? She told me that I have to go "knocking" for her and that this is their custom. They want me to bring money and stuff but I'm too nervous and I don't want to screw things up," he continued. "Sis, I really need your help."

Cliff said he was not fully versed on the process but he knew that he had to take gifts to the household. I was thrilled at the prospect.

With about six weeks to prepare myself I began gathering as much information as possible so that I could represent the brother and our family properly. The bride to be was a Ga woman and the granddaughter of a Chief. The Ga people come from the Greater Accra area. The brother was an Afrikan who had been born in the United States and had repatriated.

Now here is where I immediately began to have problems. Being from the Central Region of Ghana and Fante country, they do things a little different from the Ga people. First mistake. I asked my Fante friends about how to go about this knocking process and what we would need. They told me to take an envelope with about ten thousand cedis (worth about $3.00) in 1997) and a couple of bottles of schnapps (local liquor) and present that to the family when I accompanied my friend.

"Is that all?" I asked.

"Yes," came the response, "that's all that's necessary." "Isn't that kind of small?" I asked. "I sure think the bride would be worth more than that."

"It's just ceremony," they said. "After that they will have a wedding."

But for some reason I wasn't quite satisfied with those answers but if that was the culture, that was the culture.

On my next visit to Accra I talked with my friend Rosemary about what I was preparing to do because she is a Ga woman also.

"My sister," she said in a shocked tone, "you will be disgraced if you go like that and they will not let your brother have their daughter. She is a Ga woman and the granddaughter of a Chief. You have to go right or not at all."

"Help me," I implored, "I have never done this before and I don't want to look like a foolish foreigner."

This was the analogy she used.

"Just imagine that you're walking past a flower garden and you see this beautiful flower and you want to smell or to know it. You can't just go in and pluck it, you have to go to the gardener and speak with him. You "knock" on his gate."

"Sir, I have seen a beautiful flower in your garden and I would like to have it." At that time he will invite you to come and discuss the matter in full detail.

So my friend Cliff's fiancè was the flower and the gardener was the family.

"And you never go to the gardener/family with empty hands", she continued. "Plus, this was a very special flower, the grand-daughter of the Chief."

Rosemary also told me that I would have to take money, at least thirty to fifty thousand cedis ($15.00 to $25.00 US at that time), several bottles of imported liquor, a case of minerals (soda), and a couple of cases of beer.

"You want to make a good showing or you will be disgraced and the girl will be very unhappy, for the family will not let your brother have her," my friend continued.

"Don't worry girlfriend, I'm going to do this right, after all, I've come home and if this is the way things are done, I have no choice but to do it right."

We both got a good laugh out of that one.

"You can get in touch with me if you run into any more prob-lems," she said.

"Don't worry, you can count on it."

As the day grew nearer everyone was growing more than a little excited.

Nana, my better half, kept pumping up my balloon.

"That's my girl. Always in the mix! You go girl. Go gettum, go git dat bride baby," he teased, "go knock down dat door."

Nana was always messing with me, pumping up my balloon, encouraging me and true to form I was always getting into stuff!

Even the bride to be went over the procedure with us assuring me that everything would be all right.

On the day of the ceremony, nothing went right. The car broke down, the basket to put the liquor in was too small, my friend, the groom misplaced the money: you name it, it went wrong.

Not to be outdone, I put my creative juices to work. I sent to a local shop on the avenue and bought a large blue plastic basket, picked some large leaves and flowers out of the garden to line the basket with. We got together the money but couldn't find a decent envelope to put it into. Back to the garden I went and got a large banana leaf, which I folded into an envelope and put in the money;

Tied some colorful ribbons on basket and we were good to go. Or so I thought.

The car still had not been fixed and the time was passing. The last thing we wanted to do was be late. It was all right to be a little or respectfully late, as I call it but not hours late. But the ancestors were on our side. There was a hotel in the area that had a car service, so we sent someone to charter a car for the occasion. It couldn't have been more perfect. At the designated hour, we were more than a little antsy waiting for the taxi to arrive.

Man, oh man, did we get a surprise when this baby-blue Mercedes Benz pulled into the yard. Baby-blue basket, baby-blue Benz; it couldn't be more perfect!

When we arrived at the home of the family several friends of the family were waiting to escort us inside. We were a few minutes late because we had forgotten to put film in the camera and had to stop and buy some. But everything was fine. As we entered the house, the groom to be, another sister, (acting as his family) another friend and I were shown to our seats. A member of the family came out and offered us water as we waited. Next, an elder Aunt or Senior Mother (as aunties are called here in Ghana) of the bride came in.

She was very stern looking as she walked around shaking the hand of each of us.

"You are welcome to our home," she said, "the others will come."

She then went and sat down on the other side of the room, looking carefully at each of us.

Boy, I sure wouldn't want her angry with me, I thought to myself.

After a short time the rest of the family entered and each of them in turn greeted us. After welcoming us to the house, the head of the family officially welcomed us and asked,

"Is anyone in pursuit of you?"

We looked questionably at one another, before I responded, "Oh no, no sir, no one is chasing us."

Once that was out of the way he continued. "Then what is your mission? Why have you come to see us this day?"

I thought that a little strange to ask, for I thought they all knew why we were there. But as the Senior Sister and acting as the head of our family, I proceeded to explain our mission. Introducing myself as the head of our family, I explained that my brother was a very serious and responsible man, who had passed their garden and wanted to take one of their beautiful flowers home.

The family members laughed.

"Oh, you are truly a Ghanaian. You have tried."

The ice was broken.

"Yes," I continued, "my brother wants to marry your daughter. And as the custom demands we have come forward to meet the family. We have also brought gifts of money, drinks and flowers for the household."

They were quite impressed with the presentation. And when the leaf was opened and they found the money inside everyone laughed and talked about how different it was. Now that the family had accepted us, I asked if we couldn't see what our gifts had bought. Her mother then brought in the girl. Everyone ooowed and aahed and carried on about how nice she was and how pretty she was and how she would be a perfect wife for our brother.

We had a wonderful time. Refreshments were then served.

But she wasn't our brother's wife yet. He could not take the flower from the garden today. The family now had to digest everything and let him know what else he had to bring. After all, we had only brought the "knocking" gifts to get him in the door. Next, he would have to bring much more and they would let us know in due time just what that was. Well, one thing was sure, we had made a good first impression. We left congratulating each other on a job well done!

Several days later he was called to the family house to meet with the girl's Mother, Senior Mother, Junior Mothers and Grandmother (Junior and Senior Mothers are the Sisters of the Mother or Aunts as we know them in the west).

At this time he received his list, as follows:

Six 1/2 pieces (6 yards) of cloth, a steam iron, pots and pans, a suitcase to put her things in, dishes, tablecloth and napkins and a little money for the family.

Up to that point we were fine, almost. My brother had to dig deep and come up with these things or the flower would not be his.

"But why money?" I asked.

"It's just a token but you must give her Mother something for she brought her into the world and raised her to be the kind of woman your brother wants to marry; and her Father took care of her and provided food and shelter and discipline; her Brothers and Sisters because they were also involved in the process of raising her. Her big brothers protected her and looked out for her and her sisters were there also, so she was never alone. And her Grandmother, being the elder and a wise woman has counseled her along with her mother on how to be a good person, woman, and Wife that any man would be proud to have.

So Dad got 15,000 Cedis, Mother got 10,000 Cedis, Grandmother got 5,000 Cedis and each of the brothers and sisters got 1,000 Cedis each for a grand total of approximately $20.00 US.

When Cliff brought all that was required, he went home to await his new bride. Later that evening she was brought to him at her new home.

They were both given token gifts from her family. She was given a fan in which to cool him off when he came in from work hot and tired or was angry or upset and he was given a small cane to beat her with, if she did not behave as a proper wife.

This is where I disagree with the custom! However, in spite of what I think, traditionally, she was his wife. There would be a reception at a later date in which friends and family will get together to celebrate. It is not necessary to have a western style wedding unless you want it. There are no blood test required, nor licenses to secure. They are legally wed in the eyes of God and the community.

I was happy for them both and elated that I had been asked to be a part of their ceremony.

Returning home to Elmina, I'd see them again when they had the reception.

CHAPTER SEVENTEEN

ALL ROADS LEAD TO ONE AFRICA

All roads lead to One Africa...or so it would seem and all kinds of people show up at our door.

They know about us through a friend or a friend of a friend, who has told them that they must, just must, stop in One Africa's place once they're in Ghana...and many of them do just that. It's surprising the number of people that we see coming through our gate considering we had not been advertising.

People show up at all hours of the day or night, acting like we had known them for years.

One Africa's House as many people call it has become a meeting place for hundreds of people. They come for many reasons and we are there to welcome them. As brother Bongo Shorty always says,

"Someone will be there to welcome you."

And we are happy and blessed to be the ones.

We have performed weddings at our place.

Sister Kamali, a sister from the Bronx that we met at our place during an Afrikan History Month celebration called me a week or so after her visit to One Africa.

"Do you remember me," she asked. "I'm the one that helped you to clean up after all the people jumped on the bus and tried to leave your place a wreck. I really had a wonderful time. Thank you for hosting us."

"Oh yes, I do remember. How could I forget the expressions on the faces of some of those students when I ordered them off the bus to clean up their mess and thanks for your help also."

"They'll never forget that visit," she continued "and neither will I.

I just wanted to let you know that I'm getting married. I have found the man of my dreams. His name is Justice and he's a Computer Programmer in Accra. He's so wonderful, nice and thoughtful."

"Really," I said, for this came as kind of a surprise to me. "When did all this happen? Are you sure this is what you want to do?" I asked her.

"I met him a couple of weeks ago and we want to get married before I return to America!"

"Girl, that Love Bug really bit your butt," I laughed, "and that is a whole lot of butt to bite too, if I remember correctly."

We cracked up, laughing so hard that it brought tears to my eyes.

Now this was ironic, for she had come to Ghana with her girl-friend, who was looking for a husband and she had come along to do some shopping and to get a new perspective on things going on in her life. In fact, this whole marriage business was the talk of Ghana, as she had not been in Ghana very long and had immediately found the man of her dreams.

"We're going to City Hall and tie the knot," she continued.

"Have you ever been married before?" I asked.

"No," came the response.

"And how old are you?"

"I'm 34," she said.

"Well seestah lady, you're old enough to know better and to make your own decisions but since this is the first time, why don't you do it right?" I suggested.

"My money is kind of funny and I can't afford to do anything elaborate," she continued.

"What else is new? But Seestah Lady, what if I told you we could do a beautiful wedding for between one hundred and one hun-dred and fifty dollars, reception and all."

"Impossible," she laughed.

"Trust me girl, this be Ghana and I'm a Magician. You just get your dress and your man and come on down to our place at the appointed time. We'll take care of the rest. We might be able to get a honeymoon thrown in," I told her.

I talked it over with Nana, who thought it was not a bad idea.

"That's what One Africa is about, making good things happen for the family when they return home."

We then contacted Kohain, our neighbor & Rabbi and asked him to perform the wedding. The word went out and we notified members of our Afrikan American community to sit in as the family of the bride. We also invited our other Ghanaian friends. Arrangements were made with Kohain's wife Mabel to cater the affair, including the wedding cake. We were on.

Several days later, girl friend showed up with her husband to be, the Matron of Honor (the friend who was looking for a husband) and the Best Man. She was so happy. In fact, she had told me that she had been reading *Essence magazine* on the plane from New York and had come across this beautiful wedding dress that cost close to one thousand dollars.

"Buy some material and take the picture to a seamstress in Accra, she'll hook you up and it won't cost no thousand dollars either," I had told her the week before.

Lo and behold, the dress was fabulous and made for less than fifty dollars.

We did all the things families are supposed to do. We questioned the intended husband, asked about his background, etc. The brothers took him out for his last night on the town as a single man and explained to him some of the things he might encounter being married to a strong, independent, born in America Afrikan sister.

The sisters prepared the bride that night also. And we had a ball! The wedding was scheduled for 6:00 a.m. the following morning. Before daybreak we prepared the lawn, set up the wedding tent, covered it with Kente Cloth, put straw mats and Goat skin rugs on the ground for the bride and groom to stand on. We put up an altar and set the Frankincense to burning. We had also decorated a new broom for them to jump over.

The day couldn't have been more perfect or the bride more beautiful. She wore a white dress embroidered in gold with a gold crown and veil that I had made that morning. I was standing in as the mother of the bride and Nana as the father, who gave her away.

Sister Kiniya, who had also repatriated from Norristown, Pa. with her husband Brimah: a Ghanaian lecturer at the University of Cape Coast were also co-opted as family members. Dr. and Mrs. Rod and Scherazade King, who were also teaching at the university, were there and served as the official photographers. And Brother Bongo played the drums. The wedding was on.

As we stood under the tent listening to Kohain perform the ceremony, birds chimed in singing in the background. The day was clear and the sun was just coming up. In the distance stood the Elmina Castle Dungeons...but today was a glorious and happy day.

After they took their vows they leaped over the broom. Everyone was happy or at least almost everyone. Since they had arrived, the Maid of Honor had displayed a little attitude and had been making snide little remarks. She wasn't really happy about this whole affair.

"She's ticked off because she's not the one getting married," the bride told me.

"Well, that's not your fault, she'll get over it," I replied, "don't mind her, this is your day, don't let anyone spoil it for you."

After the ceremony, we had a wedding breakfast. And began preparing for the reception.

Because everyone's money was funny, we had to spend it wisely. Instead of driving all over town with the horns blowing, the car was decorated and a "Just Married" sign was put on the back of Brother Brimah's car. The newlyweds were then driven, horn blowing and ribbons flying to the end of our road, about four hundred feet and then a 1/4 kilometer up the highway to the Oyster Bay's Hotel entrance and back to the reception at Kohain's place, next door to One Africa.

When they got out of the car everyone cheered, but we didn't throw rice though because it would have been wasteful, considering the numbers of people who could not afford to even buy rice. We had to be conscious of our surroundings. Living in a small village community made us acutely aware of the plight of our people, not only in our community, but also in many places in Afrika as a whole. We had come home. We couldn't change the fact that so many people went to bed hungry every night but we could do the best that we could to help and not contribute to their suffering. Throwing rice was out.

It was a wonderful day. Our gift to the newly weds was a honeymoon at our place. The last time we saw Justice, he came for a visit to inform us that he was on his way to America to be with Kamali. They were still quite happy, the last time I spoke with them.

ALL ROADS LEAD TO ONE AFRICA

We've even had babies born on our place!

Brother Mukadeem El Shabazz and his Queen Ebae re-located to Ghana several years ago and wanted their first child to be born on the soil of "Mother" Afrika.

We had met sister Ebae while she was living in Accra, waiting for brother Shabazz to join her from Atlanta. When he arrived they came to visit with us and decided that they'd like the baby born at One Africa's, in one of the chalets. Nana and I were in agreement provided that we had the midwives in attendance.

We thought we had another week or so before the baby came but the baby had other plans. I was just about to leave for Accra when Ebae went into labor and I had to change my plans. After twenty-five hours of hard labor, walking up and down the compound all day, with assistance from the expectant father, brother Shabazz, two midwives and myself, Freesoul Shabazz was born.

I was totally exhausted. You would have thought that I had given birth. It certainly felt like it. It gave us a good laugh though, when both the mother and I fell back on the bed in exhaustion. I had been holding her while she/we pushed.

The midwives had said earlier that if the mother didn't do something soon, they were going to take her to the hospital to deliver. That must have been the magic word. In less than fifteen minutes Freesoul came into this world. He was long and bright with a head full of black hair, long, thin fingers and bright, black eyes that were wide open with an expression on his face that seemed to say, "What's going on here or so this is earth, heh?"

Everyone started shouting, laughing and screaming in victory, because for a while we didn't think it was going to happen there. In fact, brother Shabazz had just left to go and find a car to take his wife to the hospital when the baby made his grand entrance. As he walked up, he heard the noise and busting into the room found himself the daddy of a fine, fine son.

In all the excitement, no one remembered the camera (and Shabazz is a photographer). But the memory would be etched in our minds forever.

Once again, another adventure, another blessing in the life of One Africa, and the people who come through our gates. Unfortunately, after two years, Ebae returned to America, taking Freesoul with her and basically severing their relationship. The move cut deeply into Shabazz for he wanted both his Queen and his son with him in Afrika. And if, she would not stay then, "Give me our son. Let him grow here at home with me. Then let me take the place of the necessary babysitters and Day Care Centers you will need in America," Shabazz often implored.

But that wasn't to be. Shabazz remains here to this day mournfully celebrating his return home and throwing himself into the conscious development of our people and himself through his establishment of The Healing House, an Afrikan Holistic approach to health, economic development, unity and spiritual consciousness. We've buried and/or sprinkled the ashes of dearly departed loved ones on the ocean as per the request of family members and planted tress in memory of others who have passed.

ALL ROADS LEAD TO ONE AFRICA

And this case was no different.

A sister landed in Ghana with the remains of her brother-in-law, without a clue as to how or where she would put him to rest. But she met a friend of ours in Accra, brother Kwesi who told her, "You need to contact One Africa, they can help you out." So ashes in hand she and Kwesi showed up at our gate.

"Hey, One Africa how is et, my bruther, my seestah. It es good to see you again. I miss this place tooooo much when I am not here," Kwesi laughed. The place is sweet-o. You meet my friend sister Gerry Chisolm from the U.S."

Introductions were made all around and we made small talk while a drink of water was given, as is the tradition before getting down to any business. With all the formalities out of the way, Nana asked them, "Is there anyone in pursuit of you?"

Looking at Kwesi, with a funny look on her face, Sister Gerry asked, "We aren't being pursued, are we?" Everyone laughed.

"Well then what is your mission?" Nana continued.

"You really have the custom down," said Kwesi. "No one can ever say that you're not really Ghanaians."

"Well my brother, we're home, so we have to move according to the culture. Right?" I queried to no one in particular.

"Well," Kwesi interjected, "sister Gerry has just arrived from the U.S. and has brought the remains of her brother-in-law, Liu Kafele, home for burial. Since she has never been here before she needs some help on what and how to do this. That's why I brought her to see you and Nana Okofo."

"So where is the body," I asked.

"Right here in my bag," was her reply.

"Oh."

For a moment I was lost for words.

"Ah ha," I said, "very interesting. So how can we help you?"

"It's kind of a sad and unfortunate story," sister Gerry said.

A couple of years before her sister Halima, whose name means "gentle strength" and her husband Liu, whose name means "voice worth dying for," were married in a Traditional Nubian Ceremony performed on 11 August 1993 at sunrise by Dr. Ben Jochanan.

"It was a beautiful ceremony, held in Karnak Temple – The Great Northern Temple of Wa'rit in Luxor, Egypt (Kemet), North East Africa."

"They vowed at that time that if anything happened to either one of them, the surviving spouse would cremate their remains and bring their ashes home to Africa for burial. Brother Liu wanted half of his remains returned to Egypt and the other half to Ghana. They were certainly not planning for anyone's death, but that was their wish. They were very happy together, living in North Carolina and making plans for their future.

On the 23rd of March 1995, brother Liu, went to work at the construction jobsite to collect his paycheck but while he was there, a confrontation broke out between the boss and a couple of the Mexican workers. Tempers were hot and there was shooting, when it was over my brother-in-law, who was an innocent bystander lay dead.

All night my sister waited for him to return home, tossing and turning – unable to sleep, trying not to worry. She called around but

243

no one had seen him. But, when 4:00 a.m. arrived and he still was not home she knew something was wrong.

A little after 4:00 a.m. a police car pulled up in front of their house, as the two policemen neared the house she heard one of them say, "this must be the home of the deceased.

When she opened the door for the policeman, he informed her that Liu had been shot and killed. That's how she learned of the death of her husband."

There was no funeral but an "African Homecoming of Life Celebration." When the celebration had been completed, she began to make preparations to bring his remains home.

She was devastated and missing Liu terribly. About six months prior to his death she had suffered a miscarriage and lost their first child. So you can just imagine her surprise when she went to the doctor a couple of months after he had died and was told by the doctor that she was pregnant again. She was ecstatic: it truly was a miracle. And she didn't want anything to happen to this baby. So her plans of coming to Afrika with his remains were once again put on hold.

Seven months later she gave birth to a beautiful baby girl, Onikiah Jodenee' Afua, whose name means, "divine miracle, sacred one loved by all" and born on a Friday.

But she could still not make the journey because the baby was too young. Another delay, but her sister assured her that everything would be ok and that she would take his ashes to Afrika for her. It might take a little while because she didn't have the money just yet, but she would work on it to make it happen.

One evening she was at a function in which they were holding a raffle. The first prize was a round trip ticket to Ghana, West Afrika.

When she was approached to purchase a raffle she initially refused.

"I never win anything," she said.

"There's a first time for everything," the seller assured her.

So after a little more coaxing she bought, one ticket. When they called her name she was speechless. In fact, she was shocked and almost passed out. When it settled in that she had won a trip to Ghana, she started dancing and jumping around in excitement. She could now take the remains of her brother-in-law home to Afrika.

"So here I am," she continued. "And when I met Kwesi and told him what I wanted to do he immediately told me about One Africa."

"What a sad but wonderful story," I said quietly.

Everyone agreed.

"We'll do what we can to assist you," Nana continued. "But in the meantime let's get a bite to eat and reason on it some more later on. You're home, just make yourself comfortable."

Later on that evening, as the sun was setting, I came upon the sister standing at the waterfront, gazing into the distant waters.

"This is a beautiful, peaceful and spiritual place. It has so much history," she said. "The crashing of the waves against the shore is calming to the spirit. This is truly paradise!"

"Yes it is! In the distance are the Elmina Castle Dungeons. Did you ever imagine that you'd be standing, looking at the place where they took your ancestors away from more than four hundred years ago," I asked her.

"Not really," she replied, "not really. It is truly a blessing to be standing here today. Liu would have loved your place."

As we stood there in deep contemplation a plan began to form in my mind.

This was a very spiritual place. In fact, the remains of another brother had been brought here by Baba Andy and buried under a coconut tree and a place had been set aside as a memorial for our daughter and sister, Elmina Dennis, who had passed away the year before and our cousin, Sharon Thomas-Holden.

Sister Zakia from Harlem had even brought some personal belongings of Elder sister Alma Johns and had also buried them here, when she had joined the ancestors. Why not the brother Liu?

When I spoke to Nana about it he agreed.

"It seems appropriate," he said, "and if the sister Gerry has no problem with it, neither do I."

When I brought it back to her, she was overjoyed. We decided to perform the ceremony the following morning. Everyone who was participating would be dressed in white. There would be drumming and dancing and celebrating, for that's what the brother wanted.

We got started at 6:00 a.m. with the pouring of libation and the offering up of prayers of thanksgiving.

The drums were being played softly in the background. The final resting place had been prepared and as he was being put into the ground the sister began to slowly dance. As she danced the beat of the drums grew louder and her dancing became intense. She twirled around and around, lifting her arms to the sky, leaping through the air, the movement of her body as though she were possessed. The air was electrified and as the spirit took hold I also began to dance. We danced for what seemed like hours. Twirling & twirling the green of the grass and the blue of the ocean began meshing together. The beat of the drums...the drums...the drums pounding to the beat of your heart. I finally stopped to rest but sister Gerry continued. She danced until she fell out in exhaustion across the gravesite. She had done what she promised to do. She had brought him home and performed the rites in celebration of his passing.

She left the following morning, promising to keep in touch. We never saw or heard from her again.

As fate would have it, several years later, while I was in New York I had the occasion to meet Sister Halima, brother Liu's Queen and their little Princess, Onikiah, who is now five years old. We met at a United Afrikan Movement meeting in Harlem.

In July 2000 Sister Halima traveled to Ghana to visit the site where her beloved Kingman was resting.

ALL ROADS LEAD TO ONE AFRICA

There is never a dull moment around our place and this morning was no different. I had just finished cleaning up the breakfast dishes when there was a knock at the door and the voices of children. Several of the children from our village were outside and they were very excited.

"A visitor is come, a visitor is come," they shouted, jumping around excitedly, "Obruni, Obruni (a white man) is looking One Africa."

"Calm down and stop all the noise," I shouted from inside the house. "I will come small-small (in a short time)."

Oh crap, I thought, here we go again. All the way to Africa and I can't seem to get away from White folks. Damn!

When I walked through the door my mouth flew open as I stared at this big white man, with a receding hairline, dressed in a short sackcloth dress and wearing gladiator sandals, with heavy metal clamps around his neck and wrists connected to heavy chains, and a black teardrop in the corner of his eye. In attendance there were two weepy looking white girls – they were not in chains. They were his traveling companions. One of them had paid for their trip.

At first I couldn't speak. I was dumbfounded. After recovering from my initial shock, and I was able to speak once again, I asked.

"Is this some kind of joke? And what do you want here?"

I didn't even remember his name or if he had even given me one; but he said someone had referred him to One Africa from the Cape Coast Castle/Dungeons.

He stated that he had seen Jesus in a vision and Jesus told him to come to Afrika and apologize to Afrikans for what his ancestors did to us during the Trans-Atlantic Slave Trade."

"What?" I nearly choked. "Ok. It's too early for this. Are you on something? Is this some kind of game, first thing in the morning?" I asked all at once. "But what the hell do you really want anyway?"

He was slowly beginning to tick me off.

"I think you better leave," I said.

"Oh, I'm so sorry to startle you," he said, "but I'm looking for One Africa. The man at the Cape Coast Castle said I could find him here."

The people at the castle were always sending people to us. They usually weren't white folks though.

"Well, I'm Mrs. One Africa and he's not at home. Again, what do you want?"

"My name is Lawrence and I've come from Boston, Massachusetts in the United States. I have come with a message for the people of Ghana. Jesus came to me in a vision and told me that I must go to Afrika and apologize to Afrikans for what my people did to your people as a result of the Mid-Atlantic Slave Trade."

"I was supposed to participate in PANAFEST," he continued. "I was invited but no one contacted me to tell me that it had been cancelled. I was also to appear on Ghana TV."

So much for his vision from Jesus! It sounded like some kind of made-for TV put-on.

247

"Really! Where did you say you're from again?" I asked.

He responded, "Boston, Mass.," and in a rather proud and cocky manner, "I am of French ancestry."

"You're kidding me," I retorted. "You mean you came all the way from Boston to Afrika to start apologizing to Black folks? If you think apologizing is necessary you should have started in Boston, one of the most racist cities in America, not come all the way to Afrika. Besides, my man, you're in the wrong country. The French did not occupy Ghana."

My tolerance level had reached its peak and the man was beginning to get on my last nerve with his two female companions "Amen-ing" everything he was saying.

"Oh I've gone to other Afrikan countries too," he said proudly, "and met with Heads of States and other officials as I have been directed by Jesus. I have photographs and newspaper clippings from my visits," he continued.

Sure enough, there he was in many photographs taken in other African countries being welcomed as he apologized for the sins of his ancestors.

Give me strength, I thought to myself.

"Right," I said in an exasperated tone.

I had finally reached my level of tolerance with this charade.

"Yeah, I think you'd better talk to Nana after all, I'm not down with this nor do I have time. If you want to hang out at the beach until he comes, suit yourselves. But I have other things to do right now."

He smiled and thanked me before clanking off to the beach with his two ladies in waiting following behind him.

I stood there shaking my head as they walked away. I had seen it all. Bongo and Mama D were also around and they were as surprised as I was and all agreed that White people do some crazy shit.

Lord, give me strength. Where were these people coming from and why did they all manage to show up on our doorstep? Did I do something wrong, Creator, did we do something wrong? This had to be another test in the process of returning home. Was this yet another test from the Universe, from the ancestors and the Creator? I wonder if I'm passing?

Was it my Karma that I seemed to be attracting White folks?

Nana finally came home and being a lot more tolerant than his wife entertained our visitors, as they explained or tried to explain the purpose of their journey.

Trying to be helpful, Nana escorted them back to the castle but while there they ran into a confrontation between the guy in chains and some of our brothers from America who wanted to throw him into the ocean and felt that he was making a mockery of our holocaust. Another group of Frenchmen were also in the castle on a tour and they also wanted to beat him. When he tried to explain to them his mission, they were damn mad and said that they didn't feel that their people owed anyone an apology and who did he think he was, for he was not speaking for them.

"You're a madman, go back to America," they shouted.

Well, they got my vote on that score.

Things really got very harried for a while, before Nana left the castle with the white boy and his ladies in tow. I'd had enough of the charade for the day and returned home to what is normally the peace and quiet of One Afrika House.

However, when Nana came home we got into a big argument and that night was the first time in all the years that he and I had been together, that we had a physical confrontation. In fact tempers flared so high that we had to be separated.

All over some crazy White folks and their foolishness.

ALL ROADS LEAD TO ONE AFRICA

Another time, our sister and friend, Dr. Beryl Dorsett, a retired educator and administrator was visiting Ghana. In fact, it was one of her many trips to the motherland, where she had been enstooled as the Nkosuohemaa (Development Queenmother) of Atwima Apatrapa, a village in the Ashante Region and stool named Nana Ama Serwah-Nyarko.

The Dorsett Memorial School in the Ashanti village of Asuoyeboa is the first primary school in an Ashanti suburb of Kumasi and was named in her honor. She and her associates are also in the process of having another school built. This is one hard working and dedicated sister and when you travel with her to Ghana you are expected to donate some of your time, energy and expertise in working on one of the many projects that she has going on in her village.

To date, through the efforts of her and her associates both in America and those that she has brought to Afrika, the village now has a Health Clinic, that is equipped with dental and other medical supplies valued at over $50,000.00 and also serves people from neighboring communities. They have developed a small farming project, provided potable water, built three ovens and trained the women in bread baking and leadership development. She has also organized a sponsorship program for the children in the village and in the school, and has provided computers for the Dorsett Memorial School. She also brings medical people to service her village.

Nana Ama is practicing "Practical Pan Africanism" in every sense of the word and is supportive of the efforts of those of us who have repatriated. Whenever, she comes home, she makes it a point to take her people through our *Door of No Return Ceremony* and to visit our home with her group for lunch or just to stop in.

On one such visit she brought the wife and the daughter of brother Daryl Felix Edwards, who had joined the ancestors. Ed, as he had been affectionately known, had been a Community Activist and felt that it was his mission in life to make lost and misguided brothers and sisters aware of their ancestral heritage. After his retirement he continued in his efforts to bring the message to his people. He believed in a higher power and the brotherhood of mankind. It was the expressed wish of brother Ed to be cremated and his ashes scattered on the coast of Afrika. And the family came prepared to carry out his last wishes.

The problem though was that they had no boat and had considered standing on the beach and doing it but the strong winds off the Gulf of Guinea made that impossible to do.

"Nana IMAHKUS" (as Dr. Dorsett calls me), "we need your help. I figured if anyone knew how to do this you and Nana Okofo were the ones who could give us some guidance in this matter. The family doesn't have a lot of money, so we need to keep it simple but nice and it has to be done immediately, as we are only here until tomorrow."

"Well, we will need a boat to carry the remains out to sea but unfortunately our boat is out of service," I told her, "but Nana will check things out and get back to you."

As we didn't have much time, Nana immediately went to see the Chief Fisherman in Elmina, who pulled together his crew. We had to provide them with 'T' shirts and Akpeteshie (a local strong drink made from sugar cane) for the crew and petrol for the boat. We also made arrangements for a Traditional Priest and Drummers.

Early the following morning, everyone who was attending the Memorial Service met on the beach, behind the Elmina Castle Dungeons. The remains of Brother Ed were given to the crew captain.

The crew looked so nice in their bright gold "T" shirts as they rowed out to sea in a precise rhythm, the sound of drums softly echoing in the background, the sun slowly rising on the horizon. As brother Ed's remains were being taken to sea a simple ceremony was conducted on the shore. As the signal was given from the shore brother Ed's wishes were carried out by his wife Ismay and his daughter Denise, as his ashes were sprinkled on the water, off the shores of the Gulf of Guinea. Later that morning, Dr. Dorsett (Nana Ama) and her group departed for Kumasi.

ALL ROADS LEAD TO ONE AFRICA

We often get student groups and other community groups staying at our place. They come to get involved in community services and to complete their Rites of Passage.

One year we had a group Leadership Excellence from Oakland, California, led by Shawn and Nedra Ginwright. We had been in touch for months prior to their arrival and the entire group was excited about making their first journey home to Afrika. But unfortunately, tragedy fell upon the group and one of their sixteen year old youngsters, died suddenly of a massive heart attack while playing basketball three months before the trip.

It was a sad day for the group arriving without him. But they paid tribute to him by having shirts, which they wore while in the land, tye dyed green and orange with the map of Afrika and the following inscription:

> "Camp Afrique '99. This camp is dedicated to the
> loving memory of brother Steven Avila-Webster,
> transitioned 21 April 1999."

Before the group left One Africa, an Almond Tree was also planted on the oceanfront, in his memory. It is still there and growing.

Since we had been speaking about folks who have traveled (as they call it when someone dies in Ghana), I'd briefly like to talk about how funerals are handled here.

ALL ROADS LEAD TO ONE AFRICA

Another time, we had a visit from a brother from Los Angeles. And he was on fire - He was home in Mother Afrika: something he had wanted to do for a very long time. He had brought his two Pit Bull dogs and was staying in a small room in town.

When we asked him what his plans were, he didn't have any; didn't know what he was going to do; had very short money and dreams of arriving in paradise.

We were happy for him but more than a little concerned, which we expressed.

"Brother you need to have a plan unless this is a vacation," we told him.

"Hey, don't worry about me, I'll be fine and I'll check in from time to time," he said.

"Well brother, just remember that our doors are always open," we assured him.

Three months later we received this note from him:

"It was my intention to contact you long before this late date. But everything just moved so fast; I got sick, sold my Pit Bull dogs, got a loan and decided to go back to the states. I must now re-think my next exodus. I must seek a new exodus location. I love Afrika and always will but my diet must be first worked on before coming back. You folks have the best program and I believe God is truly with you."

And what can we say to that except, prepare yourself financially, spiritually and physically. Do your research - talk with folks who have done it and then just jump in the pool. Keeping in mind that preparation and unity is a key to our collective success in the repatriation process.

ALL ROADS LEAD TO ONE AFRICA

Sister Zakia and Baba Andy Henderson from Harlem, New York came to Ghana and on the advice of Prof. Leonard Jeffries visited us at our home with her small group of youngsters. The children were delighted. They slept outside in hammocks, climbed coconut trees and beat drums until the wee hours of the morning. This was the first time in their young lives that they felt safe after dark and did not fear being shot, robbed or molested. And did not fear for Lions and Tigers.

After several visits, Sister Zakia was made a chief in the village of Assin Kruah in the Central Region. She is now called Nana Ata Nkum I.

Just before her enstoolment, she and the Queen Mother from her village grafted an Almond tree in our yard. It was suppose to grow a certain kind of fruit. No fruit other than the almonds ever appeared but the tree split and formed two limbs instead of the one.

As I watched it growing over the years, it brought to mind the re-connection of two sisters coming together after a long separation and it still stands tall today.

Nana Atta has also adopted Nana Okofo and I as her parents.

ALL ROADS LEAD TO ONE AFRICA

The group was coming to participate in the Pan-African Historical Theatre Festival (PANAFEST), a bi-annual broad based cultural event in which artists from numerous fields of endeavor (music, art, theatre, dance, etc.) as well as scholars dedicated to the enhancement of the ideals of Pan Africanism and the development of the African Continent, come together. There were about twenty-five people in the group that Imhotep brought, quite a few of them old Garveyites, and for many their first trip to the continent.

After arriving in Accra, the group journeyed to Fort Amsterdam (Fort Amsterdam is an old slave fort, built by the Dutch in 1631 for the sole purpose of housing kidnapped Afrikans). It sits on top of a hill, over looking the Gulf of Guinea, in the village of Abandze.

After a very emotional visit to the fort, the group moved to the bottom of the hill, where a Durbar (an assembling of local chiefs, elders and towns people with drumming and dancing in anticipation/celebration of a special event), was in process to enstool Imhotep as an Mpontuhene (Development) Chief. There was an air of excitement and restless anticipation in the group.

Nana and I arrived shortly after the group had been seated. After greeting everyone, we were shown to our seats, to enjoy the festivities. The sound of drums vibrated and pulsated the air as traditional dancers evoking the spirit of the ancestors welcomed the group home. A sister sitting nearby started to moan, shake and make strange sounds. As her eyes rolled back in her head, she slid gracefully from her seat onto the green grass. Everyone was stunned as we silently watched her. As though awakened from a deep sleep we moved all at once to assist her.

Some of the women from the village church, dressed in their white, who were in attendance at the function, rushed over and began fanning her. One woman was hitting her lightly on the forehead as they all chanted, "Jee-sus, Jee-sus," while gently shaking her. "Jee-sus, Jee-sus," they continued as she began to come around. But just after they said she would be all right, the sound of two different voices started coming out of her mouth. "Jeesus, Oh Jeesus" they excitedly began chanting again and looking from one person to the other. "What is dis?" they inquired. "I don' know dis!" said another sister.

Just like she started, the sister stopped shaking and opened her eyes, looking around at all of us with a very confused look on her face.

"Is she alright?" group members inquired very concerned. "Do we need to take her to the hospital?" someone asked.

But that was not necessary for she appeared to be getting it together. "You had us a little concerned," I said, kneeling on the ground beside her.

"I don't know what happened. One moment I was fine and then suddenly a very strange sensation came over my body. I don't remember anything else until this very moment. But I feel fine now," she stated.

No one had any answers regarding her behavior, other than the fact that this was a very emotional time, returning to the land of your ancestry. Assured that she was ok, the program continued.

254

After the Durbar the group continued on to Cape Coast, where they checked into their hotel. That evening after dinner the group went to the Cape Coast Castle Dungeons, where the evenings PANAFEST program was going on. At the close of the program Nana and I were going to take the group "THRU THE DOOR OF NO RETURN" Commemorative Ceremony. Unfortunately, we were well behind schedule because although the PANAFEST performances were finished, there were still a lot of people in the castle/dungeons and the mood of the folks inside was "party-party-party". There was also a drinking bar in the old English church overlooking the castle courtyard at that time and although it was time for the castle to close, the people just were not leaving.

Sister Lena, who had fallen out earlier in the day at Fort Amsterdam, was sitting in one of the chairs rocking back and forth, not saying a word to anyone, just looking kind of dazed. When asked how she was, she just kept a blank expression and kept rocking. We called the group leader who was very concerned with her behavior. As it was getting very late, the group leader suggested postponing the ceremony until the following day and conducting it at Elmina Castle/Dungeons instead. Besides, Lena really looked like she needed to go back to the hotel. As we started getting the group together to leave the castle, she began speaking normally as we made our exit, but looking as if she didn't quite know where she was. She just smiled and said that she was feeling a little tired. Her roommate was close by supporting her and assuring everyone that Lena was fine.

"She'll be alright by tomorrow Sister IMAHKUS, it's just been a long, hot and emotionally draining day," her roommate said.

"That's cool, just let us know if you need any help my sister," I said.

With that, the group boarded their bus to return to their hotel and Nana and I went home...exhausted! We would meet the group at the Elmina Castle/Dungeons at 9:00 am, the following morning.

* * * * * * *

I left home about 8:00 o'clock the following morning to get things ready at the Castle/Dungeons.

Entering into the Women's Dungeons, I began lighting the seven candles that I had brought for the ceremony. As I was lighting the last candle, I began to feel chills running up and down my spine. And as much as I wanted to move I seemed to be stuck in that spot. I could hear people moving around and talking, although I couldn't see anyone. As the voices got closer, I heard blood-curdling screams coming from deep inside the underground dungeon exit leading to the door of no return. Suddenly released from whatever had been gripping me, I made my way to the outer courtyard. I stood in a corner as though in a dream and watched Nana, Imhotep and other members of the group moving swiftly through the various rooms in the castle. It was like watching a video being played in fast forward.

The screams, that had stopped abruptly, started up again, screams that vibrated your entire being. The screams had been coming from Sister Lena who was now being carried from the inner dungeon by members of the group. As they took her to the forecourt at the front entrance to the Elmina Castle/Dungeons, she continued to scream and moan, rolling her head from side to side.

It was suggested that someone go for a traditional priest/priestess. Nana Okofo and Nana Gypie immediately took off and found a traditional priest in Elmina and apprised him of the emergency. But after arriving at the Elmina Castle and evaluating Sister Lena's condition, he recommended that they go and get his wife who was a priestess. He felt she would better be able to handle this situation.

The Nanas again returned to town, seeking out the Priestess. When they found her she told them that she needed certain herbs to be able to treat sister Lena properly. Upon her arrival the Priestess informed us that she would have to get these herbs into Lena's nose without getting any into her eyes or her mouth. She stood watching sister Lena intently for a moment before quietly and slowly circling her three times. A very strong spirit was on sister Lena but the Priestess did not know why. Suddenly, she sprang forward, grabbed sister Lena's head and pulled it back, while discharging the herbs into her nose and chanting words that none of us understood. This action caused Lena to start gagging.

After a few minutes something large, and yellowish/green, like scrambled eggs erupted from Sister Lena's mouth. The Priestess said this had to come out as she had been carrying it with her since she left America. Voices started coming from sister Lena and this time it was as though they were arguing fiercely with each other. One voice was very high-pitched and excited, while the other voice was very low and deliberate. The Priestess continued to speak softly to sister Lena and gradually the voices subsided. The priestess said that we needed to watch sister Lena very carefully as the awesome spiritual and historic experience of returning to those dungeons was a strain on her. Sister Lena had to fight hard to resist the spiritual pull that was trying to take her over. She needed rest, as these encounters were deeply troubling and exhaustive. This was the third time that something like this had happened to her on this trip. Each time she was in or near a castle/dungeon.

Nana and I agreed to take her back to our house while the rest of the group continued their tour. They would pick her up on the way to their next stop. Back at the house she seemed more relaxed, sitting near the water chillin' out.

When Imhotep and the group arrived to pick Lena up she was reluctant to leave. In fact, as Mama D was escorting Sister Lena to the bus, she kept holding back. She started crying saying, "I don' wanna go, I don' wanna go!"

But Imhotep insisted she stay with the group because she was their responsibility. As the two women continued moving towards the bus, Mama D abruptly stumbled backwards as though she had been pushed. Mama D, a large, robust, statuesque sister stopped for a moment with a quizzical look on her face but started forward again. Again she stumbled backwards, but this time she silently turned around, holding sister Lena's arm, and went back towards the house. Lena started to make those strange sounds again.

This time we sent for the Okomfo, the traditional priestess from our village and one of the strongest and most powerful Okomfos in our region. When she arrived, Sister Lena was lying on the grass. The voices were arguing back and forth and Lena was in a trance like state. The Okomfo spoke some words that none of us understood but the voices began to get higher and higher pitched as though arguing with the Okomfo, who responded to them. During her examination she learned that there were two Afrikans in Lena's family tree. Although seldom spoken of by her family, they were there! After the Okomfo examined her, she said that Sister Lena should pray constantly, for she was carrying two spirits of her Afrikan ancestors that she had brought with her from America. And each time that she went near any of the sites where kidnapped Afrikans had been housed, those spirits started arguing as though trying to break away. They had come back to their homeland and she was the vessel that had returned them. The Okomfo calmed them and said that the sister needed to remain where she was to relax and meditate at the ocean side. It was decided that I would bring her to the shrine at Lartey, where the group would meet us.

That afternoon Lena and Nana Okofo had an opportunity to sit and reason. She revealed some of the difficulties she had encountered in first wanting to make this trip, and over her reluctance to come, but a strong force was pulling her, making it impossible for her not to come. Upon paying her deposit she was still unsettled and tried again to withdraw from the trip but it was too late to get her deposit refunded. So against all obstacles, she made the journey.

Later that evening as we were preparing to go out to a Bazaar near the Cape Coast Castle Dungeons, Lena said that she wanted to go along. We didn't think it was a good idea but she insisted that she was fine. After a brief visit we quickly returned home, for Lena was getting that far-off look again. Several friends from Accra, Sister Adjoa, Efua and Mamalena, also returned home with us. Sister Adjoa and I retired to bed early, while the other sisters crashed in the Hall (living room).

Nana and the sisters were in the Hall talking when sister Lena started to go into a trance again. The voices were back. Hearing the noise, Mama D came out of her room to see what was happening. She sat next to Sister Lena to make sure she was all right. The next thing Nana knew was that all four sisters had grown quiet. They were sitting on the floor in a circle with a dazed look in their eyes. When he spoke to them, no one responded. At this point Nana decided he needed some additional help. In trying to enter the bedroom where sister Adjoa and I were sleeping, the door was shut in his face with such force that he decided not to try and open it again. Nana said he started praying over the sisters and saying various psalms from the Bible, trying to get Sister Lena and the others to pray with him. It was a long night!

When I finally awoke and went into the hall, it appeared to be

full of fog and the sisters were lying silently on the floor. Nana was also on the floor propped up against the back of the couch. As though my entry interrupted something, everyone got up and started talking at the same
time.

"What Happened?" "What's going on?" "Somebody turn on the lights!"

I just stood there wondering, "Did I miss something?"

Daybreak was just beginning and the room was starting to clear of the fog. It was then that Efua and Mamalena decided to get back to Accra in a hurry. Whatever had happened, they had seen and experienced enough. Sister Efua said she would not be back again...and she hasn't.

With the sun coming up on the horizon, sister Lena had a new calm about her. The tension that had been so evident before had disappeared and there were no voices. She seemed to be a different person!

A few days later we took off for Lartey, which is located in the mountains of the Akwapim area of Ghana, about five and a half hours' drive from Elmina. When we finally arrived it was late in the night. Everyone was asleep except the watchman. We were given a place to sleep and advised that the Priestess would see us in the morning. For some reason I wasn't feeling comfortable in my very "unfamiliar surroundings" and suggested to sister Lena that we could leave if she wanted.

Just before daylight, we started out of the compound but we didn't get very far. We stopped under a tree to reason and in a very calm but distant voice sister Lena said to me,

"Sister IMAHKUS, you can't run away. You must stay and face the truth. If you run you will never know."

Besides being concerned for her, at that point I didn't particularly want to know anything more. But it was really too late to turn back, so we returned to the house to wait for the Priestess.

At about 8:00 o'clock we were taken to the Priestess' compound. After introductions were made all around, I related some of the experiences of the past week. Lena related what she remembered and how she had felt during those times. The Priestess didn't seem surprised. In fact, what was even more amazing was that she told us the exact same things as the Okomfo from our village, even though we had not yet told her. There was no telephone or any means of communication between Lartey and Elmina. So how did she know?

Throughout the entire discussion sister Lena continued to remain calm. At the end of our discussion we were turned over to some younger sisters in the compound and given cleansing and spiritual baths, using many types of herbs. Sister Lena and I were then separated and other rituals were performed to ensure sister Lena's safe return to America. As I watched sister Lena virtually glowing, I felt as though I had just awakened from a dream. Saying our goodbyes to the Priestess we continued on our journey to catch up with sister Lena's group in Kumasi. Just another day in the life of One Africa!

Sister Lena visited with us again several months later. She was still doing fine. She admitted that after viewing the videos back in the states, she could not believe what she was seeing. It was hard to believe what had happened to her but seeing was believing. If there had been no video, she would not have believed it at all.

Note: During most of Sister Lena's episodes, Minister Clemson Brown founder of Trans-Atlantic Productions, Brooklyn, New York, the official Videographer for the trip, was there and video taped most of the incidents.

Brothers and sisters returning from the Diaspora sometimes become possessed and very emotional. They may also be transporting the spirits of kidnapped ancestors from the Americas. Subsequently, we have been told that when doing commemorative "Door Of No Return" ceremonies in the castle/dungeons that it is advisable to have a traditional Priest in attendance or close by.

SANKOFA...

ALL ROADS LEAD TO ONE AFRICA...
AND MANY BLESSINGS!

How often have we heard "What are the blessings of returning home?" Every time I have to answer that question, I look around me and smile.

In December 1995, we had a visitor, sister Fannie, who had spent time in our home; I was taking her to Kotoka International Airport in Accra, so that she could return to America. As we rode along we discussed many things. The issue of our land development came up and sister Fannie wanted to know what we were going to do with "all that land".

Nana and I had discussed the possibilities of building several Afrikan style circular houses. We had been inspired to do this by an elder sister, Lucille Davis, who had repatriated to Ghana in the early 50's.

Coupled with the fact that operating a Guest House would also give us a little additional income, which was not a bad thought at all.

Additionally, a Ghanaian friend, brother Mustapha, who had built a beautiful Afrikan Style, Beach Resort, called AAMAL; Academy of African Music and Arts at Kokrobite – 30 kilometers from the heart of Accra, also sparked our inspiration with the simple but beautiful, functional and traditional architectural design I found there; we were Gung Ho – we just didn't have that kind of ready cash or started up money for such a project.

It was then that sister Fannie suggested putting up the money to build a Chalet and when she returned to Ghana she'd have some place to stay and when she was not here we would rent it and divide the proceeds. She wanted to come back to Ghana from time to time but didn't want to stay in a hotel and would feel more comfortable around people that she knew. It was decided that she would give me her check and I would discuss it with Nana. If he agreed, then we would deposit the check and get started. If he didn't, we would tear up and check and nothing would be lost.

I was still finding this a little difficult to believe but here it was and I was quietly getting excited at the prospects. So after seeing sister Fannie off I returned home and explained this latest development to Nana. We both agreed that this was a blessing; One that we certainly could live with and were thankful for. After informing sister Fannie of our decision we began construction on two chalets.

Today our place is called *One Africa Guest House* and we have six Traditional Afrikan Style Chalets named after great honorable Afrikans and ancestors Prof. John Henrik Clarke, the honorable

Marcus Mosiah Garvey, the honorable Harriet Ross Tubman, Nana Yaa Asantewa, brother Malik El Shabazz (Malcom X) and Queen Mother Moore; with all the the comforts of home on the Gulf of Guinea. What are the blessings????

* * * * * * *

Several times a month since 1995, our elder seestah Sybil Williams-Clark has painstackingly clipped articles (and underlined that of significant importance) from New York newspapers like the Challenger, Amsterdam News and other Afro-cenric periodicals and sends them to us here in Ghana. We affectionately call her our "News" Director, continuing the legacy of our elder, Dr. John Henrik Clarke.

Note: Sitting nearby in Paradise is Nana Atta Nkum I (Seestah Zakia Alston-Henderson), who on 19 December 2001, repatriated home after surviving the September 11th disaster in New York City, by 30 minutes. The train she attempted to catch (which would have gotten her to school on time) closed its doors in her face leaving her standing on the Subway platform at 125th Street in Harlem; that was the last train to enter the Chambers Street station under the World Trade Center before it collapsed.

All Roads Lead To One Africa...

CHAPTER EIGHTEEN

WIDOW HOOD RITES
Performed by the Akan people.

Since we had been speaking about folks who have travelled (as they call it when someone dies in Ghana), I'd briefly like to talk about how funeras are handled here.

It's a joyous occasion. The few funerals that we did attend, I thought we were at a party. It was one grand celebration. And depending on your position in the society, the affair can be most grand. The difference though from America, is that all funeral services are held on the weekend throughout the country. Very few funerals are held during the week. Every Friday, Saturday and Sunday is set aside for funeral observance. And you will always know that a funeral is going on because everyone dresses in funeral colors: red and black or orange, or brown and black or plain black.

Friday is Wake-keeping, where everyone sits in mournful silence and speaks in hushed quiet about the dearly departed.

Saturday is the funeral service (celebration), where food and drinks are served, music is played and donations made to the family. It's the place to meet friends, future husbands and wives. In many instances Professional Mourners are called in to mourn the dead.

On Sunday, everyone goes to church for the Thanksgiving Service. But for the Thanksgiving Service, everyone wears black and white or navy blue and white. If the deceased person has passed the age of Seventy (70) years, especially the Akan and Ga, they will dress in white. But, the Ashanti stick to black, black & red or any dark color or solid red. In Cape Coast and Elmina the Fisher Folk conduct their wake keeping on Monday evenings and burial on Tuesday, as that is the time that they do not go to sea.

There are also certain rites that are performed after the death of one's husband or wife. And within each clan there are varied ways in which rituals are carried out. For example, when a person has died, the widow/widower is given spice mint to put under their pillow until after the burial because the spirits of the deceased will sometimes re-visit and the scent of the mint will keep them away.

On the day of the funeral/burial, (which is usually performed on Saturday), while the body of the deceased is being conveyed to the cemetery for burial, the widow/widower is silently taken to the seaside and does not look back and does not speak.

Upon arrival at the seaside the widow is given toiletries from the man's family and from the woman's family if it is the widower.

The persons performing the rituals are the only ones who may speak during this time; and they are the Elders and another person (man or woman), who has gone through the Widowhood Rites.

At the seaside, a raffia rope is tied around the waist of the widow/widower before they are bathed in the sea, three (3) consecutive times. On the third submission into the sea the widow/widower tears off the rope and casts it into the sea, symbolically meaning that you are breaking away from the dead.

The widow/widower is then washed in plain water seven (7) times. They are then wrapped in the white cloth and given new native sandals, which has also been provided by the family of the deceased.

Before returning to the funeral gathering, food that has been prepared of chicken, yam and egg is touched to the lips of the widow/widower three (3) times. The person performing the ritual says that the widow/widower should not pass through this ordeal again and that these rites are pacifying the soul of the widow/widower. At this time the widow/widower may now speak. They are then given the plate of food to eat.

Then whatever work the bereaved does, a pen and paper is then put in front of them. The person performing the rites then writes something on the paper and then puts down the pen. The widow/widower picks up the pen and writes something down three times.

Thereafter, three coins in any denomination is given to the widow/widower and they must touch their body from the top of their head to their feet and then to the ground.

This is also done three consecutive times.

When this ritual is completed, the bereaved person will toss the coins over their head to an assembled crowd, symbolizing that they have just touched money and thrown away evil. The person performing the ritual says that they are clearing all the evils from the person.

Whomever, picks up the money must spend it immediately for that money is considered taboo if held and should not be kept but spent on whatever it will buy.

After this ritual is completed the widow/widower is taken back to where the family and friends are gathered and shown around in their white cloth and sandals. The Elders and person, who has completed widowhood rites, then proclaim them to be clean.

The family and friends gathered will pass by and shake the hand of the widow/widower, congratulating them on passing through the Rites.

For one (1) week, the widow/widower uses the toiletries given; bathing before 6 a.m. and 6 p.m., for one week performing the bathing ritual on themselves at home in plain water. After the week has passed they can go back to bathing at any time.

Previously the bereaved person stayed in mourning for a year but now that period of time has been relaxed, unless the person chooses to mourn for a year. It is their individual choice.

Not being familiar with this custom when we initially arrived, you can imagine my embarrassment when I stepped out dressed to kill in my beautiful red and black Kaba and Slit that I had just had made. Everyone stopped me and wanted to know where the funeral was.

"What funeral?" I responded. "I'm going to a friend's party."

"But did she die?" They wanted to know.

"Of course not," I responded.

"But why are you wearing red and black?" they asked.

"Oh, these are my favorite colors," I said. "I love red and black."

"Oh my seestah, here in Ghana if you dress like dis, people will think you are going to funeral."

I immediately returned home, changed my clothes and packed my dress away for the appropriate time...another lesson learned in the returning home process.

SUNSUM
(The Soul)
Symbol of spirituality.

CHAPTER NINETEEN

"THRU THE DOOR OF NO RETURN"

Someone will be there to welcome you!

The "THRU THE DOOR OF NO RETURN – The Return" is a commemorative ceremony, conducted in the Cape Coast Castle/Dungeons, spiritually created and developed for brothers and sisters of Afrikan Descent when they make their pilgrimage, returning home to "Mother" Afrika.

Someone should be there to welcome brothers and sisters home to "Mother" Afrika, back through the door of no return but not as tourists, even though the Afrikan born in America has been identified as one of three major tourist markets in the Ghana Tourism Industry (the European Market, the North American Market and Us).

But are we Tourists? Of course not! We are a historically unique group as a result of the Trans-Atlantic Arab European Slave Trade.

And returning home to the last place that our ancestors as enslaved Afrikans stood in their homeland is a unique and horrific experience for us, something that we must go through in re-connecting with our past.

Since 1992, Nana Okofo, Bongo Shorty and I have been conducting a special Commemorative Ceremony entitled "Thru the Door of No Return - The Return." Kohain, upon his return home joined us in 1994. In 1997 Brother Shabazz also joined the team of returning Afrikan descendants or ascendants, as we prefer to be called. For we are ascending to our proper place in our return home, not descending to anything.

Some of our Ghanaian counterparts have tried to duplicate our ceremony but they can't; not really. Only those of us who were born under the lash of slavery and oppression, having gone through the experience of living in the United States and struggling to survive in an extremely, racist society; where the color of our skin puts us in harms way and, jail has become big business with black men and women making up the largest percentage of prison dwellers, and where a white man has never been convicted of raping a Black woman; only those of us who know and have felt the pain of survival which continues to cut deep into the fiber of our being can relate to the significance of our return.

So not just anyone can do it for it requires someone who understands what the return home to Mother Afrika means to us physically, spiritually, emotionally and economically.

It's impossible for someone whose burning desire is to go to America and who believes that if we Afrikans born in America can afford to buy a ticket to fly you must be rich! Or that our ancestors were blessed to have been taken into slavery for we got to be born in Amerikkca.

Returning home through those doors is not a tourist visit for us. It's a pilgrimage. Those dungeons are sacred and hallowed grounds where we come together to collectively embrace the spirit of our ancestors, to begin the healing process, by releasing some of the pain and anguish of five hundred years of separation from our ancestral homeland.

Our sovereignty is still and always will be Afrika. Like the leaves on the tree, we have just been disconnected from the roots - the re-connection, the re-birth hurts but it's necessary.

The ceremony consists of an opening introduction and background summary, followed by a re-enactment of the capture of enslaved Afrikans, which is conducted by a local cultural group, Tweampong Traditionals.

After the re-enactment, brothers and sisters are led into the respective male and female dungeons where a candle light vigil is conducted. This is an emotionally stimulating and moving experience as we connect with the spirits of our ancestors and one another. The emotions displayed in those dungeons are varied.

Sisters and brothers go into themselves, they moan, cry, scream, and roll on the floor, releasing pent-up pain and suffering, others are quiet and remorseful. But there is healing, and the bonding of brothers and sisters, who have come together for the first time as a result of this pilgrimage...mothers and daughters, fathers and sons, and entire families...few, are untouched by this experience.

I can't count the numbers of sisters that I have cradled in my arms as the hot tears streamed down their cheeks and the pent up emotions of long suffering and the joy of returning home once again overwhelmed them.

It is also our opportunity to collectively pay homage to our ancestors and to give thanks and praise to The Almighty Creator for returning us safely home, across the watery graveyard of our ancestors. – The Atlantic Ocean.

To date thousands of brothers and sisters from the Diaspora and other parts of Afrika have participated in this ceremony.

On another occasion close to three hundred (300) sisters filled the Cape Coast Castle/Dungeons at one time: the largest number of sisters to be in that chamber of horror since slavery ended in Ghana. Although the room was packed, the sisters kept coming! The walls vibrated that day as our ancestors embraced us.

On another occasion, thirty-six members of the McCray family came together in those dungeons. An elder sister, successful in her professional life and grateful for her blessings, notified every member of her family to secure their passports, get their shots and be ready to return home to "Mother" Afrika on the designated date, they came during Afrikan History Month. They paid for nothing else.

The enormous out pouring of love and sorrow was overwhelming. The sister's mother, the glue that had held their family together for all of their lives was the only person missing...she had joined the ancestors the year before. But her spirit was in that room with them that day. What an emotional and rewarding experience that was.

After a Women's conference in Accra, forty Afrikan women from twenty different Afrikan countries, America and the Caribbean came together in the Dungeons and it was a heart wrenching experience for all of us. We knew so little about our collective trials and tribulations and how closely connected we really were, but the spirits of our ancestors raised up that day and made us one. The tears flowed as we embraced one another and as we walked through that door of no return, the same question was on the lips of every sister. "God, Why? What have we done?" But most of all we were grateful for the re-connection.

* * * * * * *

During the filming of the full length video "Through The Door Of No Return" by Sister Shirikiana Aina, in which Nana and I appeared and were consultants, I was once again brought face to face with another aspect/view of what our ancestors suffered as a result of the Trans-Atlantic Arab European Slave Trade - God, how we suffered... But despite all odds, we survived.

Here I was a descendant of those ancestors who had been forcibly taken away, sitting in a small fishing boat, at night, slowly sailing away from the Elmina Castle Dungeons on the Gulf of Guinea. The Life Jacket I was wearing felt like heavy chains on my body: the eerie reddish-orange glow of torches flickered against the castle/dungeon walls catapulting me back into the 15th century. I was once again being stolen away from my "Mother" land! Over my shoulders loomed the blue-black darkness of the night covering the vast ocean, where lights from fishing Trawlers/vessels glimmered in the distance. A dreadful feeling of fear and confusion like I'd never felt before in my life, gripped me as my heart palpitated rapidly in my chest, snatching my breath away. Suddenly, the fishing boat veered sharply – I let out a loud gasp bringing me back to the present.

The shoot was finished and we were returning to the shore. There was Kwesi, one of the cameramen and his crew still trying to re-capture the truth of our past, so that our people and the world could see, and hopefully feel the holocaust of Afrikan people, and there was the rest of the boating crew. I was never so relieved.

But I had once again been blessed beyond my expectations. How many descendants of those enslaved Afrikans, taken away to the West have returned in this century and had been blessed to see, experience, and feel some of what our ancestors must have felt on those waters?

God knows being in those dungeons is an awesome experience in itself, for the healing process, our re-birth truly begins there. But to be on the open sea takes it to yet another realm. For me, it drove the point clearly home that I am rightfully a descendant of those who were taken into captivity more than four hundred years ago and was subjugated in a strange land, by people who knew me not. We are truly the people that the Holy Scripture speaks of (Acts Chapter 7):

> 'And God spoke on this wise, that his seed should
> sojourn in a strange land; and that they should
> bring them into bondage and entreat them evil for
> four hundred years'.

The Slave Trade to the West began in 15th Century with the Portuguese and ended in the 19th Century.

And, I am so grateful that the Creator and the spirit of our ancestors have put in my heart and on my shoulders the responsibility of being one of those to be at the door to welcome brothers and sisters returning home. "Someone will be there to welcome you!"

Yes, there is also an economic component to this and it has provided us with the opportunity to use our God-given creativity to create our own means of survival, while providing a spiritually enriching and positive outlet for brothers and sisters to collectively participate in their return home, and in our healing process.

An Afrikan Proverb says,

**"Until the Lions have their own Historians,
tales of the hunt will always glorify the Hunter."**

Well, we have come to glorify God and our Ancestors!
This is our "Rights of Passage": **THIS IS OUR TRUTH.**

Epa

Symbol of captivity and slavery

He who allows himself to be handcuffed at any time will become a prisoner or slave.

CHAPTER TWENTY

A HISTORICALLY UNIQUE GROUP

Having repatriated home to Ghana the land of our ancestry, we had many questions and concerns. As a result, some of us who had repatriated got together and formed "The Returning African Descendants Committee" (re-named "The Returning African Ascendants Committee") to establish and set up a mechanism for dialogue with the government of Ghana regarding our recognition and status as returning Afrikan Descendants based on our historically unique experience as Afrikans born in the Diaspora as a result of the Trans-Atlantic Arab-European Slave Trade.

Consequently, some of our issues of concern were formulated and sent to President Jerry Rawlings and the NDC administration for clarification and discussion. Our concerns outlined:

ı Dual Citizenship
ı Protection against unlawful deportation
ı Removal of Visa requirements for Returning Afrikan Descendants entering Ghana
ı Land Grant Allotment & land purchase as opposed to long term leasing
ı Establishment of a formal program and written policies governing Returning Afrikan Descendants.
ı Waiver of requirements for granting Residence Permits in favor of Returning Afrikan Descendants with financial self-sufficiency.
ı Special incentives for Senior Citizens/Retired Diasporan Afrikans desiring to return home.
ı Establishment of a special Diasporan Afrikan Immigration Desk.

We, like those in America who had heard President Rawlings speak were elated and encouraged by statements he made during his visit to the United States in 1995 in support of Dual Citizenship as well as his declaration of the definite role that Afrikans in the Diaspora must play in the development of Mother Africa and Ghana in particular. His proclamation was like water on dry ground. For like brothers and sisters of the Diaspora, our returning to Africa was at best a dream or fantasy but certainly not a practical reality. We had acted without guarantees or security but rather on the visions of our forefathers and upon faith. One day soon we would have the guarantee and security of Dual Citizenship or better yet restore our Afrikan citizenship, which would be irrevocable and constitutionally inscribed, not only by Ghana but by every member state of ECOWAS (Economic Community of West African States) and the AU (African Union).

After our first letter was sent to President Rawlings in February of 1996, our newly formed committee consisting of Nana Okofo, Kohain Nathanyah HaLevi, Rabbi; Sister Kiniaya El-Awwal & myself from America and Sister Daisy Melbourne (Sister D) and Leon Morrison (Bongo Shorty) from Jamaica, West Indies, sent the following memorandum to the Speaker of The Parliament:

> We, as returning African Descendants from the Diaspora, residing in the Republic of Ghana, and committed to the progress, liberation and salvation of people of African ancestry, both at home in Africa and abroad, are appealing to the Parliament of the Government of the Fourth Republic of Ghana for DUAL CITIZENSHIP.

> Having been born and lived most of our lives in the Americas (United States & the Caribbean) as a result of the Trans Atlantic Arab European Slave Trade, traumatically separated and kidnapped from land, language and culture, suffering numerous generations of countless atrocities and basic disrespect of human dignity and human rights, have made the conscious decision to return to the land of our ancestry to live, work and be part of the development of Mother Africa

274

in general and Ghana in particular but most of all to re-
claim our African citizenship which we never
voluntarily surrendered. Over 100,000,000 million
Africans now live in the Western Hemisphere alone
who are former sons and daughters of Afrika's soil,
whom documented history confirms were captured,
sold, enslaved and disenfranchised. Although it is
unlikely that a large percentage of this population will
ever return permanently to re-settle in the land of their
ancestors, even a small percentage is a sufficient number for which Afrika needs to develop policies in anticipation of the remnant who shall return as prophecy has
declared and our living testimony confirms. "Yahowah
says, the time is coming when people will no longer
swear by me as the living Elohim (God) who brought
the people of Israel out of the land of Egypt. Instead,
they will swear by me as the living Elohim (God) who
brought the people out of Israel, out of the northern land
and out of all other countries where I had scattered
them. I will bring them back to their own country, to the
land that I gave their ancestors. I Yehowah have spoken". Jeremiah 16: vs. 14-15.

We are aware of the following:

1. that requests, petitions and attempts for Dual Citizenship have
   been made in the past by various individuals and organizations of Africans in the Diaspora,
2. that some African nations have taken bold steps to address the
   issue of Dual Citizenship (Gabon, Cote d'Ivoire & Zaire).
3. that the Organization of African Unity (OAU) has attempted
   to take action from a continental perspective by setting up a
   committee of eminent persons to pursue a viable strategy for
   reparations which included on its agenda, developing policies
   for Dual Citizenship.

Our petition to the esteemed honorable body of the Parliament
of Ghana, is that the shining Black Star of Africa, the standard
bearer of Pan African ideal and principle, act with unwaver-
ing courage and take the bold step not only to welcome your

brothers and sisters, sons and daughters home but to adopt measures and legislative policies to re-enfranchise us back into the family, from the various countries where our ancestors were forced to work and build; experience and equity that can prove to be invaluable assets at our disposal.

Those of us who were born in the United States of America and the Caribbean, who seek to re-claim our Afrikan Citizenship, should be allowed to do so and retain our Diasporan citizenship. Not as an act of double minded-ness but to take advantage of what our ancestors have worked so hard to earn, to use those resources to help benefit the re-development of Afrika. Such an example has been set in North Eastern Afrika by the state of Israel, whose Parliament has established a "Law of Return", as well as a policy governing Dual Citizenship. This allows Jewish people from all over the world to be enfranchised and feel spiritually, morally, consciously and financially connected and responsible for the well-being and security of the state of Israel.

Afrikans in the Diaspora have suffered over 500 years, not as Americans, Jamaicans, Brazilians, or Christians, Muslims, Hebrews or Traditionalists, not even as Capitalists or Socialists but as Afrikans. We have paid the price and continue to pay the price no matter what the cost, to be who we are, Afrikan people. We have not abandoned Afrika and Afrika should not abandon us. Yes, our years in bondage have certainly benefited the Americas, the United States in particular, as documented history can attest to but that same spirit, talent, experience and dedication should be utilized in the growth and development of Ghana and any other Afrikan country welcoming its children back home. Dual Citizenship benefits not only the returning Afrikan Ascendants but Ghana as well and is in reality an honorable and appropriate beginning to affirm the verbal invitation and welcome that has already been extended by President Jerry John Rawlings and Osagyefo Dr. Kwame Nkrumah (1st President of Independent Ghana) before him. It is a small gesture that speaks loudly for the governing fathers who are the lawmakers of the land to adopt and approve policy and procedures for Dual Citizenship which would set the standard for other Afrikan nations and lead to the day when all Afrikans everywhere can enjoy simply a One Afrikan Citizenship.

BENEFITS TO GHANA/AFRICA in granting Dual Citizenship

- Increased tax base and revenue collection
- Increased investment potential
- Increased technical assistance and development
- Increased Human Resources (skilled, educated & trained)
- Increased international lobbying base
- A great step towards Pan Africanism becoming a reality as well as an ideology...

> It is our prayer that serious consideration will be given to this appeal and we look forward to your righteous pursuit thereof.

Copies of this proposal were also sent to the Presidents of the United States & Ghana, the Prime Minister of Jamaica, the Ambassadors to the United States & Ghana, The National House of Chiefs, the Congressional Black Caucus, The National Coalition of Blacks for Reparations in America (NCORBA), The National Association for the Advancement of Colored People (NAACP), The Secretary General of the United Nations, the African Union (AU) and others. The receipt of this memo was acknowledged by the secretary of the President on the 29th July 1996.

The following February 1997, we received a letter from the Secretary to the President advising us that an official team had been set up by the President to meet with us and other Africans of the Diaspora who had returned and settled in Ghana. On 9th April we met with the Presidential Committee to discuss our concerns.

In the opening of the meeting we declared our moral and historical right as Africans to return to our ancestral homeland and expressed that the focus and interest of our representatives were three major areas of interest: "The Right of Return," "Dual Citizenship" and the "Diasporan Desk". We then proceeded to go over the line items of our document in response to the concerns of the returnees.

It was then that we learned that Dual Citizenship was being considered for Ghanaians only. Although the act to amend the constitution had only been instituted, Parliament had yet to pass it into law. Once again it looked as though we were being omitted.

Dr. Lee *(who had repatriated in 1957)* responded that what we were most concerned about was the "Right of Return" and that it did not take an act of Parliament for Ghana to publicly state and declare on the world stage that Afrikans in the Diaspora have the moral and Historical "Right of Return" to their ancestral homeland. In response, the committee stated there were legal limits to our aspirations and patience needed to be exercised. *Have we not been patient? I thought to myself, here we go again! We had been patient, for the last five hundred years!*

We were then advised that groups of Afrikans in the Diaspora, resident in Ghana should submit a memorandum to the relevant committee of Parliament with the view to having our expectations addressed when the legislation regarding Dual Citizenship was enacted. The presidential committee advised us that it was necessary to submit a memorandum, taking apart the current law and re-writing it to address our situation. In re-writing the memorandum we needed to be cognizant that preparing the policy would not cause problems in the Ghanaian community, but would remove obstacles and not create unsolvable problems.

The Returning African Descendent group was now being charged with developing the technical language and/or document, formalizing the "Right of Return" into a policy, to address our situation as Returning Afrikan Descendants for submission to the Parliament and the President.

According to a presidential committee member, he felt that "Afrikans in the Diaspora needed to show more committed interest and mobilize more support" as it related to Dual Citizenship. It was difficult to argue against this statement for it was in fact true that we needed the support of brothers and sisters in the Diaspora to make our presence felt. Didn't we have to mobilize ourselves during the Civil Rights era? Didn't we have to mobilize ourselves for anything that we wanted to achieve in the Americas? Was Ghana any different, when it came to our struggle as Returning Afrikan descendants on the continent?

We would need a lawyer and upon completion of the memorandum, we would meet with the Minister of Interior, who would in turn submit our document covering Africans in the Diaspora to the Parliament.

We further discussed:

1 The problems and delays with securing a visa in places like the US and Jamaica for visits to Africa and the need for either waiving or relaxing visa requirements for Diasporan Afrikans, making visas available at the airport and the possibility of ECOWAS recognition status for Returning Afrikan descendants as has been done for other Afrikan countries. The committee responded that the legislation on Dual Citizenship would adequately address this issue.

1 In our request for special incentives for senior citizens/retired persons returning home, the committee felt that senior citizens might be a liability. We informed them that retirees from America in most instances retire with sufficient income and health coverage that would enable them to care for themselves thus making them an asset as opposed to a liability. The committee had to admit that they were ill-informed on this matter but could see no way possible to make special arrangements as it would introduce an element of liability which the government would not be able to contain and that such a policy would create resentment among indigenous Ghanaians who do not enjoy such as a policy.

1 In response to the proposal for Land Grant Allotment and purchase of land for Returning Afrikan descendants, we were informed that it would be impossible and inappropriate to meet these requests as all lands in the country had rightful owners and as such free-land could not be obtained anywhere for allocation to Returning Afrikan descendants. Besides the existing land tenure systems cannot be set aside in order to make special provisions to meet the expectations of Returning Afrikan descendants, which has no place in the law. Therefore, Returning Afrikan descendants should therefore abide by the existing practice in acquiring land, utilizing the useful experiences from groups of Afrikans from the Diaspora who had already acquired land through the normal process and who were successfully operating.

1 As regarded protection against unlawful deportation without just and legitimate cause, we were further informed that every

resident Ghanaian including Diasporan Afrikans were subject to the law and as long as they remained law abiding, they had nothing to fear. Thus a Diasporan Afrikan legally resident in Ghana could not be deported without just cause, as there were appropriate legislations to protect their fundamental rights.

After addressing the balance of our other concerns, the meeting was adjourned, to be re-convened in June.

Our committee immediately began the task of re-writing the memorandum and upon completion and review from our lawyer submitted the following to Parliament May 23 1997:

* * * * * * *

MEMORANDUM IN RESPECT OF "RIGHT OF RETURN" AND CITIZENSHIP FOR PERSONS WHO ARE DESCENDANTS OF AFRICANS BORN IN THE DIASPORA AS A DIRECT RESULT OF THE TRANS-ATLANTIC SLAVE TRADE.

A BILL SEEKING TO AMEND THE GHANA NATIONALITY ACT

SUBMITTED BY: THE RETURNING AFRICAN DESCENDANTS COMMITTEE

OBJECTIVE

The objective of the Bill is to establish the "Right of Return" for persons who are descendants of Africans born in the Diaspora as a direct result of the Trans-Atlantic Arab European Slave Trade and to amend the Ghana Nationality Act to facilitate the acquisition of citizenship of Ghana by persons identified as members of a "Historically Unique Group".

280

RATIONAL

1. Pursuant to the enslavement and forced migration of Afrikans during the Trans-Atlantic Arab European Slave Trade from the fifteenth (15th) to nineteenth (19th) centuries and
2. Pursuant to the historic Atonement Ceremony of 9th December 1994 by a representative number of Traditional Rulers of Ghana, on behalf of its people, acknowledged that persons who are descendants of Afrikans born in the Diaspora as a direct result of the Trans-Atlantic Slave Trade are a "Historically Unique Group" and
3. Considering the apparent past, present and potentially forthcoming contributions to this group toward national development goals; let it be therefore recorded that:

   a. Members of the "Historically Unique Group" have accepted invitations to come home and promote the idea of Pan Afrikan development. The great number of individuals who repatriated themselves from the early 1950's to present, yet are still looked upon as aliens has amply demonstrated their selflessness. In acknowledgment of this dichotomy and in recognition of their historical identity, numerous Traditional Rulers have chosen to play their role in re-enfranchising and re-uniting the African by bestowing Chieftaincy and Queen Mother status to many returning Afrikan Ascendants from the Diaspora.
   b. Many skilled persons from this "Historically Unique Group" have expressed a desire to return to Ghana to contribute financially, culturally and spiritually to its national development.
   c. Diasporans as citizens of Ghana, holding citizenship in any other country would form a powerful lobby and could significantly influence foreign policy in the country of their birth, to the benefit of Ghana.

4. **AMENDMENT (LAW OF RETURN)**

   Therefore the Ghana Nationality Act shall be a amended to read as follows:

(1) Every descendent of an Afrikan born in the Diaspora as a direct result of the Trans-Atlantic Arab European Slave Trade is a member of a "Historically Unique Group" and subject to compliance with sub-section 2 and 3 of this act is entitled to citizenship of Ghana.

(2) Every adult (21 years or older) member of this "Historically Unique Group" who is not a citizen of Ghana on the date of enactment of this law may acquire citizenship of Ghana by completing an application and adhering to other criteria established by the Minister of Interior.

(3) Every child of a person referred to in sub-section (2) shall be entitled to Citizenship of Ghana and shall attain such citizenship upon the granting of citizenship to at least one of his/her parents.

(4) The qualifications for naturalization of any person who is not a member of this "Historically Unique Group" as defined in sub-section (1) as subject to the laws already in affect.

Between the period that the act written by our committee was submitted to Parliament and the actual passage of the law, we prepared petitions supporting our bid for Dual Citizenship, which we sent to the Diaspora; had visitors to Ghana sign, which were in turn forwarded to Parliament. Additionally, each of our organizations held meetings with other groups and diligently worked in getting the word out, rallying support for this issue. Unfortunately, we also met opposition from some of our people, who had been inappropriately informed that a Dual Citizenship Bill had already been passed into law, and subsequently refused to sign our petitions. When asked where they had acquired this information, for those of us on the ground had not been informed and they themselves had had to obtain a visa before they could enter the country, they responded that certain Ministers had informed them of this. Needless to say, this was not the fact.

The following pages speak to the new/amended law.

IMMIGRATION REGULATIONS, 2001

In exercise of the powers conferred on the Minister for the Interior by section 55 of the Immigration Act 2000, (Act 573) these regulations are made this 19th day of July 2001.

The following is the Legislative Instrument 1691 (L.I. 1691) of the Immigration Regulations, 2001 that was enacted in November 2001 as it relates to Africans in the Diaspora entitled "the Right of Abode."

Right of Abode

Application for Right of Abode

13. (1) A person who wishes to be considered for the grant of Right of Abode should submit an application as in Form E in the Schedule to the Minister through the Director.

(2) A Ghanaian national who by the acquisition of another nationality can not hold a Ghanaian nationality because of the laws governing the acquired nationality and who wishes to be granted right of abode shall not be required to produce documentary evidence of financial standing.

(3) A person of African descent in the Diaspora who wishes to be considered for the grant of right of abode, shall be subject to a verification process which requires among other things:

    (a) an attestation by two Ghanaians who are notaries public, lawyers, senior public officers or other class of persons approved by the Minister to the effect that the applicant is of good character and that they have known the applicant personally for a period of at least five years;

    (b) a declaration by the applicant to the effect that the applicant has not been convicted of any criminal offence and been sentenced to imprisonment for a term of twelve months or more;

    (c) production by the applicant documentary evidence of financial standing;

(d) the applicant satisfying the Minister that the applicant is capable of making a substantial contribution to the development of Ghana and

(e) that the applicant has attained at least the age of eighteen years.

(4) An applicant for right of abode shall submit the application in person

(5) For the purpose of verification under sub-regulation (3), the applicant must have resided in the country

(a) throughout the period of twenty-four months immediately preceding the date of the application; and

(b) during the seven years immediately preceding the period of twenty-four months referred to in paragraph (a), for a period amounting in the aggregate to not less than five years.

*   *   *   *   *   *   *

The **Citizenship Act, 2000 covering Dual Citizenship** went into effect for Ghanaians; however, it **DOES NOT** cover persons of African descent in/from the Diaspora.

The law states as follows:

CITIZENSHIP ACT, 2000, ACT 591

PART III - DUAL CITIZENSHIP, RENUNCIATION AND DEPRIVATION OF CITIZENSHIP

DATE OF ASSENT: 29th December 2000

Dual Citizenship

16. (1) A citizen of Ghana may hold the citizenship of any other country in addition to his citizenship of Ghana.

Additional information on Immigration and Citizenship laws may be obtained from the Government Printer, Assembly Press, Accra.

Afrikan Americans and other Afrikans born in the Diaspora **DO NOT HAVE DUAL CITIZENSHIP.** **Visas** are still required to enter Ghana.

Multi-Entry Visas are also available. If you are planning to leave Ghana to visit another Afrikan country during your trip, or plan to re-visit Ghana in the near future, you must have an additional Visa in order to return to Ghana. Consequently, it is advisable to purchase the Multi-Entry Visa, instead of a Single-Entry Visa. Check with the Ghana Consulate for more details.

After a careful review of the newly enacted Immigration regulations, many of us are of the opinion that we have gained very little from the newly revised law, especially those brothers and sisters who initially entered Ghana. They must reside in Ghana at least seven years before they can even apply for the "Right of Abode."

What have we truly been given? Are we as our enslaved ancestors only receiving the crumbs from the master boss's table? When will our total recognition, our total acceptance as Afrikan people returning home come into fruitition?

Although Ghana has passed a law granting the "Right of Abode" to persons "of Afrikan Ascent in the Diaspora," it is our contention that the "Right of Abode" is meaningless to us.

Our demand as a "Historically Unique Group" is for the "Right of Return" according to International Law and the United Nations Declaration of Human Rights. The law states that "if a person does not "**voluntarily surrender**" his "nationality" or "citizenship", he or she remains a citizen of the place of origin."

Consequently, we Afrikans born in the Diaspora, remain full citizens of Afrika in spite of the fact that we had not recently resided there.

We as Afrikans born in the Diaspora are Ascendants of those, our ancestors **violently kidnapped, and forcibly removed,** from their homeland, Afrika and according to definition we remain "domiciled" in Afrika.

The legal definition of "**domicile**" is the "place of one's origin and nationality in which he or she intends to return to, even though he or she may reside elsewhere".

No Afrikan country has "Legislatively" granted us the "Right of Return" or "Dual Citizenship" to date.

In Ghana, at the very least, we demand "Dual Citizenship" as was granted to Ghanaians who are resident in America and other parts of the Diaspora, that recognize "Dual Citizenship" laws.

* Ascendents = we as Afrikans born in the Diaspora as a result of the Trans Atlantic Arab European Slave Trade, are rising, not descending.

It is in our power to define ourselves and who we are, and what we are doing.

CHAPTER TWENTY ONE

HARVEST TIME

For those who don't think that I've delved deep enough into certain areas, a wise elder once said to me:

"Every truth is not to be told."

Some of it you will have to experience first hand. What I'm saying is that living in Ghana ain't easy but neither is living in New York, Detroit, Chicago, LA etc., but as our choice of battlefields, we've chosen and been blessed to be on the front line in my ancestral homeland, Ghana.

Those who don't know quite how to make this move have to prepare themselves financially, spiritually and physically - do your research - talk with folks who have done it – then just jump into the pool. There are no guarantees except the one that will bind us together, guaranteed "Unity" in coming home...It's Harvest time.

Unity is not an emotional affair – it is a structural and scientific necessity. Without unity we are doomed to destruction. What Africa/Ghana needs is trade not aid. We need current/modern equipment and technology to compete on the global market, not cast off used clothes, antiquated materials, equipment and ideas. We don't need more missionaries! We need a Common Market to sell our products at a fair price.

One of our biggest structural problems despite tremendous natural resources is that Afrikan currencies have very little value in the world market compounded by the fact that Afrikan states do not set the price of products they buy and sell. Prices are dictated overseas.

People power movement based on the principles of Afrikan Unity can solve the problems facing Afrika. It is a sad commentary, that we have not been in Afrika in our numbers but more Afrikans born in America and other parts of the Diaspora are waking up and beginning to have this connection with the land of their origin "Afrika." It's only sad because it took us so long to recognize and access our blessings. We must also not forget that back in the sixties, brothers and sisters from the Americas found their way home to Ghana. What are some of the lessons that those of us returning home today can learn from their experiences. Why did they return to America?

After being systematically divided and separated by design: like no other ethnic groups in amerikkka; we have been violently wrested from the land of our origin. History teaches that any group of people that do not identify, for whatever reason, with the place that they came from, will not know where they are going and will not enjoy life and develop to the fullest. We must be culturally, psychologically and economically linked up to our roots.

In spite of the achievements in the Civil Rights struggle and in education, sports, entertainment and wealth, full acceptance continues to elude the Afrikan masses in the United States. Afrikans born in america for the most part still remain at the bottom.

Why? Because the United States is the land of immigrants and all immigrant groupings are connected in one way or the other to their land of origin. The Jewish people do business with Israel, the Italians with Italy, the Chinese and Japanese with their people overseas.

But we have historically been deliberately mis-educated and brainwashed through religiosity, negative press and cannot connect and relate with the land of our ancestors. Because of the negative press that has been embedded in the minds of Afrikan people there is a lack of cultural relationships and most important, trade with Afrika.

Thank the Creator for the winds of change. More and more Afrikans born in the United States and the other parts of the Diaspora are returning home but not every experience is a success story.

Too often the Ghanaian perception of us as "rich" people creates problems for they don't see us lacking or having had to struggle to even get here. To them we are "rich," and many don't understand why we have come back "home" to "suffer." Little do they realize that we had been suffering for a long time in the United States, in spite of how it looks to them. When we explain how we were not able to own our homes (without a twenty-five or thirty year mortgage) or afford to build of our homes, they don't believe us.

But if we are not careful in our return home on how we handle our finances or who we entrust in assisting us in handling our affairs, as the proverb says," a fool and his/her money will soon part."

Some people will do almost anything to get to America and Europe, which they believe to be the greatest places in the world and if they can just reach there everything will be all right. Unfortunately too many of them do not return, even if they want to. With the day-to-day survival in the Diaspora of paying rent, insurance, car note, utilities, etc. there is little money left to afford a ticket, which is extremely expensive.

Additionally, as the custom is here in Ghana, once you have "Been-to" America or "Been-to" Europe or anywhere in the west you can't return with empty hands. You are expected to bring gifts for family and friends or you will bring disgrace down upon yourself. Been-to America, Been-to Europe and don't bring back anything – SHAME!!

We need each other and Afrikans of the Diaspora have a key role to play in the redemption and unification of Afrika. Honest trade amongst us is crucial and must be done in the true context of Afrikan Unity. It must be seen as a means of creating "overstanding" that will lead to the creation of an "Afrikan Common Market," in order to institutionalize "Unity" and guarantee that this "Unity" will last.

And we've networked!

Networking and sharing is an important key, an important tool, which helps us to help each other and ourselves. We can show by example the possibilities of returning home. We can be an inspiration to others who wish to return home but don't know where to start. We can share our fears, our tears, our laughter and joy with other brothers and sisters. In this way, we are doing our small part towards the redemption of our collective selves and our people.

That is why our home, *One Africa,* affectionately called "the Halfway House" (halfway between where you are going and where you have been) has become an important focal point for brothers and sisters from all walks of life visiting Ghana. It is a special, spiritual retreat where we share ourselves, sharing the Who, When, Why, Where, and How of returning home, sharing our experiences and our blessings.

It is also a museum that speaks to our past experiences living in the United States and tells the real truth about our struggles. It gives us the opportunity to also share this part of our history with our Continental born Afrikan brothers and sisters as well as the many people that visit us from all over the Diaspora.

From one day to the next people come...referred by others or having just heard that we are here. The remains of brothers and sisters have been brought to our doorstep. We have performed traditional wedding ceremonies and offered a retreat for those looking to do so.

Remember, that everyone will not welcome you "home" with open arms and will call you foreigner/*Obruni*/Whiteman. Yes, it hurts but our brothers and sisters on the continent do not know us - as we do not know them – we've been away for a long time. An elder also gave me another meaning for the word *Obruni*. It means coming from beyond the horizon...and have we not come from beyond the horizon? If each one teaches one, we will all learn much.

We must remember that the system of oppression didn't teach Afrikan Unity, it taught separation, subjugation and self-hate. To many people we look like big dollar signs. We sound like the images (white) that have been put before them. Rich America - Rich Europe - not about being Black/Afrikan within those places that we have called home. Appalled at too many beggars? People, who do not have, beg. Don't they beg in the United States of amerikkka - the "greatest country in the world?" Get real!

In 1992, a year after we arrived in Ghana, *Essence Magazine* did an article on Ghana. Nana and I appeared in a section called "Cousins." Hundreds of people have visited us as a result. Even today people come through the gates of our home waving that article. They've held onto it for years. The seed was planted and they had begun sowing (saving) towards their day of return. Others have been inspired by our bravery and sense of adventure: our not being fearful of leaving the United States, the homeland of our oppressors.

It is important for us to look seriously at our westernized attitude and modify it so that it coincides with and compliments our Afrikan personality and culture. Where we are aggressive, bold and assertive, being a product of the American society - having to fight for our rights, "fighting on arrival & fighting for survival," our brothers and sisters on the continent are essentially very humble and will do almost anything you ask of them. Many of them are looking for advice, ideas and involvement in something that will help them to help themselves. And they are very friendly but do not be fooled. There must be clear overstanding (understanding) of the motives involved on both sides.

Many of us coming out of the United States come as educators, administrators, and service providers with a lot of modern ideas. Therefore the two sides/people should be able to complement each other – eliminating conflict and confusion.

We must stay away from the notion that Afrikans are imperfect and can do nothing. That is the biggest lie that has ever been perpetuated upon our people. I have met some of the most talented people in the world in Ghana and other parts of Afrika. Ghanaians can fix anything, build anything, and design anything, i.e., like our Mercedes Benz that couldn't be fixed. We sold it to a mechanic for less than five hundred US dollars only to see it running smoothly, freshly painted around town a few weeks later. That was seven (7) years ago and it is still running!

With our technological know how from the Diaspora and their skill of hand, mind and body we are unstoppable as a people. Afrika has its modern urban environment and you can live as modern or as simple rural as you want to. The environmental conditions have improved greatly in some areas while other areas lag behind.

Having been away from "Mother" Afrika for so long we thirst for the Afrikan tradition, the culture and the political overstanding (understanding) of our people.

Afrikan culture and tradition is the backbone of the family structure, where we live, work, dream, harvest and celebrate together. Where we are functioning as a unit, providing and taking care of self and community – growing and selling our own food and raising our own children.

Creating the ideals of practical Pan Afrikanism by truly demonstrating in 'word' and 'deed' – using the principles of reciprocity. If you plant you reap/harvest, you eat. Otherwise you suffer.

We must come back to the land and get rid of our "imported" mentality. Afrika in truth needs to import nothing for she has all the natural resources for full-scale industrialization, which we as Afrikan people cannot have without "Unity."

We continue to be a divided and exploited people looking for the opportunity to bring one another down. This attitude continues to be passed down from generation to generation and unless it changes we will continue to be exploited, used and abused by the exploiters of our people.

The Western society teaches us to separate ourselves from the family and community. Go to work for some large company instead of coming together to create our own large company. We leave the community/Mother Afrika with our talents and skills, leaving no one to care for her. With all the talent gone "Mother" suffers from brain drain, while we make someone other than ourselves rich and prosperous. So we must take seriously the notion of returning home to "Mother" Afrika for we have something to give one another.

"It won't be easy but anything worth having is worth fighting for," my Daddy used to say.

When we fall down we must get up and try again, not run back to the United States because some "unconscious" person has cheated or deceived you. Learn from your mistakes (and there will be some) and gain strength for the victory, which will certainly be ours.

As Dr. Carter G. Woodson said, "History shows that it does not matter who is in power...those who have not learned to do for themselves and have to depend solely on others never obtain any more rights or privileges in the end than they had in the beginning."

We must stop laying up our "treasures in heaven where neither moth nor rust doth corrupt," while foreigners acquire our mineral and land resources, destroy and steal our arts, crafts (i.e. kente weaving) and home industries. We must become the mainstays of economic development in Afrika and Ghana in particular.

I am extremely grateful for the blessings that have been bestowed upon my family and me.

I really made it...we, made it.

We've come home and there's no disputing that. In fact in August of 1998, for the first time in the history of Afrika, Ghana held the first Emancipation Day observation, in which she welcomed and accepted back the remains of two of our ancestors; Samuel Carson who had been enslaved and died in america and three hundred year old Sister Elder Crystal from Jamaica, West Indies.

As part of that celebration a group of students, their professors from Southern Illinois University at Carbondale, several friends and myself traveled to the Upper Eastern & Northern Regions of Ghana following the Slave Route (trek) of our ancestors.

We went into the caves that had been hiding places for our people, trying to escape from the slave raiders. We visited the Slave Markets of Salaga where our people were chained to trees in the hot sun and sold to the highest bidders, we visited the deep forests/jungles and touched the "Walls of Resistance" (as I call them), which were built around villages and farm lands to protect the inhabitants from Slave Raiders.

And we visited Sandema, where the oldest Traditional Ruler in Ghana who was 115 years old and who has been on his Skin for 67 years, since 1931. (In the South of Ghana the Traditional Rullers sit on the Stool, in the North they sit on the Skin).

He told us that the knowledge of one another is what will bring us together as a people to build one common world and that your short visit should not escape your knowledge of our forefathers. "I am so sorry that you are not staying longer so that we could share other important information with you and so that you could learn more about the people who defeated Babatu and the other Slave Raiders. The remains of Babatu's weapons are still here as a testament of Bulsa Lands defeat of him.

"If I die today, I will be happy for I have had the opportunity to share the history of our people with you. I am the oldest and only surviving son of my father, who disclosed to me where to find the instruments of war used to take our people away. I am happy to see all of you, descendants of our ancestors. You are welcome back home."

We also had the opportunity to meet and share the history of our people with the descendants of one of the notorious Slave Raiders, Babatu in Yendi.

For me all of this was significant for as long as I have lived in Ghana I had not experienced the history of my people any further than Kumasi. I learned that the total picture cannot be drawn just in those dungeons alone: we have to go further. In the North I saw my people, I felt their pain, I felt their strength, I had finally come home. This has completed for me, the full circle of my return.

As I stood in the waters, in front of the Cape Coast Castle Dungeons waiting to receive the remains of my ancestors being returned home from Jamaica and the United States: returning "Thru The Door of No Return," which had now been re-named on the outside of the castle/dungeon door "Door of Return," I realized that the circle had in fact been completed and that Ghana had taken a bold step when she stood up on the world stage and claimed that we as Afrikans living in the Diaspora as a result of the greatest holocaust known to mankind, had "The Right of Return" to our "Mother" land Afrika.

We've come home. There's no disputing that.

Returning Home Ain't Easy but it sure is a Blessing.

People often ask, "What are those blessings?"

First of all I have returned home after five hundred years in captivity. I now live where I have always wanted to live, on the oceanfront of our historical homeland with a partner that wants the same things that I want. We own our home, without a thirty year mortgage to pay or the payment of rent, we pay low taxes and live a basically stress free lifestyle. I walk the streets of my town after dark, without fear.

What are my blessings?

Returning home has truly been an adjustment: an adjustment in customs and traditions, languages, foods and a general way of life. It also puts a strain on the strongest of relationships and often only one person in the relationship really wants to make the sacrifices of returning home – and it is a sacrifice. We did not make this journey without personal sacrifices. Every fiber of my being has been tested and my marriage further strained.

American born Afrikan men, mine included, are often captivated by the continental born Afrikan woman, comparing her servile and obedient manner to those of the "more aggressive, vocal" ways of American born Afrikan women and sometimes that comparison is painful.

But you've got to be able to hang in there as you work within the blessings and towards the light at the end of the tunnel. I believe that our greatest asset (my husband & I) is that we both wanted to return home, that in spite of the difficulties and strain on our relationship that neither of us wanted to "run" back to America when the going got rough.

There's an expression "when the going gets tough the tough get going." Go where? I ask myself, this is it! This is my blessing from The Creator and the Ancestors and I won't run away. But more importantly it is accepting that we as Afrikans born in the Diaspora, are a tribe unto ourself like the Fantes, the Gas, the Ashantis, the Ewes etc.

I have been told and accept the fact that Afrikans of the Diaspora are the largest tribe of Afrikans in the world and that tribalism is alive and well in Ghana.

We are the sons and daughters of our "Mother" Afrika, kidnapped and snatched away during the Trans-Atlantic Arab European Slave Trade who have come forward again and must find our niche on the continent of Afrika, our home, especially in Ghana where the largest number of slave forts, castles and dungeons can be found; Slave Dungeons that today represent our sacred monuments.

Sitting on the cliff rocks in front of our house I watch the Fisherman in their boats, pulling their nets: their voices raised in a rhythmic chant, being carried on the winds to the shore. As the white, rolling waves crashed against the jagged rocks with the Elmina Castle/Dungeons looming in the distance, I thought of the following verse:

Waves of welcome are singing
As they crash against the shore,
Waves of welcome keep singing...
Welcome home, back through the door.

That same "Door of No Return," those same exit doors through which our ancestors were marched, crawling and stumbling into the Belly of the Beast.

This return completes the circle for me, but within that circle there is still much to be done. The word must go out to those who are searching for another way, that Ghana is the place; Afrika is the place. It is time and it is possible. We must unite and use our God-given creativity and skills acquired while away from home, to develop bigger and better things for us, and our families.

I sometimes wonder if there is anything in the United States that I miss so much that I want to return; there isn't. As for family and friends, as much as we may miss them, they will have to come home...to Ghana if they want to see us again (Nana has not returned to the United States since 1991). I think of them sometimes, as the sun sets in the West along the jagged rocks and coconut tree lined coast.

But I'm distracted as the fiery ball fades behind the Elmina Castle Dungeons: the place where Kings, Queen Mothers, Chiefs, Priests and Priestesses, Physicians, Scholars and Craftsmen...were imprisoned and where under the lash of the Oppressors, a new tribe of Afrikan was being shipped to the Diaspora in the loins of our ancestors.

I look again at the Elmina Castle Dungeons (approximately two miles in the distance) and after thirteen years, I still pinch myself and ask, "Am I really here?" Sometimes I think I'll wake up and find that it's all a dream and that frightens me, because I want to spend the rest of my life in Ghana...in Afrika.

Then there are the nights when I wake up from my sleep trembling but relieved to find that my nightmares of being de-humanized in the holds of slave ships are just that...nightmares, but so real to me, and impossible to forget that which is deep in my soul.

It is my testimony that I am first an Afrikan, though born on the soil of the United Snakes of America, who has been tainted with the slaughtered, indigenous people and enslaved Afrikans. However, I remain forever connected to my people and our God-given right to be 'free.'

We, the Afrikans born in the Diaspora are descendants (ascendants) of those ancestors who were kidnapped and robbed of our heritage during the Trans-Atlantic Arab-European Slave Trade.

Please don't tell me to forget about the *Hellocaust of our people; don't tell me to let the past go and to forgive and forget. Forgiving is easy for the Afrikan, for that's our inborn nature and I can forgive but I will never forget, nor will I let anyone else forget. Our history is significant; our contribution to mankind let alone Afrikan civilization has been enormous. However, because we have listened to "forget", that is exactly what has happened to our history, power and consequently because we have studied everyone else's history, we know very little about our own and our various selves.

One of our great Historian, Prof. Dr. John Henrik Clarke said "The powerful never teach the powerless how to take the power away from them the powerful !!"

But the winds of change are upon us and we must build and secure the history and glory of our people and we must do it together. So when anyone calls you Obruni, while visiting Ghana, don't get angry, just say "Ababio" (which means he/she has been away and returned. "I'm your Sister/Brother, I'm your Mother/Father, I'm your Family and I've come home!

Our ancestors prayed for this and millions died for this, but little did we know growing up in the United States and the Caribbean that we would be the ones chosen, to fulfill their dreams of returning home.

From our house, with the vast ocean view of "Mommie Waters" before me, I watch faithfully each day the Elmina Castle Dungeons in the distance, built on a rock and jutting out like a huge accusing finger into the sea. I feel like the Gatekeeper or Sentinel, watching to assure that it doesn't happen again. Who knows - perhaps that's my portion?

"Returning Home Ain't Easy But It Sure Is A Blessing."

* Holocaust

IMAHKÜS standing in the waters of the Gulf of Guinea awaiting the arrival of the ancestral remains of Samuel Carson and Sister Crystal at the Door Of No Return" Cape Coast Castle Dungeons.

Funeral service for ancestral remains at Assin Manso during 1st Emancipation Day observance – 1998.

Nana Okofo, Ahveekhy Ben Israel, Kiniyah Awaal & IMAHKÜS welcoming the remains of ancestors Elder Samuel Carson of New York & Elder Sister Crystal of Jamaica, West Indies back through "THE DOOR OF NO RETURN "at the Cape Coast Castle Dungeons during the Ist Annual Emancipation Day Celebration in August 1998 in Ghana.

IMAHKÜS, Nana Okofo, Kohain and others at the Candle light vigil in the Cape Coast Castle Dungeons on the eve of Emancipation Day - 1999.

Dedicated to the memory of my ancestors

Too Many...

Where did I go?

Where have I been?

Enslaved in amerikkka

Surrounded by sin.

Too many years...

Too many tears,

For millions of Afrikans

Who will never hear,

The laughter, the singing, the drumbeat of home.

But I have returned,

Never more to roam...too far from home,

After 500 years

Of torture and fears

And too many tears.

Seestah Kiniya Awaal and Seestah IMAHKÜS sharing a joke just before a surprised IMAHKÜS was called by President Rawlings to speak during the Durbar of Chiefs at PANAFEST '94 held in Victoria Park, Cape Coast.

Seestah IMAHKÜS speaking at the Durbar of Chiefs as President Rawlings looks on.

300

NOTE:

We don't go looking or advertising to do many of the things mentioned in this book. People come here in search of something: help, advice, and a listening hear, a retreat or opportunity to get in touch with self and ancestors...and we're here.

We often function as Surrogate Parents to many of the Afrikan American students who pass through, often in need of an understanding ear and a soft, strong shoulder to cry on or to vent their anger, frustrations and other emotions that they oft times feel in returning home to Mother Afrika for the first time – a place to call home while away from home.

Often it is someone who we have interacted with, who has told someone else of their experience at One Africa House and sent them to us.

Nuff times folks land in Ghana with desires and/or problems and not a clue as to how and where to go to solve them. Invariably one of our brothers or sisters will direct them.

"Go to One Africa House, maybe they can help you."
And as the universe and ancestors would have it, we have, in most cases, been able to assist them or refer them to someone that can.

When you enter Elmina, immediately after crossing the small, flat bridge from Cape Coast, just look to the left, for the One Africa sign board and a long boat-shaped white house, with the colors of the Ethiopian flag painted around the crown of the house. It can be seen from the highway. There are bamboo gates with the Lions of Judah on them. There are also six Afrikan styled Chalets in the compound. As we say in Ghana,
"You're invited."

Someone will be there to welcome you!

ACKNOWLEDGEMENTS

To my other bruthers and seestahs, who have also come forward in pursuit of the same dream of returning home.

Bruthers: Kohain Nathanyah HaLevi, Rabbi, Daveed Jawara, Preston (7 Dred) Muhammed, Baba Van Kirksey, Errick Jones, George Culmer, Cliff Townsend, Elder Amram Boykin-HaLevi, Scattering Cloud, Ahveekhy Ben Israel, Dhoruba Bin Wahad, Amichai Ben Israel, Marlon Hite and Don Leon Smith, the late Ronako Flax, Malikai Halevi, the late Nana TJ.

Seestahs: Nana Ama Serwah-Nyarko (Dr. Beryl Dorsett), the late Lady Sala Shabazz, Nana Ama Manan II (E. Malkia Brantuo), Djenaba Akli, Nana Atta Nkum I (Zakia Henderson), the late Elmina Dennis, Delorse Rader, Helen Opong-Kessey, Shirley Nti, The late Queen Mother Rene Jackson, The late Queen Mother Lola Kwadjoman, Kiniaya Awaal, Gladys Rice, Malikah Faquir, Maisie Howell, Nzinga Nzinga and daughter, Annie Hall, Mamalena Diop, Victoria Cooper and Nana Esi Boah (Minon Philips), Ngone ADA AW, Bahteyah Baht Israel.

Families: Dr. Robert E. (Uncle Bobby) Lee & the late Sarah Lee & Children, Adjoa and Kofi Childs, Joey G, Byron & Sonia Lye Fook, John & Mary Ellen Ray, Thomas & Iris Bannister, Remel & Phil Moore and Sons, Nii Kwashie Adjei (Chilton Alponse) & Daughter, Debra Kofie & Children, Jafiyah and Mwanda Kumunu-Clavell & Children, Balalshange & Hastra Ashamu & Children, Elimisha Jaliwah & Daughter Aziza, Carlos Alston & Children, Dr. Rod & Mrs. Scherazade King, Nana Kweku & April Amissah & Children, Masao Mero, Janet Butler & Children, Lucille Davis & Son, Edward & Bertha Brown, Nana Kwadwo & Majewa Akpon & Son, Mona Boyd & Son, Jahbud, Denise & Son, Mr & Mrs. D, Marva & Eric, Nana Adjoa and son, Brian & Dorothy Lowe and others who have also returned that I may have left out.

EPILOGUE

The time has come for those Afrikan Descendants who have a vision of the future for Afrika to go forward and inspire our people toward a closer kinship. A closer love of self and one another: toward a greater appreciation of who we are, where we came from and where we are going. For it is only through this appreciation and acknowledgment of self-determined will, shall we be able to rise to that higher level of consciousness that will enable us to survive as an Afrikan people.

By the same token as an independent Afrikan Continent, we should have the ability to create the unity that is necessary to regain power and strength as any other continent on this planet, so that Afrika, too, becomes respected. Wherever people of Afrikan origin or Afrikan heritage go, they will be respected. Despite Afrikan Heritage and the Origin of Afrikan Civilization the current conditions remain in turmoil, etc.

In democratic America (KKK) despite over forty years of Civil Rights Demonstrations, Sit-ins, Affirmative Action and numerous amendments to laws to put Afrikan people on a more even footing with whites and other ethnic groups, we Afrikans are still on the bottom of the political, socio-economic rung of the ladder. We Afrikans born in the United States still exist in a quasi slave state. Being a non-sovereign people we continue to live in a perpetual state of slave-like conditions: meaning, we do not own the factories, produce the food or have a controlling influence in the Stock Market. In fact we are worse off today economically and legislatively than we were in the 60's & 70's. In Ghana, like most other states in Afrika — a former European Colony, neo-colonialism is on the horizon. Social and political economic problems prevail throughout Ghanaian society and for the most part, all of Afrika.

It is my belief that an overwhelming number of Ghanaians live in dire poverty because large multi-national corporations expropriate so much of the country's wealth (as well as Afrikan nations in general). Enormous profits are gained from the exploitation of mineral resources and human labor. The gold fields, diamond mines and aluminum factories produce huge earnings. However, the lions share of these profits fall into the coffers of private foreign companies. Additionally, the educational, health care, nutritional, sanitation, utilities, industrial and other genuine needs of the Ghanaian masses are barely addressed and usually go unfulfilled. Again, the same can be said for most of Afrika.

So the fight for freedom, justice and equality continues.

Where ever we go and our people are being oppressed...

Never Forget ...

THE FIGHT FOR FREEDOM IS FAR FROM OVER!

Resistance Fighters for the freedom of Afrikan people were warriors like Nana Obaa Sima Yaa Asantewa who was born in Ejisu, a central state of the Asante Kingdom in Ghana, West Afrika. Her son became ruler of Ejisu in 1880 and she became Queen Mother, a respected and powerful position in Ashanti society.

The Ashanti ruled Central Ghana for more than 200 years, mostly under severe pressure from the British, who were anxious to exploit the mineral wealth of the area. Opposition to King Prempeh I was encouraged by the British until a Civil War broke among the Ashanti that lasted for ten years and ended with the King and his supporters including the son of Nana Yaa Asantewa, being exiled to the Seychelles.

Eager to exploit the disarray, the British sent a force to the Ashanti capital, Kumasi to demand allegiance. It was Yaa Asantewa who rallied resistance in defense of the "Golden Stool," the sacred symbol of unity of the Ashanti people. As an Ashanti Warrior, she fought with legendary courage, leading her people bravely in battle against the British in 1901, against the colonial oppression of the British Empire.

The British were re-enforced from their colonies all over Afrika and sent a large, well-equipped army to capture Nana Asantewa. But her spirit was not to be broken. She fought and retreated again and again with ever diminishing supporters until more than a year later she was finally surrounded. After the battle she was captured, and together with Nana Prempeh I and other prominent Afrikans and was exiled to the Seychelles Island until she died in 1921...

THE FIGHT FOR FREEDOM IS FAR FROM OVER!

Likewise Queen Nzingha of Angola (1600-1663) fought unceasingly, against the Portuguese's enslavement of Afrikan people in Angola. She was the greatest Military Strategist that ever confronted the armed forces of Portugal. Her tactics in her fight against slavery kept the Portuguese sweating in confusion and dismay. Her aim was nothing less than the total destruction of the Slave Trade.

She was responsible for inspiring her people to continue the war of resistance against slavery. She was Angola's ablest and most uncompromising diplomat and in 1622, though not yet Queen, led a delegation to the Peace Conference in Luanda with the Portuguese.

But before the conference could begin, the Portuguese governor, hell bent on insulting Nzinga, provided chairs for himself and councilors, with the thought of forcing Nzingha, to stand humbly before him. When she entered the Conference Hall he continued sitting. While she took in the situation, her attendants quickly rolled out the royal carpet for Nzingha and one of them went down on all fours and expertly formed himself into a royal throne for her to sit upon. Being considerate of her people, she rose at regular intervals as her devoted followers allowed her to sit easily upon them.

Western historian minds unable to grasp this real meaning, saw it as a cruel and inhuman use of slaves, ignoring the fact that she was the greatest Abolitionist of Slavery and had no slaves herself and had no need for any. She was so loved by her people that they would have died for her. Such were the men, not slaves, who gladly formed a human couch for her, their leader, before the astonished Portuguese.

In 1623 Nzingha became Queen. One of her greatest acts was in 1624 when she declared all territory over which she had control as "free" country. And all slaves reaching it were forever free...

THE FIGHT FOR FREEDOM IS FAR FROM OVER!

In Jamaica, the proclamation of 1838 freed thousands of enslaved Afrikans in the West Indies. But not before the Maroons and people like Juan Dubolo, Queen Nannie and others set up strong holds in the Blue Mountains of Jamaica and fought against the English and the Spanish to remain free from slavery.

In 1655 the English took Jamaica from Spain, at the time of this acquisition the mountains were already teeming with 1,500 or more runaway slaves — whose numbers were being swelled daily with Afrikans seeking freedom.

The Maroons fought many wars over the years and were called the untamed ones: feared for their "Bush" ambushes, where they camouflaged themselves using bush, branches, trees and foliage, standing immobile, blending in with the forest and leading their oppressors into their traps. As a result of their many years of struggles, today the Maroons have their own sub-divisional government in Jamaica.

Afrikan people like the Maroons made major strides in contributing to the enhancement of Afrikan civilization...

THE FIGHT FOR FREEDOM IS FAR FROM OVER!

The Emancipation Proclamation of 1863, just a mere one hundred and thirty-seven years ago, declared over four million enslaved Afrikans in America (KKK) free, but not before they experienced many untold sacrifices and struggles and endured great hardships like their forebears.

But Emancipation had a dear price for Afrikans in the United States as violence in the South escalated and had nothing to do with their alleged criminal behavior. People like Ida B. Wells fought against the lynching of Afrikan people, which was a tool of the new caste system that was being imposed by the "White south" in the United States.

The more she studied the situation the more she was convinced that the Southerner had never gotten over his resentment that the Negro was no longer his plaything, his servant and his primary source of income. This resentment was more intense against

Afrikans in positions to compete with Whites. Lynching was a direct result of gains Afrikans were making in the South. Afrikans were a threat and lynching was a means to counteract it. Thousands upon thousands of Afrikans were subjected to these atrocities from Whites. However, the decline of these murders can be directly attributed to the efforts of Ida B. Wells.

The ongoing fight against the oppression of Afrikan people in the United States can be attributed to Warriors like, Harriet Ross Tubman, Sojourner Truth, Ida B. Wells, Frederick Douglas, The Honorable Marcus Mosiah Garvey, Dr. Martin Luther King, Jr., Brother El Haji Malik Shabbazz (Malcolm X), Dr. John Henrik Clarke, Professor Leonard Jefferies, Professor Tony Martin, Queen Mother Moore and abolitionists like Charles Lenox Remond, Booker T. Washington, Richard Allen, Gabriel Prosser, Absolom Jones, Nat Turner, Martin Delaney and many others who fought against the barbaric institution of slavery and fought for the upliftment of our people...

THE FIGHT FOR FREEDOM IS FAR FROM OVER!

We are the descendants of those brave and dedicated men and women who suffered in Ameri(KKK)a, the Caribbean and Afrika for over 500 years under the brutal Institution of Slavery. Those who have lost track of their Afrikan history will recall that our forebearers were taken away from the great continent of "Mother" Afrika and brought to the America's for the sole purpose of being used as slaves. Our forebearers were worked and treated worse than animals: they suffered, they bled, and they died. But despite death our people kept a vision and belief that one-day, their children would be free.

They dreamed that the continent of Afrika from where they came would also be free for their children, grandchildren and great grandchildren, (without Visa requirements to return home to Afrika). We are the children of their vision. Prayerfully, each of us will realize that we have a duty to perform because of the price that our ancestors paid. Their vision is yet to be completely realized. Afrikans once occupied a higher position in the world scientifically, artistically and commercially but in balancing the scale of evolution we lost our place. Someone other than ourselves now occupies the position we once held. The winds of change are upon us because God never intended that one man should enslave another. But the price for such a sin, the violation of God's law, must be paid for by everyone responsible. Afrikan descendants must work in the present so that the sorrows of our ancestors shall not be perpetuated upon us in the future.

No greater gift can be given in honor of the memory of our ancestors, than for us in gratitude of the suffering they endured, so that we might be free: no grander gift can be borne to the sacred memories of generations past, than a free and redeemed Afrika – a monument for all eternity.

"Up you might race you can accomplish what you will."

The Honourable Marcus Mosiah Garvey

"No Justice, No Peace!"

OBI-NNKA-OBI
(Bite not one another)

AN "EVERLIVING" MEDITATION

As an *Nubian person I call upon the spirit and wisdom of I ancestors and the cosmic forces of truth and justice which are with I, uniting I, strengthening I sense of responsibility and helping I to re-capture in InI minds; storing the knowledge and the love of self, learning, studying, creating, planning, building, and working together for I survival as individuals and community. The inspiration of I glorious Nubian past and the divine light of cosmic energies surrounds I and protects I from all negative vibrations, thoughts, feeling and actions, as I dedicate and commit I self/selves to affirming and claiming I humanity and I heritage. And as before, once again, become an Almighty Force in the restoration of Truth, Peace, Prosperity and Justice wherever Nubian people are found on this planet.

Hotep Maat

BALANCE

HARMONY

JUSTICE

ORDER

PROSPERITY

RECIPROCITY

RIGHTEOUSNESS

TRUTH

Dedicated to my Elder Brother, Bongo Shorty ... Life Everliving.

(Modified by Seestah IMAHKÜS from an origianl meditation by Seestah Fannie S. Clark).

* Afrikan

BIBLIOGRAPHY/REFERENCES

The Honorable Marcus Mosiah Garvey, **Philosophy & Opinions of Marcus Garvey,** 1923

*Modified from a speech of the Honorable Marcus Mosiah Garvey, Jamaican Freedom Fighter and Father of the Back-to-Afrika Movement.

Chancellor Williams, **The Destruction of Black Civilization,** Chicago, IL. 1974

Kweku Ofori-Ansa, Assoc. Prof. Of African Art History, Dept. of Art, College of Fine Arts, Howard University, Washinton, DC; **History and Significance of Ghana's Kente Cloth** - 1993

Widowhood Rites, Supi Minna & Lucy Hagar-Grant
Cape Coast, Ghana, West Afrika

Carter G. Woodson, **The Mis-education of the Negro**, 1990, African World Press, Inc. Trenton, NJ

Nvenge P. Appolinair, **African Common Market,** 1990, African Unity Press, Brooklyn, NY

The Returning African Descendants Committee
P. O. Box 1096 – Cape Coast, Ghana West Africa

Chester Higgins Jnr., **Feeling the Spirit** Bantam Books 1994

Ghana Immigration Regulations & Citizenship Act

Prof. John Henrik Clarke – Historian

***Amerikkka** – Refers to the racism of America, the Klu Klux Klan, which fights against people of color.

ANOTHER VERY INFORMATIVE BOOK
BY THE AUTHOR

POINTS TO PONDER
"A TRAVEL GUIDE"
When Considering
Repatriating Home To Mother Afrika
To Live Or To Visit,
Books can be purchased on line from AMAZON.com
BARNES & NOBEL, bookstores
or directly from the Author.

* * * * * * *

"RETURNING HOME AIN'T EASY
BUT IT SURE IS A BLESSING"

Contact Seestah IMAHKUS

One Africa Tours and Specialty Services Ltd.
P. O. Box CC 1251 – Cape Coast
Ghana, West Afrika
Tel/Fax: 233-42-40258
Mobile: 233-20 7501221, 020 8195483, 0244-830451
e-mail: oneafrica_ghana@yahoo.com
Website: oneafricaghana.com